Professional Office Business Application Development

MW00815442

Professional

Office Business Application Development

Professional

Office Business Application Development

Using Microsoft® Office SharePoint® Server 2007 and VSTO

Steve Fox
Bill Sheldon

WILEY

Wiley Publishing, Inc.

Professional Office Business Application Development Using Microsoft® Office SharePoint® Server 2007 and VSTO

Published by
Wiley Publishing, Inc.
10475 Crosspoint Boulevard
Indianapolis, IN 46256
www.wiley.com

Copyright © 2008 by Wiley Publishing, Inc., Indianapolis, Indiana
Published simultaneously in Canada
ISBN: 978-0-470-37731-4
Manufactured in the United States of America

10 9 8 7 6 5 4 3 2 1

Library of Congress Cataloging-in-Publication Data

Fox, Steven, 1970-
  Professional office business application development : using Microsoft Office Sharepoint server 2007 and VSTO / Steve Fox, Bill Sheldon.
    p. cm.
  Includes index.
  ISBN 978-0-470-37731-4 (paper/website)
  1. Microsoft Office. 2. Microsoft Office SharePoint server. 3. Business--Computer programs. I. Sheldon, Bill, 1965- II. Title.
  HF5548.4.M525F6947 2008
  004.6—dc22
                            2008034590

About the Authors

Steve Fox has worked in the IT industry for 13 years in a variety of technologies and positions, most recently in the area of Office and SharePoint development as a Technical Evangelist at Microsoft. He has co-authored *Programming Microsoft Office Business Applications* (MSPress), *Six Microsoft Office Business Applications for Office SharePoint Server* (MSPress), and *Microsoft .NET and SAP* (MSPress), and authored a number of articles for a variety of technical publications. Steve is also active on the national and international conference circuit and spends much of his time presenting and teaching developers about Office development. When not working, Steve enjoys reading, writing, and playing sports. He lives in Seattle, Washington.

Bill Sheldon is a software engineer and architect, originally from Baltimore, Maryland. Holding a degree in computer science from the Illinois Institute of Technology (IIT), Bill has been actively employed as a software engineer since resigning his commission with the United States Navy. He is a Microsoft MVP employed as a principal engineer with InterKnowlogy in Carlsbad, California. In addition to writing books, Bill also works as an instructor for Visual Basic and related courses at the University of California San Diego Extension and has published in excess of 100 articles. He is a contributing editor for *SQL Server Magazine*, and has had articles featured in several other Penton publications. Bill is an established MSDN online presenter and speaks at live events, such as VSLIve, DevConnections, Office Developers Conference, and community events, such as Code Camp and local user group meetings. Bill is an avid cyclist and wood worker, and is actively involved in the fight against diabetes.

About the Technical Editor

Andrew Whitechapel has more than 20 years experience as a software developer and architect. He is currently the Program Manager Architect for the Microsoft VSTO team in Redmond, WA where he is focused on designing strategic features of the Visual Studio toolset for building Office Business Applications.

Credits

Acquisitions Editor
Katie Mohr

Development Editor
Christopher J. Rivera

Technical Editor
Andrew Whitechapel

Production Editor
Kathleen Wisor

Copy Editor
Kim Cofer

Editorial Manager
Mary Beth Wakefield

Production Manager
Tim Tate

Vice President and Executive Group Publisher
Richard Swadley

Vice President and Executive Publisher
Joseph B. Wikert

Project Coordinator, Cover
Lynsey Standford

Compositor
Craig Woods, Happenstance Type-O-Rama

Proofreader
Amy McCarthy, Word One

Indexer
Robert Swanson

Acknowledgments

Thanks to the acquisitions and editing staff at Wiley for helping push us along and deliver a great book. Also, thanks to Nicole for putting up with my "quiet time" on evenings and weekends. Last, thanks to Andrew Whitechapel for helping us make this a better book.

— *Steve Fox*

Thanks to the team at InterKnowlogy (Robin, Paul, Kevin, Dan) who originally worked on much of this application in the Pre-Beta 2 days of Visual Studio 2008. It is a testament to your efforts that I was able to continue that work following the release of Visual Studio. To Steve, who was the sponsor responsible for making this project happen and getting permission for us to share this code with the community on CodePlex. To Katie and Christopher, who put up with my ability to test the question "when is the last minute?"

— *Bill Sheldon*

Professional
Office Business Application Development

Contents

Contents

Contents

Contents

Introduction

Office Business Applications (OBAs) are a bit of a mystery to some; developers often find it difficult to see Office as a true development platform. Nevertheless, Office has evolved quite a bit in the past few years into a strong platform that offers a number of rich technologies. Combine this with the ability to leverage the Microsoft "stack," and you have a powerful ability to use technologies like Visual Studio and SharePoint to manage processes and integrate many different types of data with the Office system to build OBAs.

For those that are willing, the journey in this book will be about developing OBAs. In fact, we'll take you through one specific OBA, a sales forecast OBA, that brings together many different parts of the Office system into a composite solution that manages process and data while at the same time uses the core infrastructure of Office and .NET as the development platform. This will likely mean taking familiar applications, like Excel, Visual Studio, or SharePoint, and combining them in ways that you may not have explored before. Although the goal of this book is to take you through a real-world application of an OBA, the more significant goal is to plant the seed for developing your own OBA and thinking through your own design.

Who This Book Is For

This book is primarily aimed at the intermediate to advanced developer who is interested in using the Office system as a platform for building composite applications. The types of skills you might possess are a familiarity with the .NET Framework, object-oriented programming, the Office applications (specifically Excel and Word), and Microsoft Office SharePoint Server (MOSS) 2007. In your travels, you may also have used Visual Studio — we'll specifically focus on Visual Studio 2008, and you may also have some knowledge in Visual Basic or C#.

As a note to the reader, our initial two chapters talk more about the concepts and design patterns that sit behind OBA. If you feel you've got a good grounding in this already, you may want to jump to Chapter 3, where we begin to talk much more about ways of creating specific parts of an OBA. The flow of the book is to take you from the client-side development of the sales forecast OBA to the SharePoint, server-side extensions, with the total sum of the book being an end-to-end working application.

Also, in many of the chapters you'll find code samples and some discussion around how to accomplish specific tasks. We tried to cover many of the key elements of creating the OBA, but we also encourage you to download the code from the companion Codeplex site and explore this either alongside the chapters or after you've read them. Either way, the code is yours for the exploration, which you can find here: http://www.codeplex.com/obasales.

What This Book Covers

This book focuses on building and deploying OBAs by using one central OBA, the sales forecast OBA, as an example. Each chapter describes a different part of the sales forecast OBA, thus giving you a well-rounded view of how to build your own OBA.

The technologies that are covered in this book range from Visual Studio Tools for Office (VSTO), a component technology within Visual Studio 2008, Open XML, to SharePoint features such as SharePoint workflow, Excel Services, Key Performance Indicators, and the Business Data Catalog. We tried to provide meaningful code samples where possible to help illustrate how these technologies connect to one another as a part of the whole composite application.

The version of Office we used for this book was Office Professional (you must use this SKU or above in order to be able to extend Office). Also, we used Windows Server 2003, MOSS 2007, Windows SharePoint Services (WSS) 3.0, and the SharePoint 2007 SDK. Even though we cover Office 2007 applications in this book, it should be noted that you can also apply the design methods within this book to Office 2003 applications as well; it's just that the process of building the extensions to the Office interface will be slightly different.

How This Book Is Structured

We structured the book in the way we did because we wanted to give you the full picture of how to build and deploy an OBA. The existing books on OBA provide views into the different technologies that help you build an OBA, but they don't put it all together into one application and then discuss the key elements of these individual pieces. That's what this book does, and that's why we feel this book will be valuable to those of you who really want to understand how to build one end-to-end.

What You Need to Use This Book

The core environment you'll need to set up in order to work through the code samples is as follows:

- ❑ Windows Server 2003
- ❑ MOSS 2007
- ❑ Office Professional 2007
- ❑ SharePoint SDK 2007
- ❑ Visual Studio 2008

Conventions

To help you get the most from the text and keep track of what's happening, we've used a few conventions throughout the book.

- ❑ We *highlight* new terms and important words when we introduce them.
- ❑ We show keyboard strokes like this: Ctrl+A.
- ❑ We show file names, URLs, and code within the text like so: `persistence.properties`.

❑ We present code in two different ways:

```
We use a monofont type with no highlighting for most code examples.
We use gray highlighting to emphasize code that's particularly important in the
present context.
```

Source Code

As you work through the examples in this book, you may choose either to type in all the code manually or to use the source code files that accompany the book. All of the source code used in this book is available for download at http://www.wrox.com. Once at the site, simply locate the book's title (either by using the Search box or by using one of the title lists) and click the Download Code link on the book's detail page to obtain all the source code for the book. The code is also available at the authors' companion web site http://www.codeplex.com/obasales.

Because many books have similar titles, you may find it easiest to search by ISBN; this book's ISBN is 978-0-470-37731-4.

Once you download the code, just decompress it with your favorite compression tool. Alternatively, you can go to the main Wrox code download page at http://www.wrox.com/dynamic/books/download.aspx to see the code available for this book and all other Wrox books.

Errata

We make every effort to ensure that there are no errors in the text or in the code. However, no one is perfect, and mistakes do occur. If you find an error in one of our books, like a spelling mistake or faulty piece of code, we would be very grateful for your feedback. By sending in errata you may save another reader hours of frustration and at the same time you will be helping us provide even higher quality information.

To find the errata page for this book, go to http://www.wrox.com and locate the title using the Search box or one of the title lists. Then, on the book details page, click the Book Errata link. On this page you can view all errata that has been submitted for this book and posted by Wrox editors. A complete book list including links to each book's errata is also available at www.wrox.com/misc-pages/booklist.shtml.

If you don't spot "your" error on the Book Errata page, go to www.wrox.com/contact/techsupport.shtml and complete the form there to send us the error you have found. We'll check the information and, if appropriate, post a message to the book's errata page and fix the problem in subsequent editions of the book.

p2p.wrox.com

For author and peer discussion, join the P2P forums at p2p.wrox.com. The forums are a Web-based system for you to post messages relating to Wrox books and related technologies and interact with other readers and technology users. The forums offer a subscription feature to e-mail you topics of interest of your choosing when new posts are made to the forums. Wrox authors, editors, other industry experts, and your fellow readers are present on these forums.

At http://p2p.wrox.com you will find a number of different forums that will help you not only as you read this book, but also as you develop your own applications. To join the forums, just follow these steps:

1. Go to p2p.wrox.com and click the Register link.

2. Read the terms of use and click Agree.

3. Complete the required information to join as well as any optional information you wish to provide and click Submit.

4. You will receive an e-mail with information describing how to verify your account and complete the joining process.

> *You can read messages in the forums without joining P2P but in order to post your own messages, you must join.*

Once you join, you can post new messages and respond to messages other users post. You can read messages at any time on the Web. If you would like to have new messages from a particular forum e-mailed to you, click the Subscribe to this Forum icon by the forum name in the forum listing.

For more information about how to use the Wrox P2P, be sure to read the P2P FAQs for answers to questions about how the forum software works as well as many common questions specific to P2P and Wrox books. To read the FAQs, click the FAQ link on any P2P page.

1

Anatomy of an Office Business Application

Over the past twenty-odd years, companies have spent considerable amounts of money (in the billions of dollars) installing and maintaining line-of-business (LOB) systems to manage all types of data, including customer data, sales and finance data, and human resource information. In many cases, these business data represent the backbone of the organization. One of the issues with these LOB systems, though, has been accessibility; the systems have been accessible to only a subset of people within the organizations. Though in some cases this accessibility might be by design, for the most part organizations can benefit by exposing much of the business data within the LOB system to their employees. For example, if salespeople have direct access to updating their sales data within the LOB system, they rely less on people who have direct access to the system and subsequently have to copy and paste data out of the system. For those that do have access to the system, there are a number of costs to the organization that are quite significant. For example, in a study entitled "The Financial Impact of Packaged Applications" (Forrester, 07/11/2006), a number of key costs were outlined such as training, temporary business backfill, or change management — all direct costs to the company resulting from an enterprise-wide LOB system implementation (see Figure 1-1). When you consider many LOB system implementations run in the twenty-five million plus region, these cost hits are no small matter.

With the growth of LOB system installations, there have also been some other changes taking place in the workplace. To name a few, many of us engage in an abundance of email communication, sending attached documents like fiscal plans created in Excel spreadsheets "across the wire" instead of posting them on a central document share; many people keep information local to their PCs (think of the problem with intellectual property leakage when these people leave the organization and IT staff wipe the drives of their machines — this information is now lost); the organization has evolved into a more team-based environment, so sharing information and knowledge has become a critical part of our daily collaborative processes; and many people are generally unhappy with the current LOB systems that are costing companies so much to implement today (some studies have found these system have user adoption issues in the neighborhood of 45% of the total user base). With these changes have arrived many new productivity tools to help manage our processes and behaviors within the workplace; in fact, it's hard to think what our lives would be like without these tools in place. Though there are many different productivity technologies on the market today, this book deals primarily with those tools, servers, and applications found within the Office platform and how these tools can integrate with LOB systems to not only mitigate the cost burdens just described (and shown in Figure 1-1), but also to begin to take better and more discrete use of the business data that lives in these LOB systems. That said, OBAs help mitigate the issues within these scenarios by leveraging the Office platform to:

- ❏ Provide a central interface into the business data within a LOB system
- ❏ Use existing technology (assuming an organization has deployed Office) to build OBAs
- ❏ Improve user adoption issues with users interacting with the business data within a comfortable environment
- ❏ Increase cost savings in, for example, training and productivity

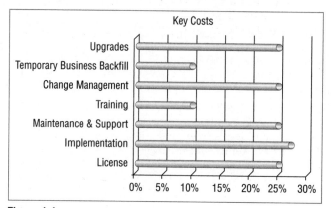

Figure 1-1

Now that you understand the high-level problem, you're probably asking yourself...

What Is an Office Business Application?

OBAs are in essence composite applications that leverage the Microsoft Office platform (or OBA Framework) to bridge the "results gap," the gap that exists when information workers don't have access to critical business data that reside in these LOB systems. OBAs are, for the most part, service-oriented, so they will require a service-oriented architecture (SOA) — or what some in the IT industry are also referring to as Software plus Services (S+S). (S+S is a broad term for integrating software that exists on the desktop with a variety of services that exist in the 'cloud.') OBAs provide access to the LOB system via a service proxy so information workers can use up-to-date business data in their everyday business lives within an environment that is both comfortable and familiar to them: the Office environment. Examples of service proxies might be Web services, Windows Communication Foundation (WCF) services, or even hosted services.

Examples of OBAs range from solutions that are specific to sales, finance, and human resources, to customer relationship management. Typically, these types of solutions are tied to some process or workflow (for example, approval of budget or interview evaluation forms) and are larger in scale — in other words, enterprise-level solutions. You can also build smaller, more discretely targeted OBAs that, for example, process annual performance review forms or generate expense forms. OBA solution design, as you'll see throughout this chapter, can also include smart-client applications (for example, documents with custom task panes or custom ribbons) to SharePoint customizations (for example, custom Web parts). It is no coincidence that these OBAs are tied to key business data that resides in the LOB system; it is the purpose of OBAs to expose this data to the organization to improve process, productivity, and business.

At a high level, we can roughly define OBAs as being composed of four main pieces:

1. The LOB system
2. Client-side customizations
3. SharePoint (or other server-side) customizations
4. The services (for example, Web services, WCF, or BizTalk adapters) that bind the LOB system to the Office client and SharePoint

Figure 1-2 illustrates these four parts of the OBA. One thing to note is that although these are the main components of many OBAs that are being built today, it is possible to build an OBA that has just a client-to-LOB system integration or SharePoint-to-LOB system integration.

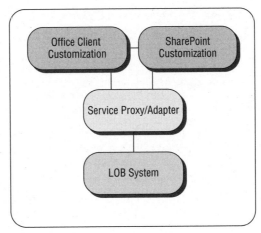

Figure 1-2

Note that in the diagram, we've made the line between the Office client and SharePoint a dotted line. This is to indicate that you could integrate these two parts of the OBA, however, it's not necessary for the solution to be considered an OBA. An example of this type of integration would be mapping a Visual Studio Tools for Office (VSTO) document-level customization to a SharePoint content type (an example that is explored in Chapter 10, "Deploying Your Client Components").

OBAs provide deep value in a number of ways. First, OBAs unlock key business data for team use through technologies such as the Business Data Catalog, Excel Services, Visual Studio Tools for Office (VSTO) customizations, and so on. Second, OBAs leverage existing functionality that is native to

Office, thus alleviating the need to reproduce this functionality in your solution design. An example of this would be building a client-side customization for Excel 2007, which would enable your end-users to take advantage of the functionality native to Excel, such as charting or functions. Another example might be building an OBA within Outlook and then taking advantage of the underlying messaging and calendaring functionality within Outlook. Third, OBAs are about enabling process, so you can customize your OBA solutions centric to a particular human workflow within the organization. The example we use throughout this book is a sales forecast approval solution (we talk more about this in Chapter 2, "Architecture Guidance and Design Patterns for Office Business Applications"), where a manager can *approve, reject,* or *amend* a salesperson's forecast through the custom workflow built into SharePoint and associated with the sales forecast document. Fourth, OBAs are about sharing information and collaboration — whether it be through document libraries, exchanging or sharing information via blogs, wikis, or MySites (where individuals can provide personalized SharePoint sites with searchable information), OBAs are all about enabling the collective — thus enabling community-level and Web 2.0 technology around Office integrations with the LOB system. This is where you'll truly begin to see the strength of the OBA technologies (which we discuss in the next section of this chapter). Finally, OBAs are about keeping information workers inside the context of their everyday environments while providing them access to the information that they need. It is here that we can distill much of the benefit of building OBAs and meet real cost and productivity savings. This cost-savings is not only realized in the context of keeping information workers within a familiar environment (thus mitigating some of the costs listed in Figure 1-1), but also alleviates engineering costs by eradicating the need for additional tools generation, support, and ongoing maintenance costs.

Types of Office Business Applications

Though the scenarios around designing and deploying OBAs can vary, there are essentially three different "types" of OBAs:

1. Type 1: Client to LOB system architecture. This represents a smart client that integrates via a service (for example, Web service, WCF service, and so on) such as a custom task pane or custom ribbon in Excel, Word, or Outlook.

2. Type 2: Client or Server to LOB system architecture. This represents the combination of a smart client and SharePoint server customization integrated, for example, via a service to the LOB system. We've discussed an example of a smart client, but the SharePoint customization might be a Business Data Catalog (BDC) Web part that consumes a service to render data.

3. Type 3: Client and Server to multiple LOB systems architecture. This represents a smart client and SharePoint server customization integrated with multiple LOB systems.

    Although SharePoint is the primary server-side platform on which OBAs are built, you can also use other servers in the Office platform — for example, Exchange Server or Communications Server.

    Though not mainstream, there is also the architecture where you could use hosted services that integrate with your LOB system. This architecture arguably could represent a fourth type of OBA.

Across these types, you can also have permutations of OBAs, depending on what designs you choose and what technologies you use to design your OBAs. To make this a little more real, take a look at a problem scenario and apply an OBA design to it.

Suppose you're a product manager, and you're trying to identify business data that helps justify the creation of a set of features for a new software application. You do not have access to the LOB system where there is key data to justify the features, so you request from your co-worker (call her Sandy), who does, to send you some data that will help in your quest. Sandy searches for the appropriate data for you and copies and pastes the data in an Excel spreadsheet. She then saves it locally in a *Temp* folder and sends the spreadsheet to you via Outlook. You are now happy that you have some data to justify the features you're going to spec, and you build your case for the new product. This is great, right? Well, not really.

First, in organizations today there are many people looking for business data that helps them create competitive products or features and our LOB systems contain much of that needed data. Second, not having direct access to the business data (and sending it around via email) is problematic. That is, if the day after the data is sent to you the data does not justify the features, all future work on that product becomes a cost, both real and competitive, to the organization. Because of the disconnect, however, you, the product manager, may not realize this until too late, or worse, not at all. Third, the process of product development is typically not done in isolation; it's a team process where virtual teams convene and agree upon the next foot forward. The costs of creating this feature set around stale data are not isolated to one person; they extend out to virtual teams and to the wider organization. Figure 1-3 illustrates this process. Note that the diagram also includes this idea of moving from the *structured* realm (where an OBA manages direct integration with the business data the processes around that data) to the *unstructured* realm (where there exists no OBA and where the business data moves further away from the source affecting more people and business decisions along the way — the results gap).

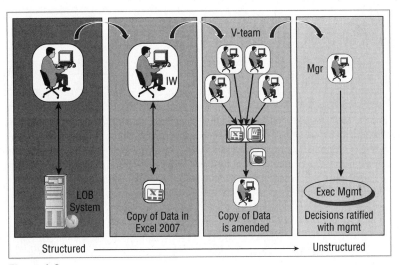

Figure 1-3

If you were to build an OBA to solve this problem, what would that OBA look like?

For this type of scenario, you might want to build a fairly simple OBA (that is, a Type 1): a smart-client Excel spreadsheet that is connected to the appropriate data source via a Web service to the LOB system. So, when you open Excel, the managed code assembly would load a custom task pane that further loads the appropriate data using the Web service connection to your LOB system. You could then select the data that you needed and populate the custom Excel template (or workbook) with the data. You might also use a custom task pane in a Word document; especially if you don't require any calculations but just require the creation of a report or inclusion of data to justify your business case within a specification template. This design, as opposed to, say, binding the LOB system data to a ListObject, might require instead using a binding method to Word content controls or OpenXML. Don't worry if any of this doesn't spring forth elaborate visions; we explore a lot of this throughout this book, so if it's not familiar now, it will be soon enough.

The OBA we explore in this book is one that is based around a sales forecast scenario; that is, a sales team that needs to submit their forecasts, have their managers review them, and then have them subsequently approved. During this process, we'll explore many different technologies that you can incorporate in the design of your own Office solution. Unlike other books that discuss related technologies using many different scenarios, we wanted to build the solution from the ground up. The reason we chose the path of building an end-to-end solution and then discussing all of the facets of releasing this solution "to market" (or to your enterprise) is that you can get a sense for all of the things that are possible when releasing an OBA to the enterprise. Thus, this book provides you with some information on the How, in both the contexts of the technology and deployment and security — from both a smart-client perspective (which you learn about in Chapter 4, "Customizing the Office Fluent Ribbon and Task Pane") and a SharePoint perspective (which you learn about in Chapters 5 through 10).

Before we dive into the solution and the rest of the book, though, let's first discuss the technologies that are available for you today to build your OBA. We say today because, as we write, Visual Studio 2008 is the tool released to market, and when this book is published you'll likely hear whispers of Visual Studio "10" and SharePoint/Office "14" futures, as well.

OBA Technologies

OBAs can be relatively straightforward in their design; conversely, they can also involve many moving parts. As I'm sure you can extrapolate from the different types of OBAs mentioned earlier in this chapter (Types 1, 2, and 3), they can range from a simple smart-client (for example, a client customization that includes a custom task pane) that uses a Web service to load data into a Word document to more complex solutions that involve custom workflow, multiple smart-client elements, consumption of SharePoint services, and so on. As an interesting example, I see the Word-based OBAs quite a lot when working with the public sector. IT departments will make custom task panes with tabs that manage data into a document that creates boilerplate forms that information workers can then fill out — thus increasing productivity and centrally storing boilerplate form data. This is, obviously, only one design for OBAs. You could, for example, use other, "thinner" presentation layers for a service, such as an InfoPath form within a SharePoint environment. InfoPath forms are great for integrating with data or Web services. Though your presentation layer can vary depending on your requirements and design, remember that OBAs are not about Office technology alone; they're also about the LOB system with which you're integrating. In large part, you'll be designing and developing the services part of the solution first, which will likely mean using the native tools within your LOB system.

This book does not cover individual LOB systems; rather, it abstracts the services away from the other layers of the OBA, which include a presentation layer, productivity layer, and services layer. Thus, the assumption is that if you're going to build your own OBA, you'll design and build your LOB system services first and then use the OBA technologies to integrate with the Office system.

That said, Figure 1-4 provides an overview of the different layers of an OBA. In effect, it shows the different technologies that exist within each and more broadly within the Office platform. Now, building an OBA does not necessarily mean using all of these technologies in your design. Use this diagram to help you understand what options are available to you when designing your OBA solution. For example, you may design your OBA using only a smart client or you may also have another Web-based Intranet presentation layer that uses SharePoint Web parts. Each presentation component would serve a different purpose, but keep in mind that the OBA would grow in complexity and support with each new moving part you add to it. The following sections take a deeper look at each of the layers in Figure 1-4.

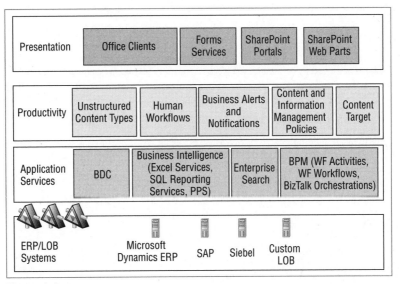

Figure 1-4

Presentation Layer

When building the presentation layer for your OBA, you have a number of options depending on your design. Your design might include an Office smart client, InfoPath forms, SharePoint-centric design, or all of the above.

Visual Studio Tools for Office (Smart Client)

An Office "smart" client (at least as defined in this book) uses the Visual Studio Tools for Office (VSTO) technology (now included in Visual Studio 2008 Professional and above) to build managed code (that is, Visual Basic and C#) assemblies (or add-ins) that you deploy to the client. These add-ins then show up when you open up the application with which the assembly is associated. These add-ins typically manifest through an extension in the custom toolbar menu (in Office 2003 client applications), custom Fluent (the branding for the Office 2007 user interface) ribbon extensions, custom task/actions panes, or other types of customization embedded within the document or triggered by an event. Figure 1-5 provides an example of an Excel 2007–based document-level VSTO solution. The solution includes a custom ribbon and custom task pane to manage data input to the Excel spreadsheet.

The add-ins that you create with VSTO come in two flavors: document-level solutions and application-level add-ins. The document-level solution is tied to a specific document (so is only loaded when you open that particular document), and the application-level add-in is tied to a specific Office application (so loads every time that host application loads). The example in Figure 1-5 is a document-level solution, so would load only when you load the particular document with which the solution is associated.

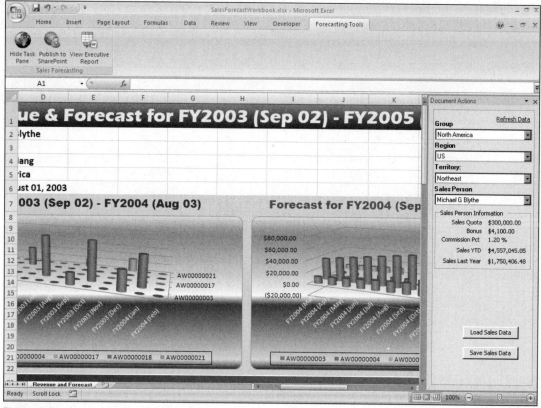

Figure 1-5

Application-level add-ins, though, are also very powerful. For example, mentioned earlier in the chapter was the fact that you could build OBAs by extending Outlook. Many companies are taking advantage of this technology to extend Outlook in many exciting ways. Creating an Outlook add-in using VSTO, you can customize the menu toolbar, customize the Outlook ribbon, create custom task panes, create custom Outlook form regions, and so on. All the while, you can integrate these objects with data sources or Web services. Figure 1-6 illustrates a custom Outlook form region (a custom contact form) that has altered the contact form in two ways. First, a data grid is linked to an external data source; second, custom logic that sits behind the form calls a service that maps the selected address of the customers in a web browser pane.

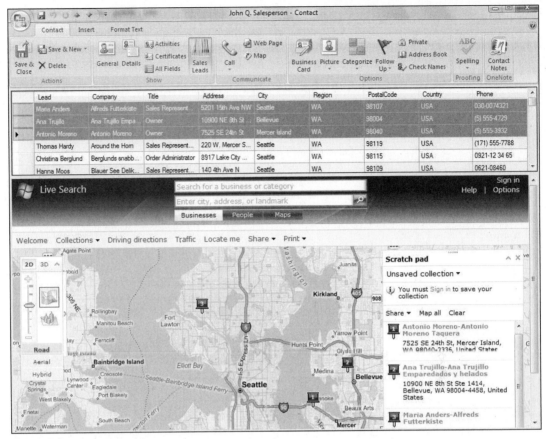

Figure 1-6

In short order, creating OBA solutions using VSTO is a great way to take advantage of many of the new features of the .NET Framework 3.5 and Visual Studio 2008 (for example, Windows Presentation Foundation [WPF], Windows Communication Foundation [WCF], Windows Workflow Foundation [WF], Language Integrated Query [LINQ], and so on) and build these into your smart-client solutions. You'll see more of VSTO in Chapter 4 and more about the other technologies throughout the book.

OpenXML

VSTO is not the only client-side technology that is conversant with Office 2007. OpenXML, a culmination of XML efforts that began in earlier versions of Office, enables server-side processing of the information that exists within a document by storing the document in XML format. This not only allows for dynamic document creation and manipulation, but it also exposes the underlying content of a document to other Office (and custom) services and processes; thus, you can program against a document without having to open it — that is, you open it programmatically without needing the host application to manage the opening of the document for you. For programmatic document manipulation, this is a huge step forward with support for the OpenXML cutting across Word, Excel, and PowerPoint. We discuss OpenXML in greater detail in Chapter 7, "Using OpenXML and Business Data."

InfoPath Forms

InfoPath 2007 is the way in which many developers are creating forms for Microsoft Office SharePoint Server 2007. InfoPath is a forms-based technology that enables you to build thin-client forms quickly, embed controls on the forms, and then tie those controls to data sources or to services, making it an easy-to-use, thin-client technology. In SharePoint 2007, there exists a forms publishing capability that enables developers to build and deploy forms direct to a MOSS 2007 site. You can further integrate workflow (as the InfoPath form exists as a document object within SharePoint), which allows you to use InfoPath forms for a wide variety of business processes. This ability to integrate with workflow makes InfoPath a technology that is doubly useful for creating OBAs. Assuming that you're building them within the InfoPath Forms Services framework for SharePoint, InfoPath forms add quite a lot of power when thinking about process-based and collaborative designs for your solution. Figure 1-7 illustrates an InfoPath form that is tied to a loan application processing workflow. In this example, the form retrieves data using the MLS (Multiple Listing Service) Web service (via the Go button) that passes the MLS number entered as a parameter and then loads property information into the form. For more information on this specific InfoPath example, you can download the OBA Loan Origination Reference Application Pack at `http://msdn2.microsoft.com/en-us/architecture/bb265266.aspx`.

Though we won't cover InfoPath in great depth in this book, you can look at a number of resources to learn more about this technology. See the "Further Reading" section of this chapter for more information. The reason we didn't use InfoPath for our OBA solution was because we wanted to build an OBA that used the Office client — and functionality of the Office client — as opposed to a thin-client solution.

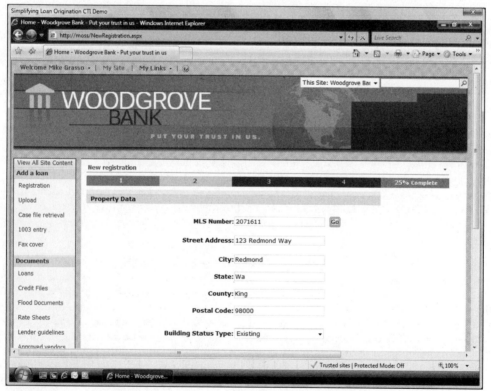

Figure 1-7

SharePoint

SharePoint is a technology that has grown incredibly over the past five years into a mature platform that enables developers to build and deploy applications not only for the enterprise but also for publicly facing sites as well. The SharePoint technology (which is referred to as SharePoint in this book) comprises two major parts: Windows SharePoint Services (WSS) and Microsoft Office SharePoint Server (MOSS). WSS is essentially the infrastructure that you can use to build sites, lists, and Web parts, for example. There is a powerful object model that lies behind WSS, and the software to build solutions based on WSS is free. MOSS is a server-based program that provides a number of out-of-the-box enterprise features that support collaboration, manage content and processes, and access information and people across your organization. You might think of MOSS as an out-of-the-box SharePoint site and tools that enable you to build, customize, and extend your SharePoint team sites and portals. When you further combine SharePoint with technologies such as Silverlight, AJAX, or other Web 2.0 technologies, you can build some very compelling user experiences on top of an already robust platform.

SharePoint portals represent a great way to provide team-based views, and subsequent role-based drill-down views, to manage process, documents, data, and information (to name a few). In this book, you build a sales forecasting portal to manage your document library, workflow, dashboard views of business intelligence, and search results — see Figure 1-8.

Figure 1-8

When building SharePoint portals and sites, you'll need to become familiar with what is known as a Web part. You can think of Web parts as one of the essential building blocks for the SharePoint site, and as such are a critical component to the design and deployment of an OBA. The Web part consists of a title bar, a frame, and content (which changes depending on which Web part you select from the Web Part Gallery); see Figure 1-9. You can choose from two primary types of Web parts: a standard Web part that comes out of the box with MOSS 2007, and a custom Web part.

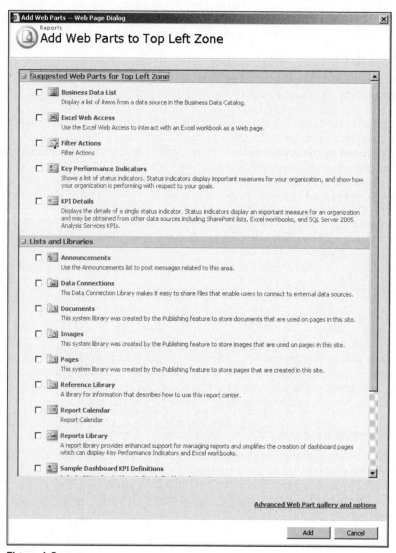

Figure 1-9

You can create a custom Web part and embed your own custom code to accomplish very specific tasks. These custom Web parts implement ASP.NET code, and developers typically use Visual Studio 2005 or 2008, SharePoint Designer, Visual Studio Extensions for Windows SharePoint Services, Silverlight, or Windows SharePoint Services to create them. Alternatively, you can use an out-of-the-box Web part (for example, Excel Services Web part) to create a business intelligence view for your OBA. Through the connection of different Web parts on one page, you can also integrate data views to make your Web parts more dynamic. For example, you can use two types of Business Data Catalog Web parts, one for a summary view and another for a line-item view, so both Web parts work together to give you high-level and detailed information.

Productivity Layer

Beneath the presentation layer lies the productivity layer, or essentially, the parts of the OBA that manage process, security, information, and so on, within your OBA solution. In Figure 1-4, we highlight a number of areas that are important when it comes to productivity. For example, when thinking about integrating smart clients into SharePoint, one of the key features in SharePoint to consider is the ability to create custom content types (an object that allows you to set properties and map the content type to a specific document or template) and then map those content types to client-side customizations. It is this type of client-server integration that begins to strike home at the power and potential of OBA solution development. That is, when you integrate the customized Excel document, for example, and a SharePoint content type, you are now integrating the Office client application features within your OBA solution — think of all the calculations and native spreadsheet functions that are now tied into your application. We've taken this approach with the sales forecast OBA in this book, so you'll learn more about this throughout the book, but the specific integration piece is covered in Chapter 10, "Deploying Your Client Components."

There's another important aspect to making the custom, smart-client document an artifact of Share-Point; you've now provided an object against which you can build custom SharePoint workflow. As our organizations become ever-more driven toward processes and accountability through those processes, creating software solutions that manage process through workflow is becoming increasingly more useful and pervasive. In the case of the integrated document, you now have the ability to tie the document into a workflow that further ties into the messaging of alerts and notifications to ensure that the appropriate people are completing the appropriate tasks. This is an important aspect of the sales forecast OBA; that is, the fact that when we take a custom document and integrate that document with Share-Point we can now manage processes around that document through custom workflow.

Application Services Layer

The LOB system business data is processed and managed through a number of key services, shown in the Application Services layer in Figure 1-4. For example, the BDC can provide a business intelligence view that can directly link to SQL Server (or other ADO.NET-based data source) or to a LOB system through a Web service. Figure 1-10 illustrates sample BDC Web parts that are interconnected and surfacing data through a Web service. Further, you use the Excel Services to create Web-based views of Excel spreadsheets — either the entire worksheet or objects within the worksheet. Key Performance Indicators (KPIs) can also be used to create score-card views to provide "quick-checks" on status for project/business health metrics. We discuss business intelligence in greater detail in Chapter 8, "Adding Business Intelligence through Excel Web Services and Key Performance Indicators."

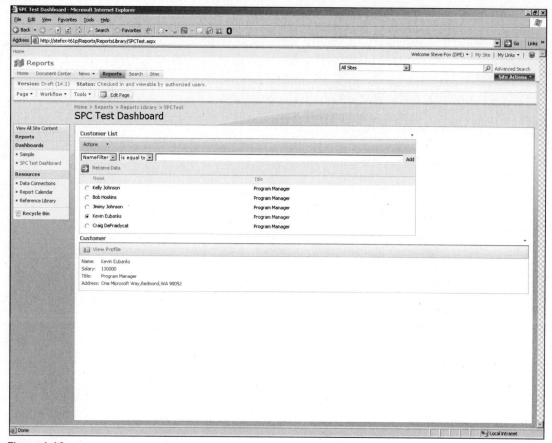

Figure 1-10

Although business intelligence is an important part of the SharePoint services, data discovery is also important, which brings us to search: a central part of any organizational portal. SharePoint's search is a shared service that provides extensible and rich information discovery through its querying and indexing engines. It supports full-text and keyword search, and it can be extended to search and index LOB system business data through the BDC. For the sales forecast solution, we felt that search was a very important component, and so we've dedicated an entire chapter (Chapter 9, "Integrating Your LOB System using the Business Data Catalog, and Extending Search into Your LOB System") to discussing how we extended search into the LOB system to query and index LOB system data.

We think you'll find this book extremely useful. There is a lot of good content that provides developers with key guidance on developing and deploying OBAs using both the client-side customization (that is, the smart client) and SharePoint customizations. We hope you enjoy reading and learning from this book as much as we enjoyed writing it. As an overview of what you'll find in the rest of the book, the next section provides a brief summary of each chapter.

What You'll Find in This Book

❑ Chapter 2: Architecture Guidance and Design Patterns for Office Business Applications

  ❑ This chapter introduces the OBA solution patterns, and then applies the appropriate pattern to the sales forecast scenario we'll use throughout this book. The chapter also discusses considerations and decisions for our design and for alternative designs that you might consider when building your OBA solutions.

❑ Chapter 3: Installing and Configuring MOSS

  ❑ One of the key aspects of the sales forecast solution is the team portal, through which all team members have access to the documents, information, and sites. This chapter provides a summary of how we created, designed, and deployed the site for team consumption.

❑ Chapter 4: Customizing the Office Fluent Ribbon and Task Pane

  ❑ This chapter introduces you to Visual Studio 2008 and Visual Studio Tools for Office 3.0. It provides an overview of how, for example, to customize the Office Fluent ribbon and create a custom task pane and then tie these user interface elements into core parts of the sales forecast solution.

❑ Chapter 5: Creating and Deploying a Custom MOSS 2007 Workflow Using Visual Studio 2008

  ❑ Visual Studio 2008 (and the Visual Studio Tools for Office component technology) is a powerful tool that provides the ability to create custom workflows for SharePoint. This chapter shows you how to create the custom workflow that was used in the sales forecast solution. It also shows you how to debug, test, and deploy the workflow in the Visual Studio IDE against and within the SharePoint environment.

❑ Chapter 6: Creating a Custom Outlook Form Region

  ❑ Custom Outlook form regions are a great way to extend Outlook into an OBA solution. This chapter shows you how you can create a custom Outlook form region that is bound to data and uses WPF to enhance data visualization. It also discusses how we tied the Outlook form region to custom SharePoint workflow.

❑ Chapter 7: Using OpenXML and Business Data

  ❑ Part of the document-creation process is using OpenXML to parse and generate server-side documents. This chapter focuses on using OpenXML to demonstrate how we did this in the sales forecast solution.

❑ Chapter 8: Adding Business Intelligence through Excel Web Services and Key Performance Indicators

  ❑ Business intelligence is a key aspect of OBAs, and it is very important in the sales forecast solution. This chapter shows you how you can create Excel services and KPI Web parts that provide business intelligence views into the sales forecast data.

❑ Chapter 9: Integrating Your LOB System using the Business Data Catalog, and Extending Search into Your LOB System

  ❑ One of the key ways of integrating your LOB systems with SharePoint is through the Business Data Catalog (BDC). This chapter walks you through how you can both integrate the BDC with databases *and* Web services using the BDC Definition Editor, a tool that shipped with the SharePoint Server SDK. This chapter also shows you how to integrate LOB system search and indexing into your SharePoint search to enhance data and information discoverability.

❑ Chapter 10: Deploying Your Client Components

  ❑ One of the critical pieces when building OBAs is the integration of the client-side customizations that you build using VSTO and SharePoint. This chapter walks you through how you integrate the sales forecast customized template with a content type within SharePoint.

❑ Chapter 11: Deploying and Securing Your OBA Server Components

  ❑ Building your OBA is one thing, but deploying and securing it is yet another. This chapter describes how you deploy both the server components for your OBA and also provides guidance on how you can secure your OBA as part of your enterprise solution infrastructure.

Further Reading

At the end of each chapter, we've provided some (of what we feel are) useful links for learning more about the areas of discussion in this book. We've taken the approach of creating an end-to-end solution for this book and walking you through the entire solution from top to bottom. We cannot, unfortunately, cover every technology that we'd like to cover that is related to OBA development (because we chose a specific design).

❑ VSTO Developer Center: http://msdn2.microsoft.com/en-us/office/aa905533.aspx

❑ SharePoint (WSS) Developer Center: http://msdn2.microsoft.com/en-us/sharepoint/default.aspx

❑ Office Developer Center: http://msdn2.microsoft.com/en-us/office/default.aspx

❑ OBA Developer Portal: http://msdn2.microsoft.com/en-us/office/aa905528.aspx

❑ InfoPath Developer Portal: http://msdn2.microsoft.com/en-us/office/aa905434.aspx

2

Architecture Guidance and Design Patterns for Office Business Applications

In Chapter 1, we introduced you to a type of composite application called Office Business Application (OBA). One of the key takeaways from Chapter 1 was that OBAs are solutions that integrate with line-of-business (LOB) systems and leverage key Office technologies (for example, Office client customizations and SharePoint server) to integrate key business data with familiar and comfortable environments of information workers. We also provided a high-level overview of some of the technologies that you can use to build OBAs. Building on Chapter 1, this chapter takes you one step forward.

Office Business Application Solution Patterns

In this chapter we discuss seven OBA solution patterns and how to apply these patterns (applying one of the patterns in detail) to the OBA (the sales forecasting solution) we refer to throughout the rest of the book. These seven patterns represent an initial list of patterns that were specifically designed for OBA development; they will surely evolve as OBA development becomes more pervasive, but they currently represent a good starting point for developers and architects beginning to engage in OBA development. What are the OBA solution patterns?

In software development, design patterns are reusable solutions to commonly occurring problems. Mostly meant to allow the designer and developer to abstract common scenarios, design patterns enable a more efficient and standardized approach to software design and development — not to mention a more "open" approach (in terms of sharing development approaches) to developing software. The end goal of the OBA solution patterns is similar: to provide guidance on how to design and construct solutions for commonly occurring scenarios.

Even though Office has enabled developers to program against it for many years, for many developers the idea of creating managed code solutions for Office using Visual Studio is new. This group, however, is certainly growing. Further, given the fact that this idea of leveraging the Office platform to build OBAs specifically is also relatively new, the OBA solution patterns can help acclimate you to the typical architecture and design pattern of an OBA. The solution patterns can help you in this manner by taking you from the abstract to the pragmatic — that is, from the conceptual to the design of a solution.

There are currently seven categories for the OBA patterns — categories because a number of the patterns have sub-patterns that roll up into a higher-level pattern. We'll refer to these as the *core* patterns within this current set of solution patterns. Figure 2-1 provides an overview of these core OBA solution patterns.

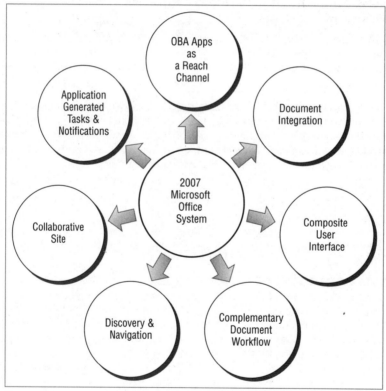

Figure 2-1

At first glance, the solution patterns may seem a little nebulous, so the following provides a high-level description of each of the patterns:

1. *OBA Apps as a Reach Channel* — The goal of this pattern is to extend the functionality of the LOB system to a broader user audience. For example, OBAs can provide many people in the organization with specific, self-service solutions, such as updating personal information. This information typically resides in LOB systems (for example, SAP or PeopleSoft), so this pattern describes a pattern that can be used to build a solution to fit such a scenario.

2. *Document Integration (and Generation)* — Many companies use a smart-client solution to integrate LOB system business data into the context of Excel or Word documents. Further, dynamic and server-side document generation (either individual or batch-processing) are also some things many companies are doing. This pattern provides guidance around document integration with the LOB system.

3. *Composite User Interface* — Because OBAs can include both Office client applications and Share-Point integration, you can create an OBA with multiple interfaces. An example of this might be an Excel 2007 interface into the data, as well as an Excel Services view into the data within a SharePoint site. This pattern describes the composition of multiple application user interfaces in an Office document or SharePoint web page.

4. *Complementary Document Workflow* — OBAs are process-centric, so workflow is an important aspect in the design of the solution. This pattern shows you how you can control and monitor document-centric processes through the use of SharePoint workflow. SharePoint workflow is distinct from the LOB system workflow, which you could also integrate into your solution.

5. *Discovery & Navigation* — Developing OBA solutions is also about integrating discovery into the overall solution. This means discovery, not only at the SharePoint portal level, but also at the level of searching and indexing LOB system business data within the results. This pattern provides guidance around a more natural way of interacting with LOB system business data to show how you can discover data by searching across multiple LOB applications.

6. *Collaborative Site* — For many developers, integrating unstructured communication or social networking into their solutions is a new piece of the puzzle. Now, workers within organizations interact in a much more dynamic fashion, calling for unstructured communication and information sharing to be incorporated into solution design. This pattern provides guidance on how to augment structured business processes with unstructured human collaboration and communication.

7. *Application Generated Tasks & Notifications* — As an output of workflow, managed processes within OBA solutions require task delegation, which further requires a communication infrastructure to manage and relay these tasks and notifications. This pattern shows you how you can use Outlook as a primary user interface to receive and act on LOB system generated tasks and alerts — as well as tie this system of communication into SharePoint workflow to create a solution that cuts across Office client, server, and LOB system.

OBA Sub-Patterns

Table 2-1 provides some additional information around the seven core patterns; mainly, describing the sub-patterns that are associated with the higher-level patterns and enumerating technologies that are associated with the patterns.

Table 2-1: OBA Patterns, Sub-Patterns, and Recommended Technologies

Pattern	Sub-Patterns	Suggested Technologies
OBA Applications as a Reach Channel	Direct integration — This is where the LOB system integration does not require a service proxy (for example, SQL Server represents the LOB system or having direct connectors to the LOB system). Mediated integration — This is where a services-oriented architecture is required to communicate with the LOB system.	Visual Studio Tools for Office (VSTO) 3.0 MOSS 2007 Business Data Catalog (BDC)
Document Integration	Application Generated Document — This process describes document generation from the LOB system. Note that you can also combine this pattern with direct or mediated integration sub-patterns. Intelligent Documents — This is where the LOB system data is integrated directly into the context of the document through objects like content controls, bookmarks, and so on.	OpenXML VSTO 3.0 BDC
Composite User Interface	Context Driven Composite User Interface — Describes smart-client components that are integrated with custom logic. Mesh Composite View — Describes connectable Web parts that can be used to create master/detail business intelligence views in SharePoint (for example, Customer summary and detail enabled through BDC). RSS & Web Services Composition — Describes a type of composite view for RSS and Web services. Analytics — Describes a type of composite view for data analysis dashboard.	Web Parts VSTO 3.0 BDC Excel Services Key Performance Indicators (KPIs)

Table 2-1: OBA Patterns, Sub-Patterns, and Recommended Technologies *(continued)*

Pattern	Sub-Patterns	Suggested Technologies
Complementary Document Workflow	LOB Initiated Document Workflow — Describes a workflow that's embedded in the document and that also includes integration with LOB system business data. Cooperating Document Workflow — Describes a workflow related to the document that supports collaborative workflow against that document.	Windows Workflow Foundation (WF) SharePoint Storage BDC VSTO 3.0
Discovery & Navigation	No sub-patterns	Enterprise Search BDC
Collaborative Site	No sub-patterns	Windows SharePoint Services (WSS) 3.0 Blogs, Wikis, MySite, Profile, Colleague Web Part, Unified Presence InfoPath 2007 & Forms Services
Application Generated Tasks & Notifications	Simple Task & Notification Delivery — One-way flow of tasks and notifications in Outlook. Task Synchronization — Two-way communication of tasks in Outlook. Intelligent Tasks & Notifications — Describes how to take actions based on the assigned task. Form-based Tasks & Notifications — Describes how to integrate technologies such as InfoPath forms to provide richer validation and automation of custom logic.	Outlook 2007 & MOSS 2007 Integration VSTO 3.0 (Custom Task Panes, Outlook Form Regions, and so on) InfoPath 2007 & Forms Services

The preceding table should give you a high-level overview of the patterns, the sub-patterns encapsulated by the parent patterns, and the technologies that map to those patterns. For more information on each of the patterns and their sub-patterns, see the following article: http://msdn2.microsoft.com/en-us/library/bb614541.aspx. It provides some additional information on each of these areas. The one thing this article does not do, however, is apply the patterns to a real-world problem and arrive at a design. For the remainder of this chapter, we describe the requirements for our scenario (the sales forecast scenario) and then apply the OBA patterns to create the solution design that we use throughout this book. Let's walk through a complete solution design from concept to code.

Mapping the OBA Solution Patterns to the Software Development Life Cycle

Before you apply the design patterns, spend a little time on the Software Development Life Cycle (SDLC). Many who are reading this probably have had some experience with the SDLC in some capacity — either wholly or as a contributor to a specific part of the cycle. For example, the Program or Project Manager will own the entire deliverable, so will be in each part of the process, whereas the software tester may contribute only to the testing of the product and not have full visibility into the whole process. Ideally, all members of a project team should have visibility into and contribute to some degree to the entire SDLC process; unfortunately this is often not the case.

At a high level, the SDLC can be roughly defined through four core parts of the overall life cycle (see Figure 2-2):

1. Research and Development (also called Design Conceptualization)
2. Design
3. Develop
4. Test

At each part of the SDLC, a number of key sub-processes have to happen in order to execute the whole product development successfully. For example, at the Research and Development phase, team leaders will collect market data, detail requirements, discuss the technologies that map to those requirements, and, generally, try to package together what it is they're going to be building. At the Design phase, one of the team members (the title ranges across companies, but this might be a Program, Project, or Product Manager) creates a technical specification (or set of technical specifications). Often, the product will be broken down into a set of features that map to multiple specifications. The goals of this phase are to map the requirements to the technologies and technical design of the product, and to provide a technical roadmap for the development, testing, and roll-out for the product. During this phase, teams will often begin creating the design document, which enumerates the implementation of the product, and the test case document, which describes the cases that the test team will test to ensure the product's integrity (both manual and automated tests are covered in this document). Though the design doc and test case doc are created at this stage, they're often finalized close to the beginning of their respective phases, because there are often changes that occur throughout the process. We haven't called this out specifically, but the implication in the SDLC is that the test team is the final body that signs off on the product and readies it for release. Therefore, a release team builds and packages the product for release to manufacturing (RTM), release to web (RTW), or other type of release.

In many cases, project teams will schedule features for product development across multiple milestones using a specific project management methodology (for example, Extreme or Agile project management). The SDLC we described is often iterated across multiple milestones until the product is ready to be released. There are, obviously, permutations of this SDLC depending on what type of product you're releasing (for example, a web-based product will release on quicker iterations than a desktop application), but there are a lot of moving parts. The key, then, to this process is starting off correctly; that is, absolutely, entirely understanding and clearly enumerating your requirements. Teams should be dedicating as much time and as many resources as possible up front in the planning process to ensure that the requirements are both accurate and complete.

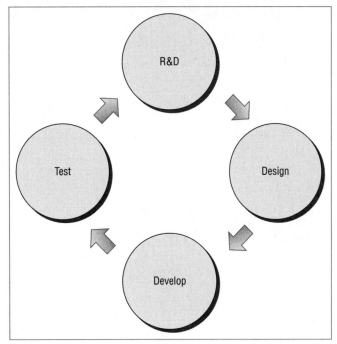

Figure 2-2

How does all of this apply to the OBA solution patterns, you ask? As we pointed out in the preceding paragraph, it's important for you to get the requirements right, and the solution patterns can help you accomplish this. They can do this mainly through taking your list of requirements and applying them to the different patterns to see what architecture is possible for your OBA, to understand the technical boundaries of your requirements, and to determine what technologies are available for you to design your OBA solution. This means that you will primarily consume the patterns during the Research and Development and Design phases. Figure 2-3 illustrates this mapping. Although it is during the Research and Development and Design phases that your interaction with the patterns will be higher, you can use these patterns as reference points throughout the SDLC.

Now that we've talked about where you would apply the OBA solution patterns, we next explain our core sales forecast scenario and requirements, and apply the solution patterns to them to understand the practical application of the patterns.

The Sales Forecasting Scenario

The main scenario that will drive all of the software development discussion throughout this book (walking you through how to code, deploy, secure, and maintain your OBA solution) is a sales forecasting scenario. Sales are important. A company needs to sell its products in order to ensure its long-term survival. Furthermore, the forecasting process is not typically done in isolation; you create forecasts that map to a broader goal with multiple team members contributing to that process. Therefore, our OBA solution will be designed to help a team of salespeople create a forecast for their accounts based on historical sales data and will involve a review and approval process. So, what are the specific requirements that map to this scenario?

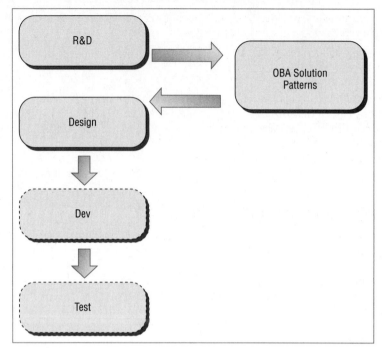

Figure 2-3

As discussed previously, the requirements are the most important part of a software development project because they give you a clear place to begin all other work. For the sales forecast solution described in the preceding paragraph, requirements would, in reality, likely be many; however, to keep things simple for the purposes of this book, we'll enumerate a number of key, higher-level requirements. These requirements are listed as follows:

1. The solution must show both historical and forecast data so salespeople can provide accurate forecasts.

2. The solution must have the ability to provide calculations for forecasting next fiscal year sales so salespeople can adjust their forecasts accordingly.

3. The solution must provide a variety of business intelligence views that show relevant sales forecast metrics.

4. All sales data must be centrally managed.

5. The solution must allow for read/write accessibility to the centrally stored data.

6. The solution must support chart creation to show historical and forecast data side-by-side.

7. There must be an approval process that allows a manager to approve, reject, or request amendments that is managed by the solution.

8. This approval process must use a notification process to ensure managers know when to approve the forecast.

9. The solution must create a roll-up view of forecasts for executive management.

10. The solution must be integrated with the organizational SharePoint site to support web-based collaboration.

11. The solution must be able to search and index sales data and company information from the LOB system.

Well, you're probably starting to get the point. In reality, the requirements list would be longer and there would be detailed descriptions (for example, we'd want to have permissions requirements, or data management requirements, maybe more detailed specifications around the management views and the notifications elements, and so on) that would accompany each of the requirements, but for the sake of getting you through this book efficiently, use these as your requirements list and then use the OBA solution patterns to create a design.

Applying the OBA Solution Patterns

Given the requirements, the next thing you need to do is to take a look at the existing OBA solution patterns and figure out which one of those patterns you will actually use.

If you look at the patterns, you may realize that your requirements cut across more than one pattern. For example, you could potentially use a number of the OBA solution patterns to help describe the design of your solution:

❑ OBA Application as a Reach Channel (Direct Integration)

❑ Document Integration

❑ Composite User Interface

❑ Complementary Document Workflow

❑ Discovery Navigation

❑ Collaborative Site

❑ Application Generated Tasks and Notifications

In fact, when you list them, it appears that in some way all of the patterns could be used to describe the design of your solution. You're probably asking yourself: is this normal?

It is normal for more than one pattern to be used in a solution, however, we're going to create a very comprehensive OBA solution to show you how you can leverage many of the features of the OBA Framework to build an OBA. It stands to reason that, because we're going to show you many different features, most if not all of the patterns should be covered *at some depth* in your design. The implication here is that for your solutions the application of the OBA solution patterns would be simpler and not necessarily apply more than one of the solution patterns listed previously. For example, if your OBA solution only requires a smart-client (that is, an Excel 2007 customization) integration with a LOB system, then you'll only need the OBA Application as a Reach Channel pattern. One way you might approach a solution design that involves multiple patterns is to break up the development of your features across the different patterns, and thus break up the specification process across multiple feature areas.

The first step in this process is to map the requirements to the patterns. Table 2-2 provides us with two columns; the first enumerates the patterns that are relevant to our OBA solution, and the second maps those patterns to the relevant requirements. The thought process behind this step is that you've taken a look at the solution patterns and having digested the patterns you now have some idea of how they would apply to your requirements. And what this really means is that you've begun to conceptualize your design. This step is not only an interesting design conceptualization exercise, but it can also manifest as a section in your technical specifications as a way to provide a template approach to the designing of your solution.

Table 2-2: Mapping OBA Solution Patterns to Requirements

Patterns	Relevant Requirements
OBA Application as a Reach Channel (Direct Integration)	Solution must show both historical and forecast data so salespeople can provide accurate forecasts. Solution must have the ability to provide calculations for forecasting next fiscal year sales so salespeople can adjust their forecasts accordingly. The solution must support chart creation to show historical and forecast data side-by-side. The solution must create a roll-up view of forecasts for executive management.
Document Integration	All sales data must be centrally managed. The solution must allow for read/write accessibility to the centrally stored data.
Composite User Interface	The solution must be integrated with the organizational SharePoint site to support web-based collaboration.
Complementary Document Workflow	There must be an approval process that allows a manager to either approve, reject, or request amendments that is managed by the solution.
Discovery Navigation	The solution must be able to search and index sales data and information from the LOB system.
Collaborative Site	The solution must be integrated with the organizational SharePoint site to support web-based collaboration.
Application Generated Tasks and Notification	This approval process must use a notification process to ensure managers know when to approve the forecast.

Having finished this table, you (and your team) would now have a sense for what patterns apply to what requirements, and vice versa. The next thing to do is to evaluate what technologies could be used to create your solution. This is likely one of a few steps toward creating an overarching architecture for the solution. Keep in mind that we are simplifying things for the purposes of illustration. In reality, you would not be evaluating just technologies, but also security protocols, scalability, technology evolution, and so on. Within this process, though, *should* be the consideration of these requirements against an existing environment (or the environment that the organization will be upgrading to in the near future). For example, in our fictional scenario, we know that the organization has recently updated to Office Professional 2007 and MOSS 2007 is also a part of the organizational infrastructure. We also know that Outlook 2007 is the predominant tool used for messaging in the organization. The organization is also on Windows Vista. Therefore, all of these need to be considered in the approach to building and designing the architecture. In summary, here's what we know about our end-user application infrastructure:

1. Windows Vista (Enterprise)

2. Office Professional 2007 is being used, which includes Access 2007, Accounting Express 2007, Excel 2007, Outlook 2007 with Contact Manager, PowerPoint 2007, Publisher 2007, and Word 2007

3. MOSS 2007 (Enterprise Edition)

The reason we ask ourselves about the existing infrastructure is because knowing the why and what of OBAs tells us what of the existing Office infrastructure we want to leverage, so we don't have to re-create custom logic that already exists within our core end-user toolset; for example, re-creating charting or analytics functionality that exists within Microsoft Excel.

Now that we've mapped requirements to the patterns and understand the current end-user environment, the next step is to understand what technologies can be used in the development process (as proposed by the patterns). This is something you've already seen (see Table 2-1), however, we'll list them here again as a part of the process:

- ❏ OBA Application as a Reach Channel
  - ❏ VSTO, MOSS 2007, and BDC
- ❏ Document Integration
  - ❏ OpenXML, VSTO, and BDC
- ❏ Composite User Interface
  - ❏ VSTO, Web Parts, BDC, Excel Services, and Key Performance Indicators (KPIs)
- ❏ Complementary Document Workflow
  - ❏ Windows Workflow Foundation (WF), SharePoint Storage, BDC, and VSTO
- ❏ Discovery Navigation
  - ❏ Enterprise Search and BDC
- ❏ Collaborative Site
  - ❏ Windows SharePoint Services (WSS), Blogs, Wikis, MySites, Profile, Colleague Web Part, Unified Presence, and InfoPath Forms Services
- ❏ Application Generated Tasks and Notifications
  - ❏ Outlook 2007/MOSS 2007 and VSTO

With these, we have a better sense for what technologies we can use in the design of our solution. The connection we need to make here is between the existing infrastructure and the technologies that we can use to build the OBA solution. Because you've read about the OBA solution patterns at this point, you know you can extend many of the Office applications that are within your end-user environment. To leverage this environment, you decide to use Excel 2007, Word 2007, and Outlook 2007, along with MOSS 2007 as a part of the overall solution design. The decision that remains now is to figure out how to extend them. To help make this clearer, Table 2-3 re-creates Table 2-2 with an additional column that enumerates the technologies we'll use and how we'll use them.

Table 2-3: Suggested Technologies

Patterns	Relevant Requirements	Technologies
OBA Application as a Reach Channel (Direct Integration)	Solution must show both historical and forecast data so salespeople can provide accurate forecasts.	VSTO: Use to extend Excel 2007 to create data management console and leverage charting and calculation features.
	Solution must have the ability to provide calculations for forecasting next fiscal year sales so salespeople can adjust their forecasts accordingly.	VSTO: To create workflow to tie Excel 2007 custom document to MOSS 2007.
	The solution must support chart creation to show historical and forecast data side-by-side.	
Document Integration	All sales data must be centrally managed.	VSTO: Custom extension will manage data view and enable user to edit/update data in Excel 2007 to central data source. (Note this is our LOB system for our OBA solution.)
	The solution must allow for read/write accessibility to the centrally stored data.	
	The solution must create a roll-up view of forecasts for executive management.	OpenXML: To parse data out of Excel 2007 document and create a Word 2007 document with relevant information in it.
Composite User Interface	The solution must be integrated with the organizational SharePoint site to support web-based collaboration.	MOSS 2007: This will be the sales forecast site, where we'll have the business intelligence views and sites for document management, collaboration, and search.
	Solution must provide a variety of business intelligence views that show relevant sales forecast metrics.	BDC/Excel Services/KPIs: Use these as main entry-points for the business intelligence views.
Complementary Document Workflow	There must be an approval process that allows a manager to approve, reject, or request amendments that is managed by the solution.	VSTO: To create the workflow and tie to Excel 2007 document for approval workflow.
		MOSS 2007: To tie the document to SharePoint so workflow can be triggered from SharePoint or from document.

Table 2-3: Suggested Technologies *(continued)*

Patterns	Relevant Requirements	Technologies
Discovery Navigation	The solution must be able to search and index sales data and information from the LOB system.	MOSS 2007: To provide the search functionality for the portal (for example, documents and so on). BDC: To provide the searchability into the LOB system.
Collaborative Site	The solution must be integrated with the organizational Share-Point site to support web-based collaboration.	MOSS 2007: Use it for the sites and web-based interface into the LOB system data.
Application Generated Tasks and Notifications	This approval process must use a notification process to ensure managers know when to approve the forecast.	Outlook 2007: Communication infrastructure for the workflow messaging. MOSS 2007: Use the SharePoint workflow infrastructure for the workflow and notifications. VSTO: To create the workflow and tie to Excel 2007 customized document.

With Table 2-3 complete, you can see how this sales forecast solution design is beginning to take shape. Again, you'd likely take deeper steps within this process, but how you would get there, at a high level, would be very similar. Now that you have the table, what do you do next?

Table 2-3 provides us with the connection point between the end-user technologies we want to leverage and the technologies that we're going to be using to build our solution. This helps us in two ways:

1. It will help us determine what the architecture of our sales forecast solution will look like; and

2. It will help us create a development environment for our solution development.

For the first item, we have enough information to create a high-level architecture. For example, we know that we're going to have both a smart-client and web-based (MOSS) view into the LOB system. We know that we're going to have some business intelligence views within MOSS that are built using Excel Services, the BDC, and KPIs. We know that we're going to have workflow that will manage an approval process for the sales forecast document across subordinate and management. Last, we know that we're going to be using Outlook and MOSS to marshal/manage the workflow communication process. How do we put this together?

Putting the architecture together will require some knowledge of the ways in which these solution pieces will work together. For example, you would need to know that SharePoint workflow must be tied to an allowable object of some sort, in this case, a custom document, or that the BDC requires different application definitions to support search or to support a summary/detail view of the data. These are obviously things you would learn in researching the technologies (all of which you will learn throughout this book). That said, assume you've now finished with reading this book and are fully prepared to create your own OBA solution. You'd likely create an architecture that looked something like Figure 2-4.

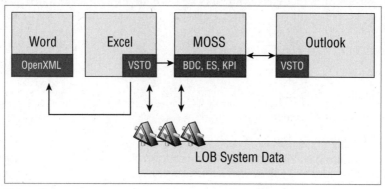

Figure 2-4

You'll note that in this high-level architecture, you have all of the end-user applications represented in some fashion as well as the technologies you've derived from the OBA solution patterns (and further explicated in your mapping of the requirements to the patterns).

> *We've represented the preceding integration with the LOB System data as managed by a Web service. In the solution in this book, we've leveraged the AdventureWorks database to keep things straightforward. Therefore, there is no need for a service proxy. We will, however, discuss service integration throughout this book.*

This is a fairly high-level architecture. In reality, you would go into much greater detail within the application architecture when going through this process. For the purposes of this book, all that we've discussed so far gives you an idea of the process you would go through, as well as how you could incorporate the OBA solution patterns as a part of that process. The rest of this book will derive from this architecture and drill into each piece in greater detail, talking at the feature and code levels. Thus, in each of the areas you'll understand how they work, and how you would use a particular technology to create that part of the solution.

At this point, the OBA solution patterns have pretty much served their purpose: they've helped you in the initial Research and Design phase in the SDLC and given you an understanding as to your options for how you will go about building your OBA solution. As a last step in this process, put together the development environment that will map to the OBA solution architecture. This will not only help you in mapping development environment design to the patterns (as a theoretical exercise), but also help you set up your environment so you can begin coding along with this book.

Development Environment

Given what we've discussed in this chapter, you would need to install a number of applications to set up the environment to build out the OBA solution displayed in Figure 2-4. The following provides a list of requirements. Note that they are listed in a recommended installation order:

1. Windows Server 2003 with Service Pack 2 (required for MOSS 2007)

2. Office 2007 Professional Edition

3. Microsoft SQL Server 2005

4. AdventureWorks sample database (our LOB system)

5. SQL Server Management Studio

6. .NET Framework 2.0 and 3.5

7. Visual Studio 2008 Professional Edition (which includes VSTO 3.0)

8. Office Primary Interop Assemblies (which should be installed as part of the Visual Studio 2008 installation)

9. Microsoft Office SharePoint Server (which requires ASP.NET 2.0)

10. Microsoft Office SharePoint Server SDK

11. Microsoft Business Data Catalog Definition Editor (setup files are included in the MOSS SDK, but you'll need to install it after you've installed the SDK)

You can also install the following applications as optional applications:

1. Visual Studio 2005 Team System

2. Visual Studio Tools for Office 2005 SE (design-time and runtime bits)

3. Expression Blend (for designers to create enhanced UI)

After you have your developer environment set up, you'll be ready to begin coding along with this book. If you just want to read along to learn how to do some of the things we discuss in this book without installing the prerequisite environment, that's fine too.

Summary

In this chapter, we first introduced you to the OBA solution patterns and the SDLC. We then walked you through how you could use the patterns in your own solution design by applying the patterns to the sales forecast scenario, the core scenario that lays the groundwork for the application design throughout this book, in the context of the SDLC. In doing this, we covered a number of steps that took you from the requirements generation stage, to the mapping of those requirements to the patterns, to understanding the end-user environment and what technologies could be leveraged within that environment, to the ultimate generation of an architecture for the sales forecast solution. Out of that architecture also fell the knowledge of our development environment.

It's important to remember that you'll likely be operating at a much lower level in reality; however, the process outlined in this chapter is quite important in the software development process, and the OBA solution patterns are quite useful. Getting the requirements right and understanding what technologies you're going to use in a solution design is vital to the success of the project.

Further Reading

❑   OBA Solution Patterns Article: `http://msdn2.microsoft.com/en-us/library/bb614541.aspx`

❑   Install Office SharePoint Server on a Standalone Computer: `http://technet.microsoft.com/en-us/library/cc263202.aspx`

❑   Expression Blend: `http://www.microsoft.com/expression/products/overview.aspx?key+blend`

3

Installing and Configuring MOSS

This chapter looks at configuring your Windows Server 2003 server, setting up MOSS on that server, and creating the necessary accounts for the sales forecast OBA. The goal of this chapter is to focus on helping you set up an environment where you can get the sales forecast OBA operational. To this end, the chapter is broken out in the following main topic areas:

❑ Baseline and optional server setup

❑ Installing and configuring MOSS

❑ Setting up user accounts

❑ Installing the business application database

Setting up a complete environment isn't something that is covered in a single chapter of any book for a load-balanced public-facing MOSS installation. This chapter contains elements that, to an experienced IT professional, may already be familiar. To someone new to SharePoint, however, and for certain specific characteristics of the sales forecast OBA environment, this chapter provides the necessary knowledge. The narrative as a whole targets an IT professional or developer who is setting up an environment in which they can leverage the sales forecast OBA components and the knowledge gained by re-creating the core environment that hosts these components.

As a result, how to create a load-balanced set of web sites that leverage a separate SQL Server cluster as well as how to handle permissions outside of the local intranet are beyond the planned scope of this chapter. On the other hand, setting up a combined domain controller, SQL Server, and MOSS host machine that will potentially also be installed with the Office client tools and Visual Studio 2008 is the target.

Baseline Server Setup

Because the goal is to create a single server, that server needs to fulfill several different roles. For starters, your environment needs to have ASP.NET 2.0 installed and enabled. Additionally, all of the steps in this chapter will be executed while logged-in using the built-in Administrator account. Although this installation could be spread across several independent servers, this chapter addresses the scenario of using only a single server instance to host both MOSS and Active Directory. The targeted environment is great for creating either a single or shared development environment. The setup is appropriate for a Virtual PC and it is recommended that the server have or be granted about 2GB of memory.

Ideally, a "production" quality deployment would include several servers. At the level where servers were seeing enough load, the most likely typical deployment would include a domain controller that might or might not also be the local DNS server for members of the domain. There would be a database server that would host the company business application data and that would also be used for the MOSS databases. MOSS would be installed either on a dedicated web server or as part of a larger web farm, and some of its key services might be deployed across different physical servers. Finally, there would most likely be a Microsoft Exchange server and possibly an Office Communications Server 2007, each of which would be installed on their own server. In fact, you should not attempt to install Microsoft Exchange, Office Communications Server 2007, and MOSS on a single server, given that all three want to control Port 80 on their host machine. Obviously, for an enterprise production environment, where scalability is required, having these services on the same server is suicidal, but even for a developer environment, attempting to co-host these server applications can lead to an overburdened server due to memory and processor requirements even before you add in Visual Studio and the Office client tools. The sales forecast OBA environment omits both Office Communications Server 2007 and Microsoft Exchange, and, instead, we are simply relying on the built-in capabilities of Windows Server 2003 to support POP and SMTP mail services.

The sales forecast OBA was built to refer to a MOSS server on a server named MOSS. This server is also the domain controller for the LitwareInc.com domain. This means that before you start customizing the server, you'll want to ensure that the machine name is correct, and, ideally, that you can assign the machine a fixed IP address on your local network. This fixed IP address will allow the machine to refer to itself correctly as a Domain Name Server. Any other client machines you choose to add for testing and demonstration purposes will eventually need to list the domain controller's DNS services as its primary DNS service.

The server needs to be configured as (what Windows Server 2003 refers to as) an Application Server. The easiest way to do this is to leverage the built-in Manage Your Server wizard that is shown in Figure 3-1. Each page of the wizard walks you through the necessary steps to set up your server.

Figure 3-1 shows that this server has been configured with four roles, the first of which is the Application Server role. Next it shows that the server has been configured as a Mail Server. When you are configuring these roles, the Mail Server role should be the last role configured. The remaining two roles, Domain Controller and DNS Server, will be installed simultaneously if you select the Domain Controller role.

We recommend installing these roles in the following order, after you have installed a baseline instance of Windows Server 2003, and fully patched this server using Windows Update:

❑   Domain Controller, which will also install the DNS Server role

❑   Application Server

❑   Mail Server

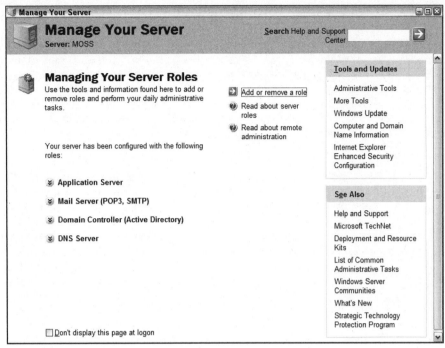

Figure 3-1

The Mail Server is the only role that is truly dependent in the preceding list, in that the authentication method selected during installation needs to refer to the domain's Active Directory services. If Active Directory, which is part of the Domain Controller role, has not been installed, the Mail Server can't refer to this model and throws errors related to authentication. The good news is that, if you do install these in the wrong order, you can simply uninstall the Mail Server role and then reinstall that role. You don't need to undo the Domain Controller or rebuild the server from scratch.

You are not adding the SharePoint role that is part of Windows Server 2003.

The sales forecast OBA can be set up on a single server implementing these roles. The most common use for this configuration is for a developer workstation. In addition to the server roles described, you will want to install a complete copy of the Office client tools including Word, Outlook, Excel, and InfoPath. After installing the Office applications, you should consider installing Visual Studio 2008. We have done the installation where MOSS was installed and configured and then the client tools and vice versa. You need to install Visual Studio 2008 either prior to MOSS or only after you have fully installed and configured MOSS. MOSS will, during the installation process, turn off your existing default web site on Port 80 and install a new web site. Until you have finished the instructions in the following section to limit this site's name resolution, and restored your original default web site, installing Visual Studio 2008's ASP. NET capabilities will conflict with MOSS. Finally, as you'll see when we discuss the MOSS installation, you should run Windows Update to ensure that the latest patches are installed.

Installing the MOSS Binaries

This section demonstrates installing MOSS 2007 from the MSDN materials. Figure 3-2 shows the installation source from the MSDN DVD. To initiate the installation of MOSS you simply click the setup.cmd file. This file will first check for key dependencies in your server configuration so that they can be resolved prior to installation.

For example, one error that may occur if you are installing MOSS without having installed Visual Studio 2008 is shown in Figure 3-3. Essentially, the settings associated with IIS are not configured to support ASP.NET 2.0. Fortunately, resolving this minor issue is simple.

You can leave this message box on the screen while you resolve the problem, or close it. Either way, once you have resolved this problem you will need to restart the installation. Access the Start menu, go to Administrative Tools, and open the Internet Information Services (IIS) Manager shown in Figure 3-4.

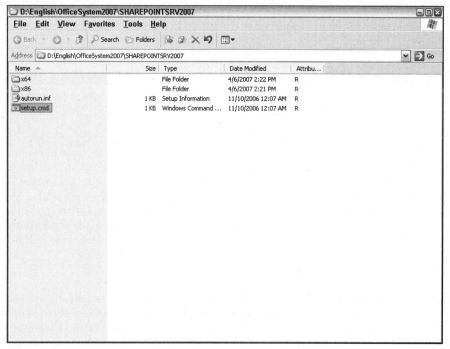

Figure 3-2

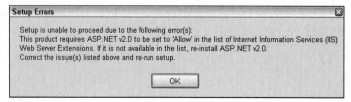

Figure 3-3

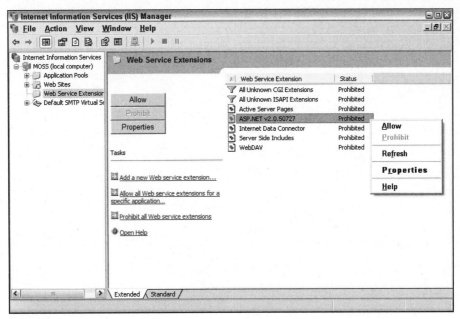

Figure 3-4

From this window you'll need to refer to the Web Service Extensions section and change the status of the ASP.NET v2.0.50727 to Allow, as shown in Figure 3-4. As noted, this type of issue is similar to a missing prerequisite, which is easily resolved. Once resolved, you'll simply restart the installation process as shown previously.

Once the actual installation wizard starts, you'll be presented with a dialog asking for your license key. This dialog isn't shown, nor is the dialog that occurs immediately following that one asking you to accept the licensing agreement. These dialogs don't actually present decision points, however the third step in the installation dialogs allows for a single choice. Figure 3-5 shows that your first choice in the MOSS installation is either to create a basic single server standalone or use the Advanced button.

The basic option will automatically configure your installation on a single server; however, it expects a standalone server. We are installing as part of a domain and though we have a single server, it is a domain server and using the Advanced button is the correct choice. The Advanced button allows for follow-on choices. Our goal isn't to cover every possible choice in this wizard, but to ensure that you can understand these first few choices. You'll see that in Figure 3-6 we've highlighted the Stand-alone choice. This is based on the idea that we are going to create a single server focused on a developer solution, or shared development environment.

In a production scenario, even if we only wanted to stand up a single server as part of the current installation, we would still select the Complete option. By selecting the Complete option you are presented with several alternatives as you proceed through the setup process.

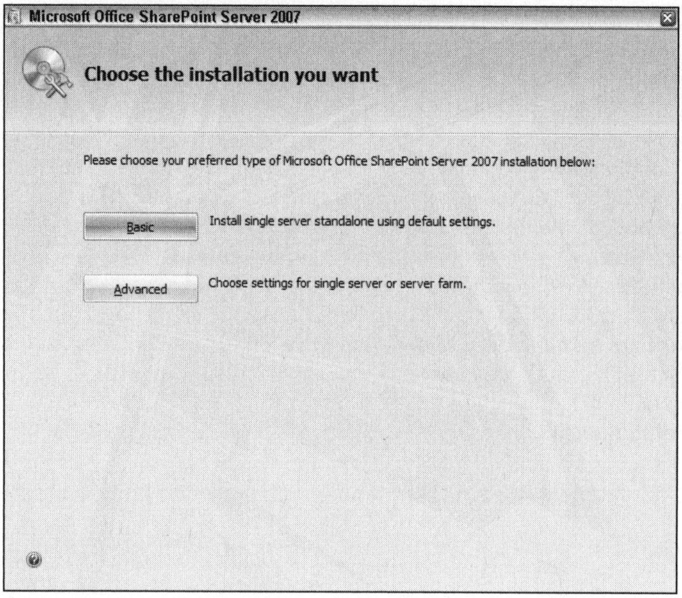

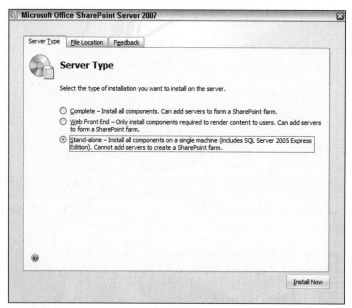

Figure 3-5

Figure 3-6

For example, by selecting the Complete option shown in Figure 3-6, you have the option to identify a local or remote database server. With the Stand-alone option, as noted in the text that accompanies the option, MOSS is bound to the local SQL Server 2005 Express database. Even though this portion of the installation is focused on just copying the associated binary data for your site, this selection will determine the expandability of the resulting MOSS installation. Using Complete gives you many more options in your production environment; however, for a machine targeting your development environment, selecting the single server installation simplifies the process.

If you do want to leverage a local or even remote instance of SQL Server, you should select the Complete option. This option will allow you to connect to a remote database. The settings involved include a custom account for your configuration database and the ability to select the port used for your administration site. These actions are outside the focus of this chapter.

As you can see in Figure 3-7, selecting the Stand-alone server option installs the MOSS binaries and then takes you to an installation complete screen. That's it. The files associated with running MOSS and with SQL Server Express have been installed onto your local server. You are not yet finished with the installation. The first installer only copies the necessary binary files from the DVD onto your local hard drive. Next, you need to initiate the actual configuration of MOSS. Fortunately, the checkbox shown in Figure 3-7 will automatically take you directly into that process.

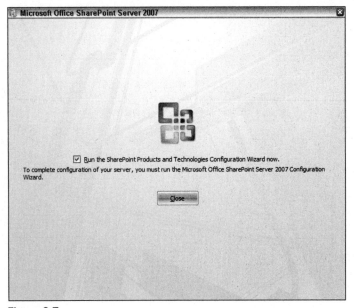

Figure 3-7

You can uncheck that checkbox and use the Start menu to access the Configuration Wizard later, after a restart or some other interruption. However, for this installation, continuing from this point into the Configuration Wizard is recommended.

Configuring MOSS

Installing the MOSS binaries doesn't actually leave your system ready to run MOSS. Configuring a system to run MOSS requires a set of databases that need to be generated based on your machine's settings. Additionally, changes need to be made to your IIS settings, and various services related to things like search and indexing need to be initiated and configured. Fortunately, MOSS ships with the Configuration Wizard, a tool that handles the default configuration automatically.

By default, the MOSS installation will run the Configuration Wizard upon completion of the installation, regardless of which type of installation you select. Typically, this is the recommended solution, however the Configuration Wizard is one of the installed binaries. As a result, the Configuration Wizard remains available after the initial installation completes and can, at a future date, be rerun. In fact, the ability to return to this wizard is a significant advantage over having the configuration separate from the installation.

Figure 3-8 illustrates the startup screen for this wizard. As is typical for most installation wizards, it doesn't really provide much information. Starting the wizard displays the informational message box shown in Figure 3-9, which might have just as easily been presented on that first wizard page. The warning is your first indication of what the configuration process is going to adjust. Note that it lists three services, two of which, as you would expect, are SharePoint related.

The other IIS should also come as no surprise. If you were installing MOSS on a production web site with other existing web applications, it would be important to be aware that the service provided by these applications would be interrupted, even if only briefly during that restart. In the case of this installation, that isn't a problem. In fact, a larger concern, which isn't mentioned in the warning, is that the Configuration Wizard is about to modify your IIS settings in such a way that MOSS will become the primary default web application on your server, a situation that you will need to address after the Configuration Wizard completes.

Figure 3-8

Figure 3-9

The Configuration Wizard itself goes through a series of steps, which are not going to be recorded here. It should be noted, however, that the same configuration steps that are automated by the wizard can be run from the command line. Running them from the command line allows you to customize the parameters to each of the individual configuration tasks, but also requires that you call the command-line tool once for each of the configuration categories. The tool's real value is that it allows you to reconfigure a portion of your MOSS installation without rerunning the entire wizard. The command-line tool is `PSConfig.exe`. It is installed as part of the installation process and is typically located in your `Program Files\Microsoft Shared\web server extensions\12\bin` folder. Typing `psconfig.exe ?` at the command line will retrieve additional help, and MSDN contains additional documentation on using this tool.

Given that you need to complete the initial configuration using the Configuration Wizard, it makes sense to allow it to automate the updates for everything from IIS through registry settings and SQL Server databases. The process takes a little while, and requires no interaction from you. It is possible that something might go wrong, but we haven't seen that occur since the Beta.

Figure 3-10 illustrates the next screen in which you'll take action. Yes, it is something of a joke in that you only click Finish, but that's not why the screen is included. It is included because you need to read the message carefully. For starters, it lets you know that when you click Finish, it is going to attempt to open your newly installed site. Next, it warns you that you'll be prompted for a username, and because the only valid user is the one you are currently signed in as, you'll need that account to access the site. Finally, it mentions off-handedly that you will be prompted to add the site to the list of trusted sites.

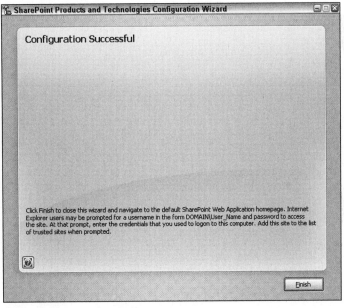

Figure 3-10

Depending on your security settings, you may not be prompted to add your site to the list of trusted sites. On the surface your site might open without an issue, that is, until you attempt to access something like the Site Settings, and they don't work. The key is, whether you are prompted, you'll need to add the site to the list of trusted sites.

In theory, the first thing that should happen when you click the Finish button is that Internet Explorer should open and prompt you for credentials. Once you have been successfully validated, you should receive a screen that looks similar to the one shown in Figure 3-11. This page is the site default whether you have used the fully qualified site name http://MOSS.litwareinc.com, just the machine name http://MOSS, or the IP address you assigned to your local machine.

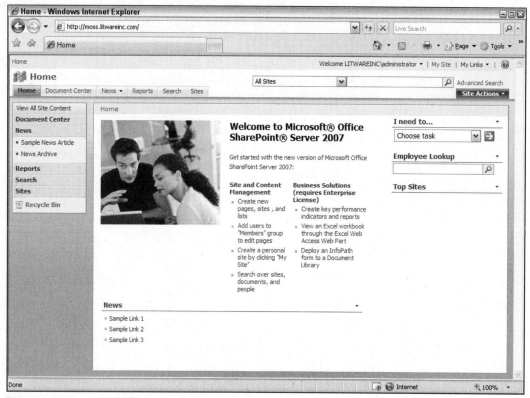

Figure 3-11

Handling an Unplanned Error

To paraphrase George Carlin in a routine that was called "Picky Eater" — Is there a picture of that in the cookbook? I bet it don't look like that. Though Figure 3-11 shows what should happen — we've all been there — your screen looks nothing like Figure 3-11. In fact, after you sign in, instead of being taken to a nice looking page, your browser throws up an ugly configuration error, similar to the one shown in Figure 3-12. Perhaps its time to roll everything back and start over... on second thought, don't.

The problem here is that, by default, when you install MOSS, it is configured with the settings that you would use in a production environment. Best practice in a live environment is not to return to the anonymous public at large details related to what has gone wrong on your web site. After all, one of the first steps in trying to figure out how to hack a site is to get it to throw an error.

Therefore, the default configuration for your new MOSS site does not return details related to any errors that occur on the server. It doesn't matter that you are local, because, in theory, in a production environment, someone might be spoofing that they are coming from a local browser. When an error occurs, MOSS makes one concession. If it thinks you are local, it lets you know how to get to the information you need. If you are only pretending to be local, this doesn't much help you.

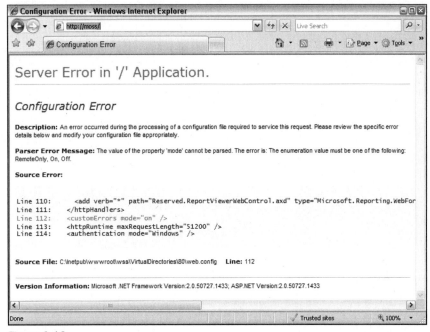

Figure 3-12

Figure 3-12 shows the default error screen that may be presented. This isn't actually your error. This screen tells you exactly where the `web.config` file you need to modify is located on the local machine. You need to modify the `web.config` in order to discover the actual error. Note that MOSS leverages actual configuration files located in folders that, by default, are assigned by port number. The item to change is on line 112 of your configuration file, and all you need to do is change the value of "on" to "RemoteOnly."

In the case of the preceding screen, we forced this error by going to the `C:\Windows\Microsoft.NET` folder and denying all access to this folder by the Network Service account. This caused an error, and once the value of the `customErrors` setting was set to RemoteOnly in the `web.config` file it was easy to see the simpler permissions issue. In all likelihood, if you receive a screen similar to Figure 3-12 following installation and configuration of MOSS on your server the issue will be relatively simple; just take a few minutes to get the details and resolve the problem.

Even if you don't have an error the first time you run your MOSS site, if you are configuring a server for use by a developer or tester, you still should make this change. In either scenario, you will want to have access to the details of errors that are occurring on your server. As a result, even if you didn't get the error, I still advise you to navigate to your default web site location, open the web.config file, and update the customErrors setting.

Customizing the Installation

Returning to the expected sequence of events, you have the default home page for your new MOSS site open in the browser. If you are not already familiar with MOSS, one thing you will notice as you make various configuration changes to your site is the importance of the Site Actions button. You can see it in Figure 3-11 in the upper-right corner. However, if your site isn't listed in the trusted sites list for your system that button won't actually do anything.

To get to the trusted sites list, use the Tools menu and select the Internet Options item. Within the Internet Options dialog (not shown), select the Security tab, and then select the Trusted Sites icon, which will enable the Sites button that is used to open the Trusted Sites dialog. Figure 3-13 shows the Trusted Sites dialog. The operation of the dialog is simple: type a URL of interest in the text box and use the Add button to add that URL to the list of sites you trust. In this case you need to add two entries to this list.

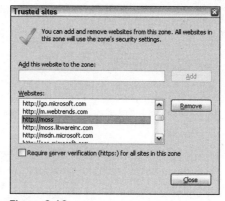

Figure 3-13

The first entry to add is `http://MOSS`, which represents a current URL associated with your web site. In fact, if you navigate away from your current default page, you'll find that this is the default address of your installed MOSS application on this machine. This is also reflected in Figure 3-14, where you'll see that the settings page currently refers to a site URL of "MOSS."

You need to add a second entry for `http://MOSS.litwareinc.com` to this list. Though your site is currently set as the default mapping for both of these URLs, later in this chapter you will change your free default machine name and other mappings and have MOSS mapped only to the fully qualified domain name. This will allow you to configure the settings necessary to support having a custom Web service running on the same machine. Similarly, Visual Studio 2008 will look to leverage the default web site when creating web projects that rely on IIS, and making this change will open that capability.

Once you have added both URLs to your list of trusted sites, you can close the dialogs and then close Internet Explorer so the settings will take effect. Returning to the home page for your MOSS site, you can click the Site Actions button from your default page and from that menu select Site Settings ➪ Modify All Site Settings as shown in Figure 3-14.

This action will take you to your second home for the MOSS configuration process. The Site Settings page shown in Figure 3-15 provides access to most of the main areas to look at when configuring your site. You are going to start by examining some of the minor issues that need to be resolved with your first visit to this page. The first item to note is that the title of your site is "Home." This really isn't an acceptable title, so to get a feel for modifying some of the settings on this page you will update this to Litware Inc. Additionally, just to jumpstart your site to a different look and feel, you are going to change the master page associated with your site.

Figure 3-14

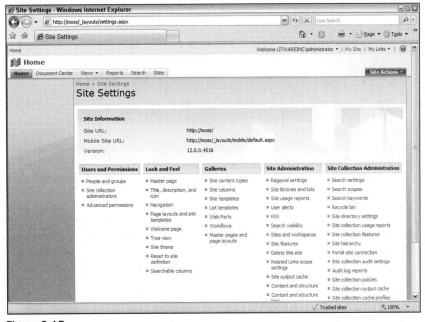

Figure 3-15

The second item to notice is the version. Version 12.0.0.4518 is an unpatched version of MOSS. Since SP1 has been released, one of the next steps is to change patch the server again. Finally, you'll note that the Site URL is currently set to `http://MOSS`, and as noted earlier, you want to change this to be the fully qualified domain name.

Notice that in the second column, Look and Feel, the second item down is the "Title, description, and icon" link. Clicking this link takes you to the page shown in Figure 3-16. This simple screen allows you to edit the title of your site, so instead of defaulting to Home, it can instead display Litware Inc., your corporate identity. There is also a logo image listed on this page; it currently links to the default `.gif` that ships with SharePoint. Yes, you can change this image; however, we suggest that you click the test link before working to change it. What you'll find is that perhaps the four people icon that you see on this screen isn't the icon you thought you would be editing. This icon is seen on many of the administrative pages, but does not actually appear in the default display, because it is replaced by the one referred to in the selected style sheet. You'll want to update the style sheet with your corporate logo.

The only change you need make on the screen shown in Figure 3-16 is the name of the site. If you want to change the appearance of your home page, then you want the top link at the top of the second column shown Figure 3-15. The Master page link allows you to apply a different look and feel to the pages that are displayed publicly as part of your site. Just as an aside, there is no matching figure, but we selected the BlueGlassBand.master pages and saved the changes. This change is visible Figure 3-16.

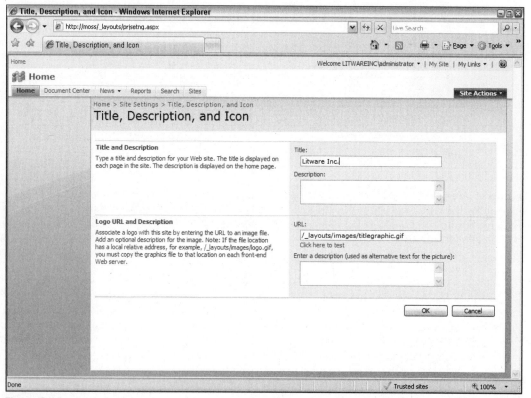

Figure 3-16

Having updated the page title and the master page, the next item of business would typically be to update the URL associated with the MOSS site. Because you need to exit the site itself to carry out this task, it makes a good time to access the Windows Update site. Checking Windows Update, you should find three patches of significance: one to the core SharePoint components that are part of Windows Server 2003, another to the components of Microsoft Office SharePoint Server (MOSS), and, finally, an update to SQL Server. These updates are pictured in Figure 3-17 and should all be installed, as well as any others that have been released since the writing of this chapter.

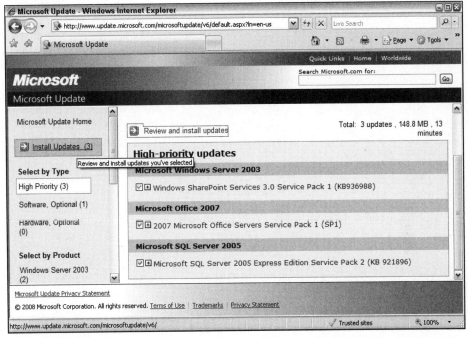

Figure 3-17

Because you have already tested the site, you know that it is working. If a problem were to occur after installing these patches you could, if needed, roll back the patches. Based on experience, however, these patches do not run the risk of breaking anything on your site. When you have installed the patches, change the default URL used by the site. MOSS and SharePoint essentially install three different web applications. In addition to the main site there is a site for administering Shared Services and a Central Administration site.

Both the Central Administration site and Shared Services site used ports that were randomly assigned during the installation process. Additionally, you can modify these settings after installation by applying the same steps you are going to use to update the default application URL. Though many site-related settings for MOSS are accessible from the Site Settings page within your application, many others are accessible only via these administrative sites. The Central Administration site is the key, because it contains a link to the Shared Services administration site, as shown in Figure 3-18.

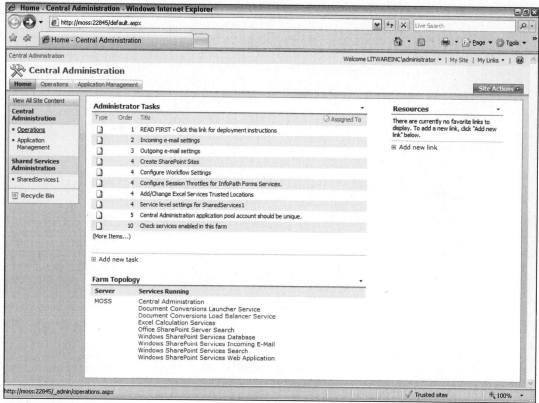

Figure 3-18

The Central Administration web site isn't one for which you need to guess at the URL or open the IIS Settings page to find. Instead, you'll find a link either on your Start menu or under the Office Servers section of the Start menu. Starting this site brings up the page shown in Figure 3-18. For the purposes of updating the URL associated with your MOSS site, the next step is to access the Operations page. The Operations page is shown in Figure 3-19.

This page contains several tasks related to managing components and the web environment associated with your MOSS installation. In this case, the only thing you want to do is change the default access mapping associated with your MOSS application. You can do this by accessing the Global Configuration section in the left column and selecting the "Alternate access mappings" link. Clicking this link opens the page shown in Figure 3-20.

Figure 3-20 displays all three of the MOSS sites that were created during the configuration process. The port numbers shown in Figure 3-20 will not match those created on your machine; they are randomly generated as part of the configuration process. The random generation isn't done to make it more difficult to locate these sites, but rather to make it more difficult for someone to create a simple script that just automatically attacked the SharePoint Central Administration port. Because each installation has a potentially different port for this purpose, it isn't possible for someone to drop an automated attack script on the web to attack a known port.

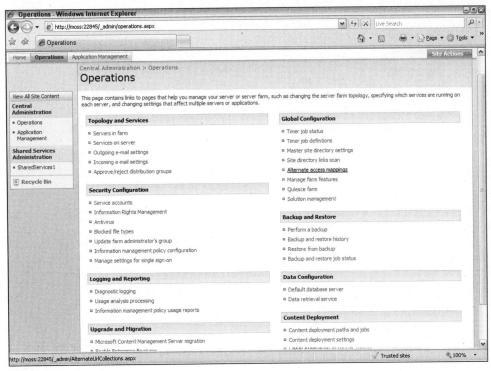

Figure 3-19

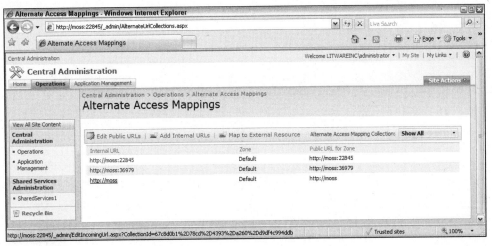

Figure 3-20

Within Figure 3-20, the only site you are interested in changing the mappings for is the MOSS site, so click the link for that site's configuration. This will take you to the page shown in Figure 3-21. The Edit Internal URLs page allows you to modify the root portion of the URL associated with your MOSS application. The site uses this value to be able to refer the browser correctly to links that might be difficult to express in a relative URL. For your purposes you simply need to update this URL to refer to the fully qualified domain name for your site, http://MOSS.litwareinc.com/.

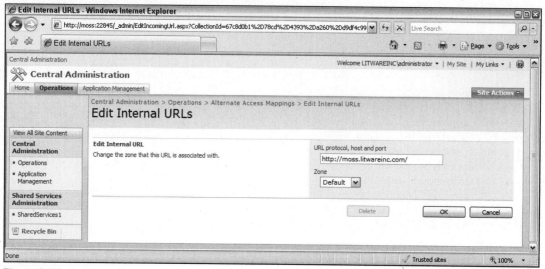

Figure 3-21

Once you have updated the URL value in this screen you can click OK. The Zone setting relates to the way the system handles security in terms of alternative authentication methods. For your purposes, the Default zone is the correct zone. After clicking OK, you can close this instance of the browser because the remaining configuration needs to be done from the IIS Manager. To open the IIS Manager, go to the Administrative Tools menu and select the Internet Information Services Manager from the menu. This opens the window shown in Figure 3-22.

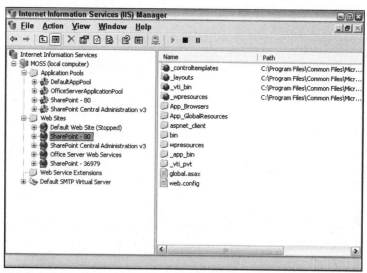

Figure 3-22

This dialog is reasonably straightforward, but you should take a second to notice what the installation of MOSS changed. This server originally had only a default web site; now you'll see there are three new application pools and four new web applications. Of these, we are most concerned with the first two web sites. The default web site has been stopped. It was stopped because it originally was used to handle all requests sent to the server on Port 80. SharePoint has taken over this role for the moment, which is why the site is labeled SharePoint-80.

You need to change when information is sent to the SharePoint web site so that only the fully qualified URLs `http://moss.litwareinc.com` are sent to this site. For example, requests made to `http://moss` should once again go to the default web site. To make this change, you need to open the properties for the SharePoint web site by right-clicking its entry in Figure 3-22.

This will open the SharePoint-80 Properties dialog shown in the background of Figure 3-23. The Advanced button, which is visible in Figure 3-23, is then used to access the Advanced Web Site Identification dialog. This dialog, shown in the foreground of Figure 3-23, allows you to control which ports, IP address, and host headers a given web site is forwarded. In Figure 3-23, you'll note that these settings indicate that the SharePoint site should accept any IP address requests that are received by this server on Port 80 for any host header or URL. Leaving the Host Header Value blank indicates that the site shouldn't screen based on a specific host header. Thus, you need to use the Edit button to open the Add/Edit Web Site Identification dialog shown in Figure 3-24.

Providing a host header value of `http://moss.litwareinc.com` in the text box of this web site indicates that it should only respond to http requests that use that fully qualified URL as part of the request. Therefore, a request to `http://moss` will not be handled by this web site. Instead, IIS will look for another handler for such requests.

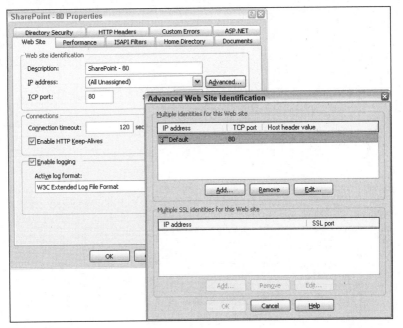

Figure 3-23

Figure 3-24

Implementing that other handler simply involves closing these dialogs to accept your changes, and, back in the IIS Manager window, right-clicking the Default Web Site and selecting Start. This will restart the default web site that has the settings that the SharePoint site previously had. Accordingly, it is now handling any requests on Port 80 that are not handled by another web site. Figure 3-25 shows the final state of the Internet Information Services Manager.

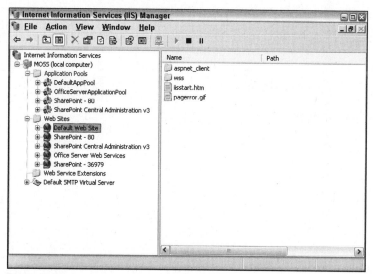

Figure 3-25

The final step in this process is testing the end result to ensure that the server is behaving as you expect. Open up Internet Explorer and attempt to access the http://moss site. Next, open a second instance of Internet Explorer and attempt to access the http://moss.litwareinc.com site. If your configuration is correct, the results in each browser should look similar to those shown in Figure 3-26.

Note that Figure 3-26 also displays the alternative template for the master page on the public-facing portion of the site. These templates provide the basis for configuring the look and feel of your site. Though it is possible to configure many portions of your site from within the tools provided by MOSS, if you want to change the elements of one of these style sheets you will need to work with either Visual Studio or the SharePoint Designer.

Redesigning the master pages and site elements isn't a focus of building the sales forecast OBA, so we aren't going to demonstrate working to make changes to the pages. The sales forecast OBA is often used on a site where the master page templates have been customized. Certainly, that is an appropriate task when setting up a new site. However, editing the pages does not change the behavior we are looking to leverage or add to the sales forecast OBA.

Figure 3-26

Now that you've reset MOSS to expect to refer internally to its fully qualified URL and have updated IIS so that it will route requests only for that fully qualified URL, you are ready technically to move forward with the configuration of your MOSS site. Before doing so, and setting up the appropriate folders to handle the sales forecasts and related documents, this is a good time to install the client tools, such as Office and Visual Studio, that you will eventually look to use on this site.

Additionally, we recommend that you set up one or more named users rather than using the domain administrator's account. This is good practice, because it is not uncommon to find that the default administrator who installed the software components has in fact inherited one or more permissions that you would otherwise need to assign. Going through the process of setting up these permissions, even on a development server, will help identify the steps necessary to set the appropriate permissions in your production environment.

Setting up the User Accounts

Typically, when thinking about adding users the reaction is to go to the Active Directory Users and Computers MMC and work from that interface. This allows you to add new users to the system. In the case of the sales forecast OBA, we want to ensure that each of our users has a valid email account. If we were using Exchange, we would add users via Exchange, which can create a new mailbox and a new user account in one easy step.

Although we aren't using Exchange, the same concept applies. From the Administrative Tools, as shown in Figure 3-27, you can access the MMC for the POP3 Service. This will open the MMC, which is not pictured, but which has a domain tree on the left side of the window. Expanding the domain tree, you will see your domain listed and will select your domain. On the right side of the display there will be a link to Add Mailbox. Clicking this link will open the window shown in Figure 3-28.

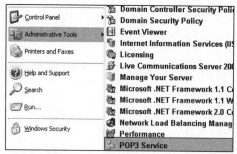

Figure 3-27

Figure 3-28 shows the Add Mailbox dialog with the information for Michael Blythe populated. The mailbox name will become the account name for this user. The checkbox labeled Create Associated User for this Mailbox indicates that, when this dialog is submitted, a new account in the `LitwareInc.com` domain will be created with the password provided. That pretty much covers it in terms of creating your user accounts. Each time you click OK, a confirmation box will be shown.

For our demonstrations we created users based on the names of the salespeople in the AdventureWorks database. For example, MBlythe is for Michael Blythe, and SJiang is for Steven Jiang. By using the names of the salespeople who were in our database, we were able to sign in as these users and attempt both to build and use the software.

In the case of Michael Blythe, his account was used to create the Sales Forecast Excel Spreadsheet, the XML Web service used to leverage OpenXML and generate Word documents on MOSS, and to create the custom Sales Forecast Approval Workflow. Steven Jiang, as the sales manager, was used as the account for creating the Sales Forecast Outlook Form Region. Because Steven was the primary consumer of the interface we worked with his account in creating it.

We later added additional accounts that had nothing to do with the creation of the custom OBA assemblies. These users, also salespeople from the AdventureWorks database, then became test accounts to ensure that the applications that worked from Visual Studio would also install and run correctly for users who weren't running Visual Studio. Additionally, although it is outside the scope of this chapter, we also tested by adding one or more client machines that didn't include things like Visual Studio as part of the installed application suite, to ensure that we hadn't built any dependency on Visual Studio.

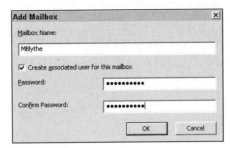

Figure 3-28

Creating the associated account is only part of the effort. Because we want to use these domain user accounts as our developer accounts, it's necessary to increase their permissions on the domain. In this case, you want to select the Active Directory User and Computers menu option from the Administrative Tools menu. From within the MMC, shown in Figure 3-29, select the Users section and then right-click one of your newly created user to access that user's properties.

When the Properties window opens, you'll be on the General tab, and you'll probably note that the POP3 Service user creation creates a rather sparsely populated user. There is no other name-related information on the user, but you are welcome to populate this data. Doing so, however, is also not necessary. You then need to access the Member Of tab to assign your new user to some additional security groups, as shown in Figure 3-30.

Because Michael Blythe was used to develop several of the OBA components, it is appropriate to grant him Domain Administrator privileges on this server as well as SharePoint Administrator privileges. Note that the privileges granted in these windows are related to the operating system, not SharePoint. Granting these permissions doesn't actually change the permissions of these users within your site. Once you've added these permissions, you need to go to your site, still authenticated as the administrator, and add these accounts to MOSS.

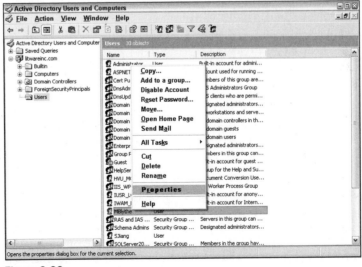

Figure 3-29

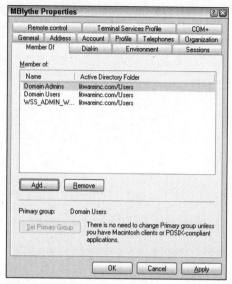

Figure 3-30

Starting from the Site Settings page, shown earlier in Figure 3-15, you will be selecting the "People and groups" link at the top of the left column titled Users and Permissions. Clicking this link opens the page shown in Figure 3-31. By default, when the page in Figure 3-31 opens, you'll be on the Home Members security group, and you'll want to change that to the Home Owners group, as shown in Figure 3-31. By default your administrator account will already have permission in this group. Your next action is to click the New button to Add Users as shown in Figure 3-31.

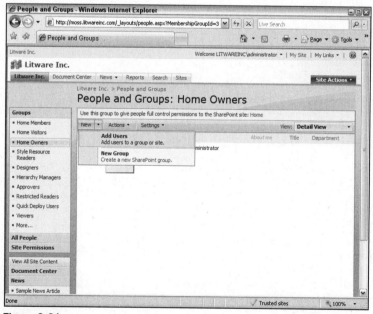

Figure 3-31

Clicking this button opens the page shown in Figure 3-32, where you can add new users. The usernames can be entered into the box and the icon of a person with a check will verify that the usernames entered are valid. From there, it is simply a matter of ensuring that you are adding the users to the group you expect. In this case we are adding both Michael Blythe and Steven Jiang to the Home Owners group, granting them access to the full site. The default group is based on the group from which you selected the New Users button, so, if you didn't navigate to the group prior to selecting Add Users, you'll need to select the correct group from this drop-down. Clicking the OK button located below the visible portion of the page finishes the process.

Now that you've added the users to the site, the next step is to add the necessary document libraries to support the sales forecast OBA.

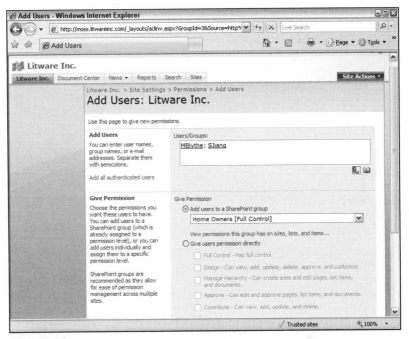

Figure 3-32

Document Library Configuration

The remaining task for your MOSS site is to update and create the document libraries used as part of the sales forecast OBA. When the site was created, the configuration process automatically created a Document Library site. To access your site, proceed to the Document Center as shown in Figure 3-33. From this page, access the Site Actions menu button in the upper-right corner of the display.

You need to be within the Document Center when you open the Site Settings, because you want to add a new document library within the Document Center, not at the top level of your site.

Opening this page results in the display of the page shown in Figure 3-34. Notice that the breadcrumb menu above the content in this page shows that you are at the Document Center's Site Settings and not the Site Settings for Litware Inc. The first step in creating the necessary libraries is to create the Sales

Forecast document library. To create a new library, you'll need to go to the fourth column from the left, Site Administration, and select the link for "Site libraries and lists" under this heading.

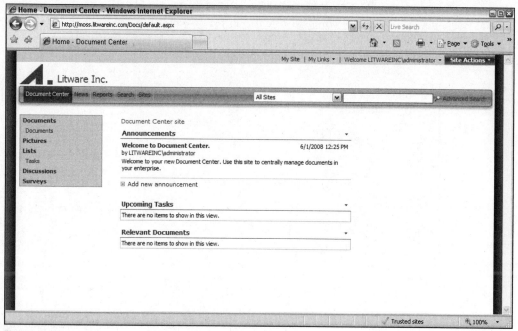

Figure 3-33

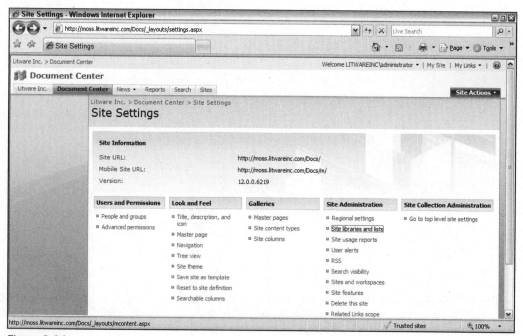

Figure 3-34

Clicking the "Site libraries and lists" link opens the page shown in Figure 3-35. This page includes a list of your current content libraries and allows you to select the "Create new content" link. The "Create new content" link opens the window shown in Figure 3-36.

Figure 3-35

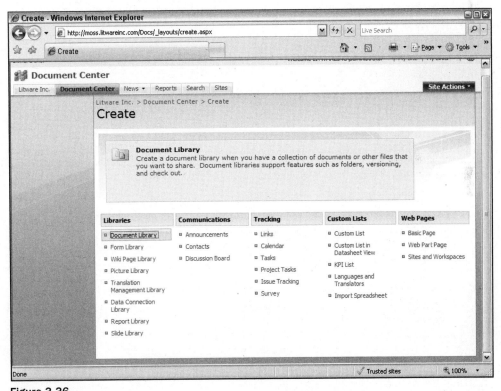

Figure 3-36

Figure 3-36 provides an array of options for your content type. In this case you are simply looking to add a new document library, which is the very first option available on that page. Clicking that link takes you to the page shown in Figure 3-37. This is the page where you will actually define your new document library. The library's name will be Sales Forecast, and, as you can see in Figure 3-37, a simple description explaining that this library will be customized to host the Sales Forecast VSTO-enabled spreadsheet has been added to the description.

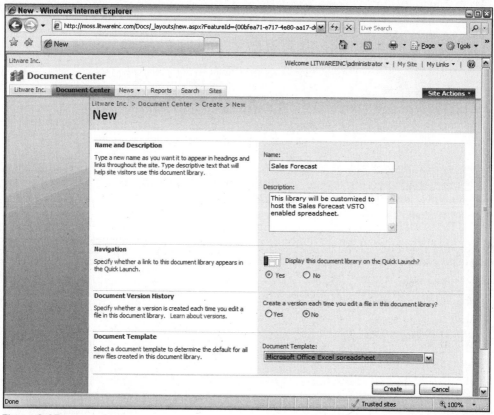

Figure 3-37

The Navigation and Version History have been left with their default settings in Figure 3-37; however, the Document Template has been customized to refer to a Microsoft Office Excel spreadsheet. Once you have filled in the necessary settings you can use the Create button to create your new document library. After a short delay, you will be taken to the screen shown in Figure 3-38.

Figure 3-38 is your new Sales Forecast document library. There remains one task for the sales forecast OBA. The logic also uses a Sales Documents document library. In this case, instead of creating a new document library, you can navigate to the existing Documents library and use the Settings drop-down, as shown in Figure 3-39, to select the Document Library Settings option and open the settings page for this existing document library. Once on the library's settings page, not pictured, you'll use the link at the top of the page to navigate to the General Settings for the Documents library, as shown in Figure 3-40.

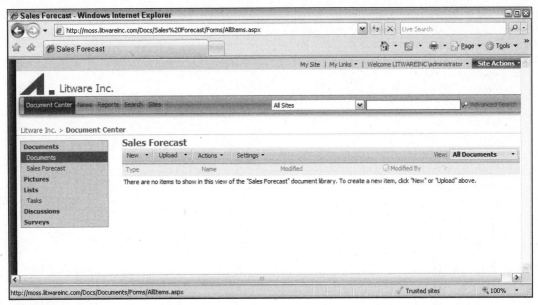

Figure 3-38

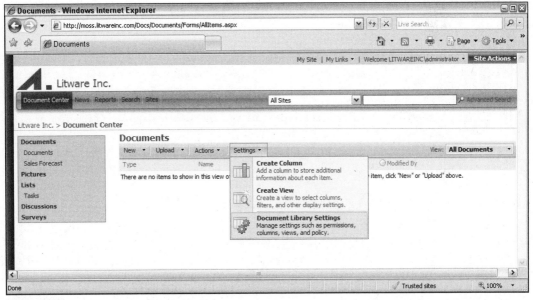

Figure 3-39

The only change you need to make on the page shown in Figure 3-40 is to adjust the name of this library from Documents to Sales Documents. You should note that when you created a new document library called Sales Forecast this name was also given to the virtual folder used to access that library. When you change the name of a document library, it does not trigger a change in the path associated with the document library.

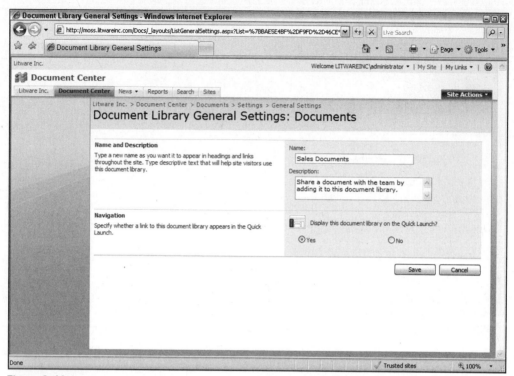

Figure 3-40

Once you have updated the name of your document library, you can return to the Document Center (see Figure 3-41). Notice that the left-hand navigation pane has been updated to reflect the new library name. Additionally, this page itself has already been set up with several useful Web parts to show users the status of any pending workflow tasks and documents that they own in any of the document libraries within the Document Center. At this point, your MOSS configuration for the sales forecast OBA is complete, however you still need to add an application database to your server.

The Business Application Database

When MOSS is installed and configured, it automatically sets up an instance of SQL Server Express Edition. Because everything is running on a single server, our recommendation is that you avoid installing a full copy of SQL Server alongside this instance. Instead, leverage the tools that ship in Visual Studio and the Microsoft SQL Server Management Studio Express, which is a freely available download from Microsoft. The installation package can be downloaded in either 32-bit or 64-bit versions, and the first page of the wizard echoing the product title is shown in Figure 3-42.

Using these tools, in particular the Management Studio Express tools, it is possible to create your development database within the same named instance of SQL Express that is being used by MOSS. Given that it will consume additional system resources, adding a second SQL Server instance to the server isn't something you want to do. Instead, by installing the SQL Server Management Studio Express, you can quickly connect to the one installed by MOSS.

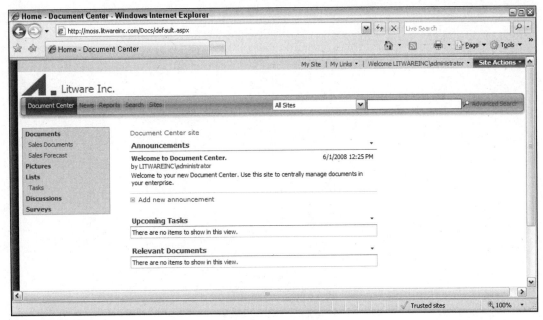

Figure 3-41

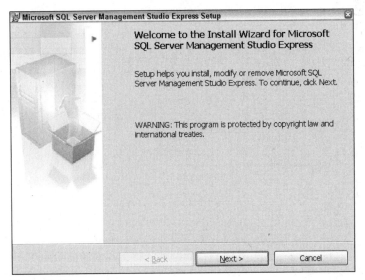

Figure 3-42

Figure 3-43 shows the startup screen and initial connection to the instance of SQL Server running on the MOSS server. Notice that, unlike the typical SQL Express installation, when installed as part of a MOSS installation the named instance is "OfficeServers" not "SQLExpress." This is important because it will impact the default location on the file system for your database files. Connecting to your SQL Server instance updates your display to that shown in Figure 3-44.

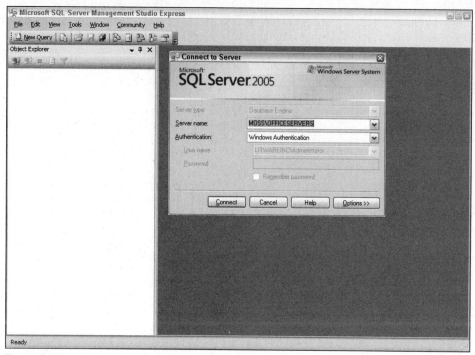

Figure 3-43

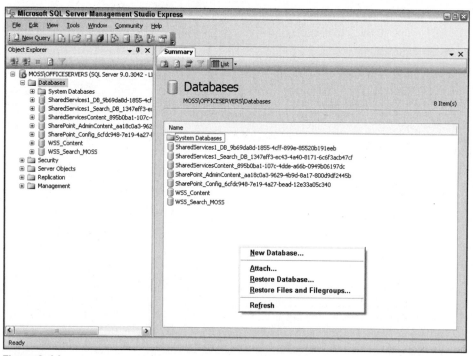

Figure 3-44

Figure 3-44 illustrates the list of databases that were created during the MOSS installation and configuration process. Directly accessing these databases isn't recommended. In fact, as the popup menu shown in Figure 3-44 hints, the main reason you are here is to install/create a new copy of your business database. It should be noted that you don't have to install a local copy of your business database. In order to ensure we've described the steps to allow you to configure a standalone sales forecast OBA server, we are going to show you how to place our sample application database on the server.

Selecting the New Database menu option in Figure 3-44 opens the dialog shown in Figure 3-45. You'll notice that the name we've used for our database is AdventureWorksVSTO. This is because the database started out as the standard Microsoft AdventureWorks database. Once you have provided a name for your new database, you can accept the other defaults, including the location for the database files. Click the OK button. This will complete the creation of your database, but, of course, at this point it is empty. To resolve that, you are going to restore a copy of the customized AdventureWorksVSTO database, available from the Codeplex site containing the sample code and related online materials associated with this book (`http://www.codeplex.com/obasales`).

The original AdventureWorks sample database was customized to support the additional capabilities related to sales forecasts and the sales forecast OBA. There are two new tables, Sales.Forecast and Sales.ForecastEstimates, which are in this database. Additionally, the database was modified to include a customer name column on the Sales.Customer table. In addition to these three table changes, there are new stored procedures in the database related to retrieving both Quarterly Sales data and Forecast data.

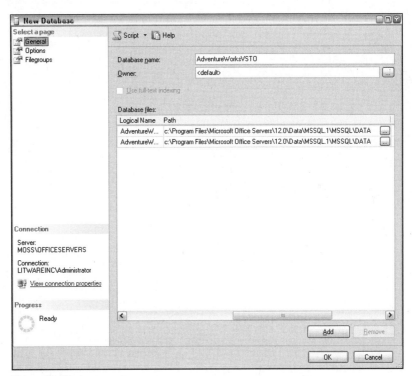

Figure 3-45

In addition to changes to the tables and the addition of new stored procedures, the data in the database was modified to a small extent. For starters, the CompanyName column in the Sales.Customer table was updated to include a company name for each customer. Next, in order to make it possible to group enough sales to show meaningful behavior in the sales forecast process, the customers of Michael Blythe were combined into 10 common companies.

In fact, Michael Blythe's sales are the only entries where the customer data was actually scrubbed in order to provide a meaningful set of results. There is no reason others couldn't be scrubbed in this fashion, but the version of the database available for download from the Codeplex site currently includes only data updates for Michael Blythe. Finally, the three order-related dates in the Sales.OrderHeader table were updated to bring sales into the present by adding months. All three columns were updated at the same time to move the order history forward, because the data isn't what we would call "live."

Once you have copied the AdventureWorksVSTO.BAK file to your local server from Codeplex you can start the database restore process, as shown in Figure 3-46. You'll use the newly created Adventure-WorksVSTO database as the target for your restored data files. In this way, if at some point you make changes and want to roll back to the original database, you will already be familiar with the process to restore the database. Selecting the Database menu item opens the dialog shown in Figure 3-47.

When Figure 3-47 opens, the location from which to restore the backup will not be populated, and, similarly, the option to select the backup sets to restore will be empty. Using the highlighted ellipsis (...) button on the right side of the From Device: setting, navigate to the folder holding your copy of the AdventureWorks.BAK file, and select this file as the device from which you will restore the database.

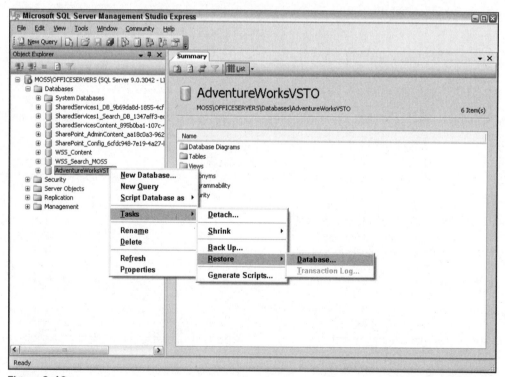

Figure 3-46

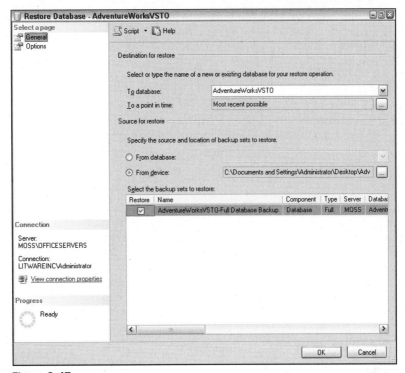

Figure 3-47

Once this is complete, the option to restore the AdventureWorksVSTO full database backup will need to be selected. When this is selected, you will need to select Options from the Select a Page list on the left-hand side of the screen. Selecting this list item changes the dialog to what is displayed in Figure 3-48.

Once again, the default displayed when you first open this screen will not match what is in the figure. The first change you will need to make is to select the checkbox to indicate that you wish to overwrite the existing database files. Next, you need to adjust the current Restore As paths. Even though you have indicated that you want to overwrite the existing database files, the paths shown are actually those to the database that was originally backed up. Because your server is using a different database path, attempting to restore without correcting these paths will result in an error.

The path for the database files you created is visible both in Figure 3-45 and in Figure 3-49. By clicking the ellipsis button shown next to the Data file you will open the Locate Database Files window shown in Figure 3-49. This figure shows the complete default path from your C: drive to your database files. You will need to update this value for both the .mdf and .ldf files referred to in Figure 3-48. Once you have updated these paths you are ready to click the OK button, shown in Figure 3-48, and restore your database.

As noted in Figure 3-50, this completes the restoration of the AdventureWorksVSTO database. It also completes the configuration of the server products on your MOSS server. Having completed the installation of the business database as well as the initial configuration of your MOSS web application, you are now ready to start developing and testing against this server. This also marks the point where we recommend installing first the Office 2007 client applications (Word, Excel, InfoPath, and so on) and then Visual Studio 2008.

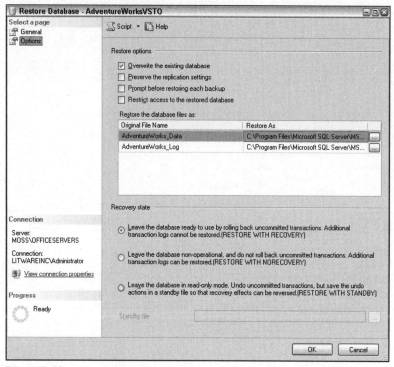

Figure 3-48

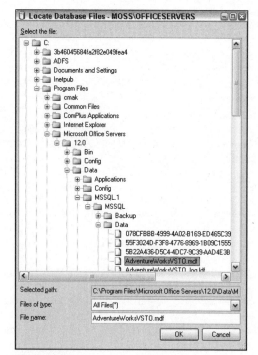

Figure 3-49

Figure 3-50

Our recommendation is to install the Office 2007 client applications prior to Visual Studio 2008. Also, we no longer recommend installing Visual Studio 2005. The Windows SharePoint Services 3.0 Tools: Visual Studio 2008 Extensions, Version 1.2 were released and we suggest adding these tools to your Visual Studio 2008 installation for working with MOSS 2007.

Summary

Setting up a developer MOSS environment with a custom domain follows a different set of steps from setting up a production MOSS server. The idea of placing this many roles on a single server isn't one that would ever be recommended for a production environment. On the other hand, for a developer who needs to focus on creating components that will run in an environment with these same characteristics, this is a very manageable solution.

This chapter covered:

❑ Installing an configuring MOSS on a single server domain host

❑ Configuring your MOSS site and prepping IIS to support both MOSS and custom ASP.NET applications

❑ Setting up user accounts for your test users

❑ Setting up the custom AdventureWorks database used by the sales forecast OBA

Though this chapter covered the initial creation of your sales forecast OBA environment, there are still several other elements that you can add to this baseline. Chapter 8, "Adding Business Intelligence through Excel Web Services and Key Performance Indicators," reviews adding business performance indicators. Chapter 9, "Integrating Your LOB System Using the Business Data Catalog and Extending Search into Your LOB System," looks at integrating the business catalog and the ability to search your business data. Finally, Chapter 10, "Deploying OBA Client Components" and Chapter 11, "Deploying and Securing Your OBA Server Components," look at installing and configuring your Sales Forecast custom assemblies and setting up the custom content type and workflows that make up your actual business applications.

4

Customizing the Office Fluent Ribbon and the Task Pane

Chapter 2, "Architectural Guidance and Design Patterns for Office Business Applications," provided an overview of the Office Business Application (OBA) solution patterns and then applied the patterns to the solution you'll be working through in this book: the sales forecast OBA. The goal was to lay out a high-level design process to think about the why, what, and how of our OBA using the solution patterns as a reference point. Following on that, this chapter begins building out that design. Specifically, this chapter discusses the Visual Studio Tools for Office (VSTO) document-level customization that you'll build using Visual Studio 2008. This customization includes a customized task pane that will act as the data manager view and a custom ribbon component that will extend the current Office Fluent UI (the new branding term for the Office UI) even further.

What Is Visual Studio Tools for Office (VSTO)?

VSTO 3.0 is a component technology within Visual Studio 2008 that enables you to build managed code solutions (Visual Basic and C#) for Office. These solutions are, in essence, managed code assemblies that access the Office object model, enabling developers to extend on the functionality native to the Office system. VSTO 3.0 also leverages the features within the .NET Framework 3.0, so projects you build using VSTO support, for example, Windows Communication Foundation (WCF), Windows Workflow Foundation (WF), and Windows Presentation Foundation (WPF).

VSTO 3.0 is quite an evolution from its predecessor, VSTO 2005 SE. VSTO 3.0 provides developers with visual designers such as the visual Ribbon designer and Outlook form region wizard, improved deployment through ClickOnce support, VBA/VSTO interoperability, Word content control data binding, and much more. MSDN hosts a VSTO developer center — a good place to start when learning about VSTO — that provides you with a number of articles and sample code. For more information, see http://msdn2.microsoft.com/en-us/office/aa905533.aspx.

VSTO supports the extension of a number of different Office applications. Figure 4-1 illustrates the New Project dialog and shows the different types of project templates available to you. You'll notice that support for Office in VSTO 3.0 cuts across both 2007 and 2003 Office applications, the most popular of which are Outlook, Excel, and Word for solution customization.

As mentioned earlier, we're going to use VSTO 3.0 to build a custom actions pane and an extended ribbon for our sales forecast OBA. The VSTO customization will be a document-level solution that is built against an Excel 2007 workbook. This customization will represent one of the key read/write interfaces for the sales data (our LOB system).

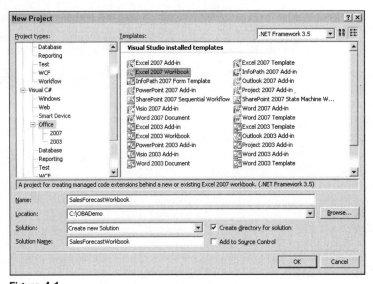

Figure 4-1

Creating a New VSTO Project

The first thing you'll need to do is create a VSTO project. Open Visual Studio 2008, and click File ⇨ New ⇨ Project. In the New Project dialog (see Figure 4-1), navigate to the Office node in either the Visual Basic or Visual C# nodes and select Excel 2007 Workbook. Provide a name for your project (for example, SalesForecastWorkbook) and click OK. Before Visual Studio completes the project creation process, it will ask you whether you want to create a new document or copy an existing one into your project (see Figure 4-2). Because this is a document-level customization, you can use an existing document or template or create a new one right within Visual Studio; many of the Office application features are available to you within the project when creating document-level customizations. For the sales forecast OBA, we used an existing Excel workbook for the project (see Figure 4-3). In the wizard, you can select Create a New Document, in which case you provide a name for your document and then click OK. If you select Copy an Existing Document, browse to the document that you want to include within your project and click OK.

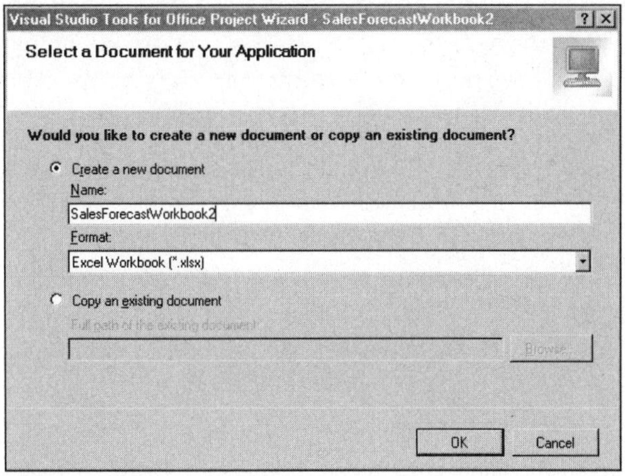

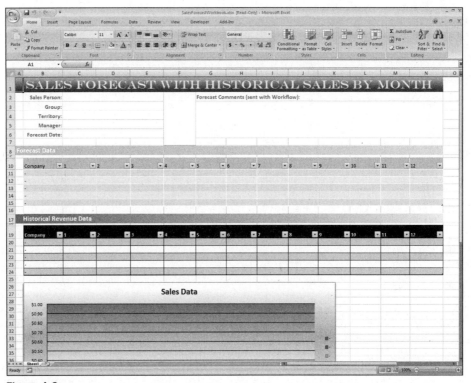

Figure 4-2

Figure 4-3 shows the spreadsheet that we used for the sales forecast OBA, which you can find in the solution files that accompany this book. You can find these project files at www.wrox.com or http://www.codeplex.com/obasales. While you have the full project files available to you, we recommend that you walk through the process of creating a separate VSTO project to help with your learning.

Figure 4-3

After you get your project set up, you'll notice that VSTO creates a core class for the project called ThisWorkbook.cs or ThisWorkbook.vb. Two key events in this core class are important: the Startup and Shutdown events. They are triggered by the host application (for example, Word, Excel, and so on) when the VSTO assembly is loaded and unloaded. For example, you'll want to make sure that, on loading the sales forecast OBA project, Excel displays the custom actions pane by default, so you'll need to have some code in the Startup method that accomplishes this task.

Note that in this book we use both C# and Visual Basic (VB) in different project files to illustrate both languages being used in different scenarios. For the VSTO document-level customization project, we used VB.

With the sales forecast VSTO project created, you'll want to do three main things:

1. Add a data source to your project;

2. Create a custom actions pane that hosts a user control that will enable users to manage data into the Excel spreadsheet; and

3. Create a custom ribbon that will provide some additional functionality to the solution.

For the sales forecast OBA, we used the AdventureWorks data source for our LOB system. You may want to use this data source or build an alternate database that you can use. It is typical for building OBAs to use services to integrate with your data source, so you may also want to add service references to your project so you can consume the data from your LOB system.

Within the second two of these, we will not only show you how to create the objects for the solution, but we'll also have some custom code for you to add to the project.

While we walk you through how to create specific items for the sales forecast project, all of the source code is available for you to download at www.wrox.com *or* http://www.codeplex.com/ obasales.

Adding a Data Source to Your Project

For the sales forecast solution, we used the AdventureWorks database as our LOB system, which you can download free of charge from Codeplex at the following location: http://www.codeplex.com/ MSFTDBProdSamples/Release/ProjectReleases.aspx?ReleaseId=4004. (Select the first option in the list of database choices.) If you choose another data source, the way in which you add the database to your solution as a reference is similar.

To add a new data source to your VSTO document-level customization project, click Data and Add New Data Source. This invokes the Data Source Configuration Wizard (see Figure 4-4). Select Database, click Next, and select New Connection. You'll want to select SQL Server as the database source, enter your server name, select the database name, and click OK. When prompted, do not copy the data files into the project. The wizard will then ask you to save the default connection string; you can either click Next to accept this string or change it and then click Next. The wizard then prompts you to select the specific tables you want to add to the solution.

After you've completed this step, click Finish. The database will now be added to your solution.

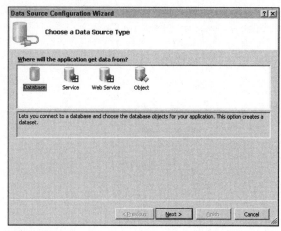

Figure 4-4

While the sales forecast OBA uses the AdventureWorks database as its LOB system, you'll frequently need to add a Web service to your project, a Web service that you create using the native tools within the LOB system. For example, PeopleSoft or Siebel provides a set of tools that enable you to create a wrapper Web service that accesses core business data within the system. Remember that a service-oriented architecture lies at the heart of an OBA. Although the creation of the Web service in the native LOB system toolset is out of scope of this chapter, once you have a deployed Web service, it is trivial to hook up the service to a Visual Studio project. For example, if you have a web method called GetCustomerDetails (a fictional method for illustration purposes only), to expose this in your project you need to add a reference to the Web service within which this web method resides. To add a Web service, right-click References, and select Add Service Reference, Advanced, and Add Web Reference (see Figure 4-5). Notice the GetCustomerDetails web method that is exposed by the Web service you created.

You can provide a name for the Web service (the default name is localhost) and click OK, after which Visual Studio adds a reference to the Web service in your project.

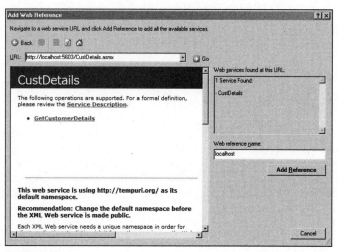

Figure 4-5

With a database connected to the solution (or if you chose to add a Web service instead, the Web service reference added to your project), you can now begin to write code that manipulates the data that you'll be pulling from the data source into the project. For example, you can create the custom actions pane and build a management view into the data.

Creating a Custom Actions Pane

A custom actions pane (or what is called a custom task pane in the application-level add-ins) is a pane that can be used to manage custom functionality. In many cases, developers use these custom actions panes to generate a manager of some sort (for example, a data manager using drop-down menus and textboxes or a manager of sections that will generate a well-structured document). A custom actions pane essentially hosts user controls, which is where the data management aspect comes into play. Also, you can use traditional Windows Form user controls or you can use the more recent .NET 3.0 WPF user controls. Either way, the process is the same: you first create your user control and then you host that user control in the custom actions pane.

In the sales forecast OBA, we use a WPF user control that is then hosted (via a Windows Form user control) in the custom actions pane (using the ElementHost class). Using this method does require a little more code to bind the data to the project; however, you are left with improved data visualization and graphics options with the WPF user controls. (Many developers argue that WPF is the wave of the future, but keep in mind that it still requires some additional coding when compared to Windows Forms. This is sure to change in future versions of Visual Studio and WPF.)

To create a WPF user control, you can either create the control in Expression Blend (a professional designer tool that enables you to build user interface experiences), or you can add a new project to the solution by right-clicking the project, and clicking Add, New Item. Then select Visual C# Items or Visual Basic Items, WPF, and select User Control (WPF). This will add two files to your solution: a .xaml file (which will contain the XML-based description of your WPF control), and a .xaml.cs (or .xaml.vb) file (which stores the code-behind for the WPF user control), which you can use to build your WPF user control.

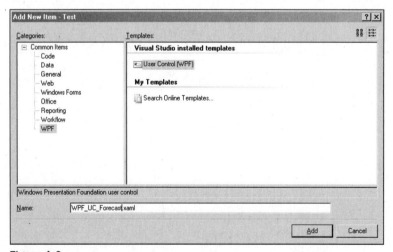

Figure 4-6

You can also add WPF user controls by adding a New Project and selecting Windows and then WPF User Control Library, or you can import a built Expression Blend project into your solution.

After you've added the WPF user control to the solution, you can now create the look and feel of the user control. You do this either by dragging and dropping controls onto the WPF designer (which auto-generates XAML for you), or hand-coding the XAML (or copying and pasting from Expression Blend) in the XAML view. Either way, you'll end up with some user interface elements that represent your WPF user control. For the sales forecast OBA, the XAML code that represents the WPF user control is as follows:

```
<UserControl x:Class="WPF_UC_Forecast"
    xmlns="http://schemas.microsoft.com/winfx/2006/xaml/presentation"
    xmlns:x="http://schemas.microsoft.com/winfx/2006/xaml" Width="300" Height="525"
Background="LightGoldenrodYellow">
        <Grid Height="525">
        <Label Height="28" Margin="26,8,0,0" Name="LabelID" VerticalAlignment="Top"
HorizontalAlignment="Left" Width="120">Group</Label>
        <Label Height="28" Margin="26,67,0,0" Name="LabelDate"
VerticalAlignment="Top" HorizontalAlignment="Left" Width="120">Region</Label>
        <ComboBox Height="23" Margin="26,35,40,0" Name="ComboBoxGroup"
VerticalAlignment="Top" />
        <ComboBox Height="23" Margin="26,95,40,0" Name="ComboBoxRegion"
VerticalAlignment="Top" />
        <Label Height="28" HorizontalAlignment="Left" Margin="26,125,0,0"
Name="Label1" VerticalAlignment="Top" Width="120">Territory</Label>
        <Label Height="28" HorizontalAlignment="Left" Margin="26,182,0,0"
Name="Label2" VerticalAlignment="Top" Width="120">Sales Person</Label>
        <ComboBox Height="23" Margin="26,151,40,0" Name="ComboBoxTerritory"
VerticalAlignment="Top" />
        <ComboBox Margin="26,210,40,0" Name="ComboBoxSalesPerson" Height="23"
VerticalAlignment="Top" />
        <Grid Margin="26, 245, 0, 0" Width="233" HorizontalAlignment="Left"
VerticalAlignment="Top" Height="115" Background="#ffcdcecd" Name="Grid1" >
            <StackPanel HorizontalAlignment="Left" Width="100">
            <Label BorderBrush="Black" BorderThickness="1" Height="23"
Width="101" Name="Label3" VerticalAlignment="Top" HorizontalAlignment="Left">Sales
Quota</Label>
                <Label Name="Label7" BorderBrush="Black" BorderThickness="1"
Height="23"  Width="101" VerticalAlignment="Top" HorizontalAlignment="Left">Sales
YTD</Label>
                <Label Name="Label8" BorderBrush="Black" BorderThickness="1"
Height="23"  Width="101" VerticalAlignment="Top" HorizontalAlignment="Left">Sales
Last Year</Label>
                <Label Name="Label6" BorderBrush="Black" BorderThickness="1"
Height="23"  Width="101" VerticalAlignment="Top" HorizontalAlignment="Left">Commiss
ion %</Label>
                <Label Name="Label5" BorderBrush="Black"  BorderThickness="1"
Height="23" Width="101" HorizontalAlignment="Left"  VerticalAlignment="Top">Bonus</
Label>
            </StackPanel>
            <StackPanel HorizontalAlignment="Right" Width="134">
            <Label Name="LabelSalesQuota" Width="134" BorderBrush="Black"
BorderThickness="1" Height="23"   VerticalAlignment="Top"
HorizontalAlignment="Right"></Label>
```

```
                <Label Name="LabelSalesYTD" Width="134" BorderBrush="Black"
BorderThickness="1" Height="23"   VerticalAlignment="Top"
HorizontalAlignment="Right"></Label>
                <Label Name="LabelSalesLastYear" Width="134"
BorderBrush="Black" BorderThickness="1" Height="23"   VerticalAlignment="Top"
HorizontalAlignment="Right"></Label>
                <Label Name="LabelCommissionPct" Width="134"
BorderBrush="Black" BorderThickness="1" Height="23"   VerticalAlignment="Top"
HorizontalAlignment="Right"></Label>
                <Label Name="LabelBonus" Width="134" BorderBrush="Black"
BorderThickness="1" Height="23"   VerticalAlignment="Top"
HorizontalAlignment="Right"></Label>
            </StackPanel>
        </Grid>
        <Label Height="28" Margin="26,363,0,0" Name="Label4"
VerticalAlignment="Top" HorizontalAlignment="Left" Width="120">Select Companies</
Label>
        <ListBox Height="88" Margin="26,391,40,0" Name="ListBoxCompanies"
VerticalAlignment="Top" ToolTip="Select up to 5 companies" />
        <Button Height="28" Width="150" Margin="0,490,0,0" Name="ButtonLoad"
VerticalAlignment="Top">Load Sales Data</Button>
    </Grid>
</UserControl>
```

The preceding XAML translates into a user control with several controls on it that will all help in some way to manage the external data into the sales forecast document-level customization. Figure 4-7 illustrates the WPF user control in the Visual Studio 2008 designer view.

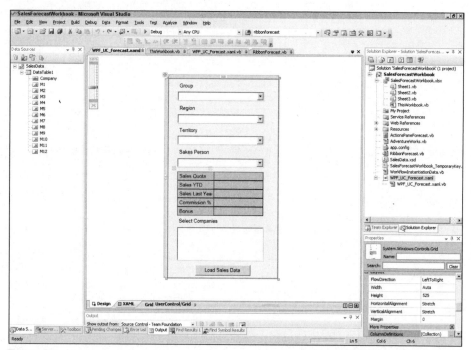

Figure 4-7

You're not done with the WPF user control just yet; you need to provide some key business logic (or code behind) to make the user control functional. For your user control, the code behind lives in the `WPF_UC_ Forecast.xaml.vb` file. It is here that you add data binding code or any code that manages events or user interactions with the controls on your WPF user control. The following sample code illustrates some of the code from the sales forecast OBA project.

In this code sample, you'll notice that we're invoking a new connection instance (AdvWorksDC) and then setting the visibility of the custom actions pane to false, which is accessed via the TaskPaneVisible property on the ThisWorkbook object, if the SalesEmployeeID is greater than 0 (essentially hiding or showing the task pane automatically using the value of the current SalesEmployeeID). We then populate the objects within the WPG user control by first creating queries to get the data we want from the AdventureWorks database (for example, salesrep) and then adding the individual items that are retrieved from the database to the WPF user control objects (for example ComboBoxSalesPerson).

```
Partial Public Class WPF_UC_Forecast

    …


        Globals.ThisWorkbook.AdvWorksDC = New AdventureWorksVSTO(My.Settings.
AdvWorksDBVSTO)

        If Globals.ThisWorkbook.SalesEmployeeID > 0 Then
        Globals.ThisWorkbook.TaskPaneVisible = False

        Dim salesrep = From persons In Globals.ThisWorkbook.AdvWorksDC.Person_
Contact _
                        Select persons.FirstName, persons.LastName, persons.
ContactID _
                        Where ContactID = Globals.ThisWorkbook.SalesEmployeeID

Me.ComboBoxSalesPerson.Items.Add(salesrep.First.FirstName + " " + salesrep.First.
LastName)
        Me.ComboBoxSale,sPerson.SelectedIndex = 0

        Dim territory = From terrtbl In Globals.ThisWorkbook.AdvWorksDC.Sales_
SalesTerritory _
Select terrtbl.Name, terrtbl.CountryRegionCode, terrtbl.Group, terrtbl.TerritoryID
_
                        Where TerritoryID = Globals.ThisWorkbook.TerritoryID

        ComboBoxGroup.Items.Add(territory.First.Group)
        ComboBoxGroup.SelectedIndex = 0
        ComboBoxTerritory.Items.Add(territory.First.Name)
        ComboBoxTerritory.SelectedIndex = 0
        ComboBoxRegion.Items.Add(territory.First.CountryRegionCode)
        ComboBoxRegion.SelectedIndex = 0

        ComboBoxGroup.IsEnabled = False
        ComboBoxTerritory.IsEnabled = False
        ComboBoxRegion.IsEnabled = False
        ComboBoxSalesPerson.IsEnabled = False
        ButtonLoad.IsEnabled = False
    Else
        Globals.ThisWorkbook.TaskPaneVisible = True
```

```
            Dim groups = From regions In Globals.ThisWorkbook.AdvWorksDC.Sales_
    SalesTerritory Select groupname = regions.Group Distinct
            For Each groupname In groups
                Me.ComboBoxGroup.Items.Add(groupname.ToString())
            Next
            Me.ComboBoxGroup.SelectedIndex = 0
        End If
        ListBoxCompanies.SelectionMode = Windows.Controls.SelectionMode.Multiple
    End Sub
    ...
End Class
```

Often, you're not just loading data into a document without having to manage some degree of user interaction with that data. For the sales forecast OBA, code was required to manage the different user selection changes that might occur as a user interacts with the data. For example, the following code limits the user's selection of companies to no more than five. This not only controls the number of companies that can be selected in the Select Companies list, but it also limits the amount of data brought into the spreadsheet from the database.

```
Partial Public Class WPF_UC_Forecast

    ...

    Private Sub ListBoxCompanies_SelectionChanged(ByVal sender As System.
    Object, ByVal e As System.Windows.Controls.SelectionChangedEventArgs) Handles
    ListBoxCompanies.SelectionChanged
        If ListBoxCompanies.SelectedItems.Count > 5 Then
            ListBoxCompanies.SelectedItems.RemoveAt(0)
        End If
    End Sub
    ...
End Class
```

In the codebehind, there is also logic that handles mapping the data that is loaded by the user into the controls to the Excel workbook. This is where you can begin to see the power of VSTO: you can data-bind via connection string or Web service proxy and then insert data to be read and written into the workbook. The data can be inserted using a couple of different methods. For example, you could load a data set into a ListObject (which represents the rows and columns of the data) and then load the ListObject into Excel. You could alternatively load data into specific cells or named ranges. Each of these has its own benefits and drawbacks.

In the sales forecast OBA, the mapping of the data from the WPF user control is controlled by the ButtonLoad_Click event. Note that to insert the data selected by the user, the sales forecast OBA uses both named ranges and ListObject. For example, in the case of named ranges we set the Value2 (the value of the named range) equal to the values or properties provided to it via the user selections. In the following code snippet, the named range values of the sales rep (NamedRangeSalesRepName), territory (NamedRangeTerritoryName), and forecast date (NamedRangeForecastDate) are assigned through the selected value of ComboBoxSalesPerson:

```
Partial Public Class WPF_UC_Forecast

    ...

    Private Sub ButtonLoad_Click(ByVal sender As System.Object, ByVal e As System.
    Windows.RoutedEventArgs) Handles ButtonLoad.Click
```

```
      ...

          Globals.Sheet1.NamedRangeSalesRepName.Value2 = ComboBoxSalesPerson.
SelectedValue
          Globals.Sheet1.NamedRangeTerritoryName.Value2 = ComboBoxTerritory.
SelectedValue
          Globals.Sheet1.NamedRangeForecastDate.Value2 = Today()
          Globals.Sheet1.NamedRangeGroupName.Value2 = ComboBoxGroup.SelectedValue
          Globals.Sheet1.NamedRangeManagerName.Locked = True
          Globals.Sheet1.NamedRangeForecastDate.Locked = True
          Globals.Sheet1.NamedRangeTerritoryName.Locked = True
          Globals.Sheet1.NamedRangeSalesRepName.Locked = True
          Globals.Sheet1.NamedRangeGroupName.Locked = True


      ...


  End Class
```

In the case of the ListObject, we create a ListObject and then map the data table (that contained the data from the user selection) to that ListObject. Once the data is in the Excel workbook, the user can use the native functionality of Excel to make changes to the data. In the following code sample, you'll note that we create a new instance of a data table (forecastDataTable) and also create a new instance of a ListObject (salesDataTable) to this new instance of forecastDataTable. We then take each company that the user selects in the Select Companies list (companyName) and use the other options that the user selected in the WPF user control as filters to load the appropriate data into the ListObject within the spreadsheet. You'll also note that in this code snippet, we create new instances of a sales row (salesRow) and sales forecast row (foreCastRow), which add the name of the company and data for each month in the fiscal year to the spreadsheet. We then make a call to UspGetSalesDataByMonths, which passes a set of parameters, gets in return the current sales (currentSales) for a specific company, and loads this data into the spreadsheet. The data is displayed through accessing the DataSource object in Sheet1 (that we've populated using the user selections and appropriate data queries) and then binding that to the salesDataTable ListObject. The final line of code then hides the task pane to the user to maximize the data view within the spreadsheet.

```
  Partial Public Class WPF_UC_Forecast

      ...


          Dim forecastDataTable = New SalesData.DataTable1DataTable()
          Globals.ThisWorkbook.salesDataTable = New SalesData.DataTable1DataTable()


      ...


          For Each companyName In ListBoxCompanies.SelectedItems
              customerNm = companyName.ToString
              Dim companyid = (From customer In Globals.ThisWorkbook.AdvWorksDC.
  Sales_Customer _
                          Select customer.CustomerID, customer.CustomerName,
  customer.TerritoryID _
                          Where CustomerName = customerNm).First.CustomerID
              Globals.ThisWorkbook.CompanyIDs.Add(companyid)

              Dim salesRow() As Object = {companyName, 0, 0, 0, 0, 0, 0, 0, 0, 0, 0,
  0, 0}
```

```
            Dim foreCastRow() As Object = {companyName, 1, 2, 3, 4, 5, 6, 7, 8, 9,
    10, 11, 12}
            Dim currentSales = Globals.ThisWorkbook.AdvWorksDC.
    UspGetSalesDataByMonths( _
                        Globals.ThisWorkbook.SalesEmployeeID, companyid,
    startDate, endDate)
            For Each companyData As UspGetSalesDataByMonthsResult In currentSales
                If companyData.Month IsNot Nothing Then
                    Dim i As Integer = companyData.Month
                                      If i < 4 Then
                        i = i + 9
                    Else
                        i = i - 3
                    End If
                    salesRow(i) = companyData.ActualSales
                End If
            Next
            Globals.ThisWorkbook.salesDataTable.LoadDataRow(CType(salesRow,
    Object), True)


            For i = 1 To 12
                Dim salesNum As Decimal = 0
                Decimal.TryParse(salesRow(i), salesNum)
                salesNum = salesNum * 1.1
                If salesNum = 0 Then
                    salesNum = 100.0
                End If
                foreCastRow(i) = salesNum
            Next
            forecastDataTable.LoadDataRow(foreCastRow, True)

        Next

        Globals.Sheet1.ListSales.DataSource = Globals.ThisWorkbook.salesDataTable
        Globals.Sheet1.ListForecast.DataSource = forecastDataTable
        Globals.ThisWorkbook.TaskPaneVisible = False

    End Sub

        ...

    End Class
```

After creating a WPF user control, the next step is to add it to a Windows Form user control; it's the Windows Form user control that will host the WPF user control through the ElementHost class. To do this, right-click the project and select Add and then select Windows Form User Control. Provide a name for your user control (for example ActionsPaneForecast) and click Add. This should by default open the designer view for the user control. If it does not, right-click the new user control in the Solution Explorer and select View Designer. To add the WPF user control, you must first build the solution, so click F6 to build (not build and debug) your project. This will build the solution and add the WPF user control (for example WPF_UC_Forecast) in your Toolbox, where you can drag and drop it onto the Windows Form user control designer surface. Figure 4.8 illustrates the WPF_UC_Forecast user control in the Toolbox that was dragged and bound to the Windows Form user control.

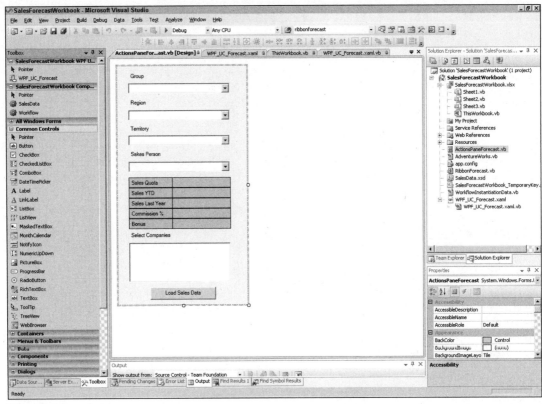

Figure 4-8

With the WPF user control hosted within the Windows Form user control, you are almost done; the last thing you need to do is to create an instance of the Windows Form user control. You can do this by adding one line of code within the Startup method in the ThisWorkbook.vb class, illustrated in the following code:

```
Public Class ThisWorkbook

...

    Private Sub ThisWorkbook_Startup(ByVal sender As Object, ByVal e As System.
EventArgs) Handles Me.Startup
        Me.ActionsPane.Controls.Add(New ActionsPaneForecast())
    End Sub

...

End Class
```

There are obviously many different customizations you can add to manage data in either your WPF or Windows Forms based user controls. In many ways, custom actions panes are a great way to manage data in and out of your Office documents. However, custom actions panes in the wider scope of VSTO functionality are but one feature; there are many others that can be employed to enhance and extend your Office client applications to build OBAs. One great addition to the VSTO family in version 3.0 is the visual Ribbon designer, which we discuss in the next section of this chapter.

Creating the Custom Ribbon

The Ribbon is the new navigation mechanism in Office 2007 — the successor to the command toolbar menu in Office 2003. Not all of the Office applications have the Ribbon; for example, Visio and Project support in Visual Studio 2008 are still limited to customizing the command toolbar menu because they do not use the Ribbon. Furthermore, Outlook 2007 is a hybrid application wherein the main interface for Outlook uses the command toolbar menu, and the individual inspectors (for example, a mail message) use the Ribbon.

The visual Ribbon designer is one of the ways in which you can extend and customize the new Ribbon structure (which, at its root, is essentially an XML structure — the designer-generated code for the VSTO Ribbon wrapper classes is used by the VSTO runtime to generate XML at runtime) — and is by far the easiest way to create the Ribbon. An alternate way to create a ribbon is through raw XML. Creating the ribbon this way means that you need to manually map the XML to callback methods.

The creation of the Ribbon, whether through the designer or through editing the native XML, must conform to a specific structure. To illustrate this, the following sample displays the default code for a ribbon created in Visual Studio 2008. (If you want to use this option, right-click your project, click Add, New Item, and then select Ribbon (XML).) This default code shows the structure to which the XML ribbon needs to conform. In this code sample, note the onAction event (bolded) that is associated with the toggleButton element; this would map to an event definition (a callback) located in the code-behind file that corresponds to the ribbon XML.

```xml
<customUI xmlns="http://schemas.microsoft.com/office/2006/01/customui"
onLoad="OnLoad">
  <ribbon>
    <tabs>
      <tab idMso="TabAddIns">
        <group id="MyGroup"
              label="My Group">
          <toggleButton id="toggleButton1"
                       size="large"
                       label="My Button"
                       screentip="My Button Screentip"
                       onAction="OnToggleButton1"
                       imageMso="HappyFace" />
        </group>
      </tab>
    </tabs>
  </ribbon>
</customUI>
```

In Visual Studio 2008, the visual Ribbon designer is very easy to use. Simply right-click your project, and click Add, New Item, select Office, and then select Ribbon (Visual Designer). This will invoke the designer with a default view that includes a tab and one group; there are no individual ribbon controls (such as buttons, checkboxes, and so on) added to the group by default.

After the default view is loaded, you can use the Office Ribbon Controls in the Toolbox to drag and drop controls onto the designer to extend the Office Ribbon. Note that you are not necessarily restricted to just extending the existing Ribbon; moreover, you can use the StartFromScratch property on the Ribbon to replace all of the Ribbon elements in the Office application save for the ones you create and the ones located in the Office button. Figure 4-9 illustrates the visual Ribbon designer along with some of the ribbon controls that we added to the sales forecast OBA.

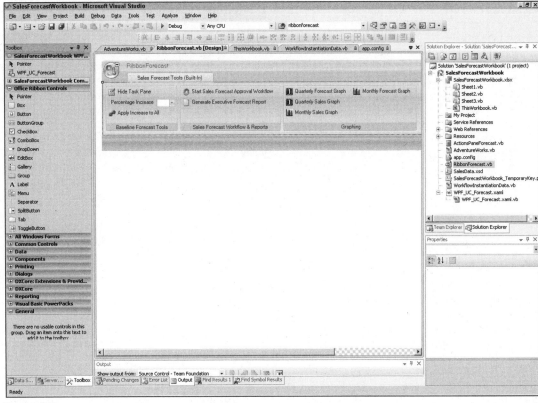

Figure 4-9

Figure 4-10

After you've added some controls to your ribbon, the next step is to add event handlers for those controls so that the controls will have some action associated with them. You can integrate events across multiple areas within your document. For example, you can change the properties of the ribbon controls (see Figure 4-10), effect changes within the document (lock content controls or create charts), or change the properties of the custom actions pane. In the sales forecast OBA, we added a number of events that were mapped to specific ribbon controls. The following code illustrates the click event that maps to the ToggleButton1 button, a toggle button control that hides and shows the task pane. The click event essentially uses the state property of the button (a Boolean based on the checked or unchecked state) and sets the property of the task pane based on that property. If you're building an application-level add-in you'll want to take note that the code for setting the visible property on your custom task pane (as opposed to actions pane at the document level) is much easier. This has to do with the way Office constructed the actions pane versus the custom task pane. The reason we call this out is because accessing the properties of the actions pane in general is different from the task pane. These differences are not limited to the setting of the visibility property; there are other

coding differences across the application-level add-ins and document-level customizations. You may also notice that we're referring to images in two places that we added as resources to the sales forecast OBA project files.

```
Public Class RibbonForecast
...


Private Sub ToggleButton1_Click(ByVal sender As System.Object, ByVal e As
Microsoft.Office.Tools.Ribbon.RibbonControlEventArgs) Handles ToggleButtonTaskPane.
Click
        Globals.ThisWorkbook.TaskPaneVisible = ToggleButtonTaskPane.Checked
    End Sub
...


Public Property IsTaskPaneVisible() As Boolean
        Get
            Return ToggleButtonTaskPane.Checked
        End Get
        Set(ByVal value As Boolean)
            ToggleButtonTaskPane.Checked = value
            If value Then
                ToggleButtonTaskPane.Label = "Hide Task Pane"
                ToggleButtonTaskPane.Image = Global.SalesForecastWorkbook.
My.Resources.Resources.EditInformationHS
            Else
                ToggleButtonTaskPane.Label = "Show Task Pane"
                ToggleButtonTaskPane.Image = Global.SalesForecastWorkbook.
My.Resources.Resources.ArrangeSideBySideHS
            End If
        End Set
    End Property
...
End Class
```

Another example of an event handler mapping to a button in the Ribbon is the starting of a workflow instance. We discuss this more in Chapter 5, "Creating and Deploying a Custom MOSS 2007 Workflow Using Visual Studio 2008," but one of the key features in the sales forecast OBA is a SharePoint workflow process that manages the state of approval for the sales forecast OBA document-level customization (that is, the customized Excel sales forecast workbook). There are three states in this workflow: approve, reject, and amend. This type of code execution is interesting for a couple of reasons. First, once in SharePoint the document is a SharePoint artifact, so creating an instance of the workflow and then kicking it off from within the document is a valuable integration with the document (the alternative is to kick it off manually through the SharePoint site). Second, this type of custom logic speaks to how well VSTO can lend itself to enterprise-level process management and integration. This is one of the core integration points with SharePoint. What the following sample code illustrates is the invocation of the SharePoint workflow when the user clicks a button on the custom Ribbon. Specifically, the code creates a new instance of the SharePoint workflow service, sets credentials for the workflow service, loads data into the workflow from the spreadsheet, and then invokes the specific workflow template (created in a separate VS 2008 project and deployed to the same server):

```vb
Private Sub ButtonWorkflow_Click(ByVal sender As System.Object, ByVal e As
Microsoft.Office.Tools.Ribbon.RibbonControlEventArgs) Handles ButtonWorkflow.Click

If Globals.ThisWorkbook.FullNameURLEncoded.Contains("http:") Then
          Using workflowWebSvc As WorkFlowSoapProxy.Workflow = New
WorkFlowSoapProxy.Workflow()

               workflowWebSvc.Credentials = CType(CredentialCache.
DefaultCredentials, NetworkCredential)
               Try
                    Dim itemWorkflowData = workflowWebSvc.
GetWorkflowDataForItem(Globals.ThisWorkbook.FullNameURLEncoded)

                    Dim workflowInfo = New XmlDocument()
                         workflowInfo.LoadXml("<WorkflowInformation>" +
itemWorkflowData.InnerXml + "</WorkflowInformation>")

Dim nsMgr As System.Xml.XmlNamespaceManager = New XmlNamespaceManager(New
NameTable())

                    nsMgr.AddNamespace("spWf", "http://schemas.microsoft.com/
sharepoint/soap/workflow/")

                    Dim documentApprovalWorkflowTemplate = _
workflowInfo.SelectSingleNode("//spWf:WorkflowTemplates/spWf:WorkflowTemplate[@Name
='SalesForecastApprovalWorkflow']", nsMgr)

                    Dim documentApprovalWorkflowTemplateIdSet =
documentApprovalWorkflowTemplate.SelectSingleNode("spWf:WorkflowTemplateIdSet",
nsMgr)
                    Dim documentApprovalWorkflowTemplateId =
documentApprovalWorkflowTemplateIdSet.Attributes("TemplateId").Value
                    Dim runningWorkflow As System.Xml.XmlNode = workflowInfo.
SelectSingleNode("//spWf:ActiveWorkflowsData/spWf:Workflows/spWf:Workflow[@
TemplateId='" + documentApprovalWorkflowTemplateId + "' and @Status1=2]", nsMgr)
                    If runningWorkflow IsNot Nothing Then
                         MessageBox.Show("The Workflow is already running for this
SalesForecast.")
                    Else
                         Dim workflowData = New WorkflowInstantiationData()
                         Dim SysArray = CType(Globals.Sheet1.
NamedRangeForecastComments.get_Value, System.Array)
                         If SysArray(1, 1) Is Nothing OrElse String.
IsNullOrEmpty(SysArray(1, 1).ToString) Then
                              workflowData.comments = String.Empty
                         Else
```

```
                             workflowData.comments = SysArray(1, 1).ToString()
                        End If
                        Dim serializer As XmlSerializer = New System.Xml.
   Serialization.XmlSerializer(GetType(WorkflowInstantiationData))

                        Dim workflowParametersDocument = New XmlDocument()
                        Using stream As MemoryStream = New MemoryStream()
                            serializer.Serialize(stream, workflowData)
                            stream.Position = 0
                            workflowParametersDocument.Load(stream)
                        End Using

                        Dim startInfo = workflowWebSvc.StartWorkflow( _
                            Globals.ThisWorkbook.FullNameURLEncoded, _
                            New Guid(documentApprovalWorkflowTemplateId), _
                            workflowParametersDocument.DocumentElement)
                    End If
                Catch ex As Exception
                    MessageBox.Show(ex.Message)
                End Try
            End Using
        Else
            MessageBox.Show("The Workbook needs to be saved before starting the
   workflow.")
        End If
    End Sub
```

We've shown you just a few examples of custom logic that are mapped to the Ribbon controls; however, you can do much more than this. For example, you can enter data into an edit box that updates all of the sales data by x%, or you can invoke other operations such as data exports or mail communications through the Ribbon, as well. At the end of the day, the Ribbon is a versatile developer tool that can really enhance the user experience and make the difference in the OBA that you create. In the sample project files that you can download with this book, we've added some Ribbon controls as stubs for you to add events (that is, the controls exist, but we added no code to the controls) so you can learn how to add event handlers to the Ribbon controls.

Summary

In this chapter, you learned about the custom actions pane and the custom Ribbon, both of which can be used to create and host custom logic for your OBA. You also learned how to create WPF user controls and add those to a Visual Studio project (remember, you can also use Expression Blend if you want to do more sophisticated UI creation).

In this chapter, we included a subset of the code that was created for the sales forecast OBA to demonstrate some of the core components of the solution in order to help provide some background on the custom actions pane and the Ribbon. As mentioned earlier, you can download the full set of project files for your use from Codeplex at http://www.codeplex.com/obasales. You can also find the link to the code at www.wrox.com.

Further Reading

Here are some additional links for technologies that were discussed throughout this chapter:

❑ Information on .NET 3.0: `http://msdn2.microsoft.com/en-us/netframework/aa663309.aspx`

❑ VSTO PowerTools, a set of complementary tools for VSTO: `http://www.microsoft.com/downloads/details.aspx?FamilyId=46B6BF86-E35D-4870-B214-4D7B72B02BF9&displaylang=en`

❑ WPF Developer Center: `http://msdn2.microsoft.com/en-us/netframework/aa663326.aspx`

❑ VSTO Developer Center: `http://msdn2.microsoft.com/en-us/office/aa905533.aspx`

❑ LINQ samples: `http://msdn2.microsoft.com/en-us/vcsharp/aa336746.aspx`

Creating and Deploying a Custom MOSS 2007 Workflow Using Visual Studio 2008

In organizations today, there exist processes around many of the things that we do. Sometimes these processes are informal and ad hoc; other times they are strict and must adhere to a set of formal steps. Within these processes, data and events must be managed in a strict and rigorous fashion. For example, if you're building a purchase order (PO) process, oftentimes customer, inventory, and pricing data will be used in tandem with a document of some sort to manage user interaction with the PO data. Further, the PO document may need to be approved by a manager to ensure that the data is correct and then marked as paid by a finance person. The point here is that the example process touches multiple people, must conform to specific organization policies and rules, reads and writes data into a workflow, and requires a set of tools to manage the ways in which the users interface with the process. To handle all of these requires a specific software application that tracks and routes information and documents to the appropriate person in a strictly defined way. Enter workflow.

In this chapter, we discuss the different types of workflow relevant to the sales forecast OBA and provide some general guidance on how you can create them. After you read this chapter, you will want to download the solution files from the sales forecast Codeplex site and explore the custom code within the sales forecast OBA workflow (`http://www.codeplex.com/obasales` or at `http://www.wrox.com`).

What Is SharePoint Workflow?

To help you build solutions that manage these formal processes, Microsoft shipped the Windows Workflow Foundation (WF) in the .NET Framework 3.0. WF provides a baseline set of technologies for you to build a myriad of workflow solutions that includes a workflow runtime engine (which executes activities within a specific Windows process, such as Windows Forms application or ASP.NET web site), a programming model, and different tools that enable you to build workflow. Using this technology, you can build what are called activities, which are the individual actions that, taken together, make up your workflow. You also have a number of services available to you when building and deploying these activities. For example, Figure 5-1 illustrates a set of activities that you might build and the different services available to you in the WF runtime. An example of an activity might be creating a custom task in response to the submission of a document to a SharePoint site or sending an email to a specific person in the organization for document approval.

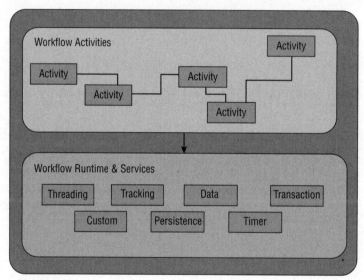

Figure 5-1

Using WF, there are essentially two primary types of workflows that you can build: Sequential and State Machine. Sequential is exactly as it sounds: the workflow is run one activity after the other until it completes. You can design a Sequential workflow with elements such as a start, activities, while loops, and a finish. You might also think of this type of workflow as being appropriate for an automated workflow process that does not involve a lot of human intervention. Sequential workflows in one sense are more straightforward to create because you're essentially creating a workflow that will execute one step at a time. State workflow is where the activities rely on a particular state for them to complete (or trigger another event). That is, the workflow responds to an event or trigger. For example, imagine you are publishing a compliance document and there are several contributors to the document. You will likely need to have external events that provide gateways for the workflow to continue. You'll need a state for the document created; you'll need another state when all contributors have completed their edits; and you'll need yet another when all managers have approved the document. Converse to Sequential, State workflow is more appropriate where there is either a high degree of human intervention or the process is longer-running. State workflows are a little more challenging to create because you first create the states, then the relationships across the states, and, finally, the activities within the states.

SharePoint Workflow

Now that you know a little bit about WF, you're probably asking yourself where SharePoint fits into the picture. As mentioned earlier in the book, SharePoint can be broken into Windows SharePoint Services (WSS) 3.0 and Microsoft Office SharePoint Server (MOSS) 2007. WSS ships free with Windows Server, and MOSS is value-add software that provides an additional set of enterprise collaboration features to WSS. You can subsequently use Visual Studio and the .NET Framework 3.0 (which includes WF) to build workflow that is specific to SharePoint. Specifically, in Visual Studio 2008, there exist a number of WF templates that you can use; the two that we specifically discuss in this chapter are the Visual Studio Tools for Office (VSTO) 3.0 project templates that you can use to build either a State Machine or Sequential workflow and deploy directly to your SharePoint server. Note: You can also use SharePoint Designer to build workflows; however, in this chapter we focus on VSTO as the primary means for creating workflow for SharePoint.

MOSS 2007 ships with a limited set of out-of-the-box workflow — see Figure 5-2. Nevertheless, you can build very powerful workflow solutions using the VSTO technology, which allows you to create custom workflow for your OBA.

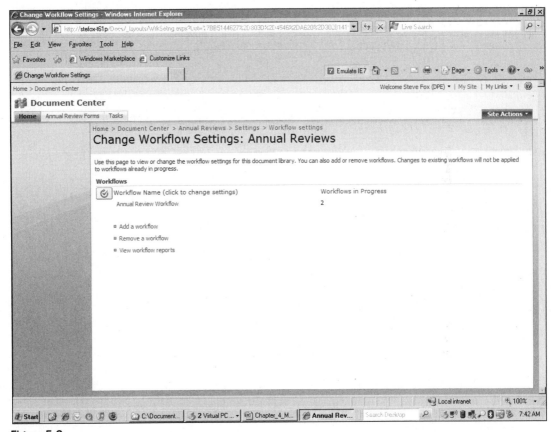

Figure 5-2

Though the out-of-the-box workflow provides some limited functionality and task routing, in the sales forecast OBA we created a custom approval workflow (State Machine workflow) for the forecasts that a salesperson creates. In this workflow, when a document is saved to the core document library, a task is created requesting the sales manager to review the forecast and either approve or reject it, or request an amendment to the sales forecast. With each option that is selected by the manager, a message is sent back to the salesperson. If the manager approves the sales forecast without any changes, the workflow completes. If the manager requests an amendment, the salesperson must go through the process of editing and saving the document again — essentially kicking off the workflow from the beginning again. If the sales forecast is rejected, then presumably the sales manager and the salesperson will discuss it offline. The lines are dotted in this case because these are not official parts of our sales forecast workflow (or at least the software that supports the workflow), but they represent actions that could result from the rejection of the sales forecast. Figure 5-3 provides an overview of the sales forecast workflow.

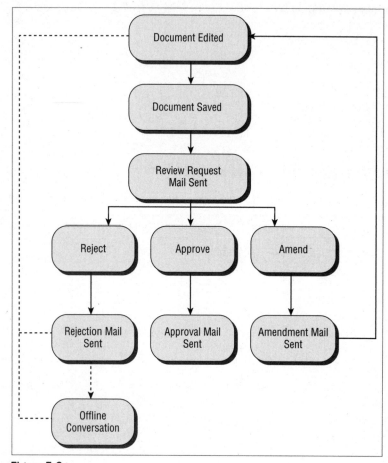

Figure 5-3

Some additional details on the sales forecast workflow that you may find either important or interesting are as follows:

❑ The workflow is tied to the specific document library in which the sales forecasts are stored and is started when the document is saved to that document library.

❑ The workflow activities live within specific states (hence the workflow being a State Machine workflow) that enable the workflow activities to be triggered at particular times within the business process.

❑ The workflow can be started manually through the SharePoint site or through the custom ribbon in the sales forecast document.

❑ The workflow triggers a custom mail that renders within an inspector that displays a custom Outlook form region, for enhanced data presentation, and routes this to the salesperson's manager for approval. This gives the manager additional information about the approval request. Rejection and amendment mails are sent with a straight text-based mail.

❑ Notifications are sent via email when the workflow actions are changed (that is, from approved, to rejected, to amend).

❑ A field in SharePoint displays the status for the workflow (for example, In Progress vs. Complete).

While this list provides a small background on workflow in general, this area is generally one that requires more practice and research than other areas. It also requires some careful design, because of the interdependencies that you create across objects within your OBA. That said, workflow is an exciting area and can bring a lot of power to your business process-centric solutions.

Creating SharePoint Workflow

For creating Windows workflow solutions in general, you don't necessarily need a SharePoint site; you could build a workflow solution using a command window. Before you can create and deploy your SharePoint workflow, however, you need to set up a SharePoint site because you will map the workflow to that site (or more precisely artifacts within the SharePoint site such as a document library or list). If you haven't created a SharePoint site before, Chapter 6, "Creating a Custom Outlook Form Region," provides an overview of how to create a SharePoint site.

To actually create and debug the workflow, you use the same tool, Visual Studio 2008 (specifically the VSTO 3.0 within Visual Studio), to build the workflow so you'll want to make sure you have this installed as well. (If you tried what we discussed in Chapter 4, "Customizing the Office Fluent Ribbon and the Task Pane," in your own environment, then you should have Visual Studio 2008 already installed.) In the rest of this chapter, we cover some of the key steps involved in creating workflow and provide some code samples from the sales forecast OBA. For SharePoint workflow, we would also recommend reviewing the samples that ship with the Office Server 2007 SDK and reviewing the full solution files within the sales forecast project files.

To create a new SharePoint workflow, open Visual Studio 2008 and click File ⇨ New ⇨ Project. In the New Project dialog navigate to either Visual Basic or Visual C# and then click the Office and then 2007 node. In the list of VSTO project templates are two choices for SharePoint workflow (see Figure 5-4):

1. SharePoint 2007 Sequential Workflow
2. SharePoint 2007 State Machine Workflow

The Sequential Workflow template is intended for workflows that follow a predefined set of tasks within a particular business process. These workflows may involve branching or looping, but they invariably follow a sequential path or progress through the activities that make up the workflow. As discussed previously, a simple document approval process is an example of a Sequential workflow.

The State Machine Workflow template is intended for workflows that move between states. This type of workflow does not follow a specific sequence of activities. Think of a customer support workflow, wherein the support ticket may have different states at different times and therefore may have specific events or activities associated with it. For workflows such as this, consider using the State Machine model.

These two workflow templates enable you to use the workflow objects included within the .NET 3.0 WF, but the VSTO workflow project templates provide additional debugging and deployment capabilities specifically geared toward creating workflow for MOSS 2007. As such, VSTO 3.0 has *significantly* reduced the amount of work it takes to build SharePoint workflow. For example, VSTO 3.0 provides you with a wizard that helps you configure the workflow for a specific list or library within SharePoint. Further, Visual Studio then deploys all of the built files to the appropriate locations within SharePoint, reducing a lot of overhead for the developer. If you have had experience programming applications for SharePoint, you will really appreciate the debugging experience!

The experience of creating the Sequential workflow versus the State Machine workflow is slightly different. For example, in the Sequential workflow, you'll create the project and then add activities to the designer to create a sequence of events within your workflow. You will first need to build states, however, and relationships across those states, when creating State Machine workflows. When creating your own workflow, we recommend trying the Sequential workflow first and then moving on to the State Machine workflow.

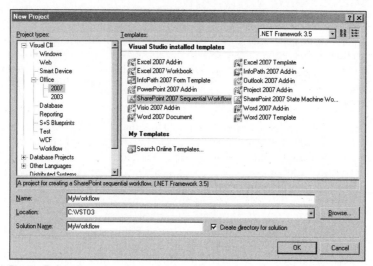

Figure 5-4

Figure 5-4 shows the VSTO workflow templates in the Office | 2007 node in the New Project dialog. To explore the other project templates associated with WF, navigate to Workflow instead of Office, and you'll find the other WF templates. After you select the SharePoint 2007 Sequential Workflow project template, you can provide a name and location for your workflow, and click OK. Clicking OK will invoke the New Office SharePoint Workflow wizard. The first dialog in the wizard will prompt you to provide a name for your workflow and a local site with which you'll want to associate the workflow. The local site is the SharePoint site to which you will be deploying your SharePoint workflow, so enter the URL to the base site, and Visual Studio will load all of the lists and libraries from that site, which you'll see in a later dialog, in the new workflow process (see Figure 5-6). After you complete this step, click Next (see Figure 5-5). This invokes the wizard mentioned earlier, where you have a number of configuration steps for your new workflow.

The next step in the wizard prompts you for the library or list (that are loaded from the site URL that you provided in the first dialog in the wizard), history list, and task list that you want to associate with the workflow when debugging your workflow. When you create your workflow, you'll want to select the appropriate list or library to which you want to map your workflow. To have the workflow automatically make the associations for you, which is recommended, keep the Automatically Associate Workflow checkbox checked. You'll likely not have more than one option for the History List and Task List (unless you've created alternate lists yourself for these within SharePoint), so you'll want to leave these as the default choices. After you've made your selections here, you can click Next to move on to the next step in the wizard (see Figure 5-7).

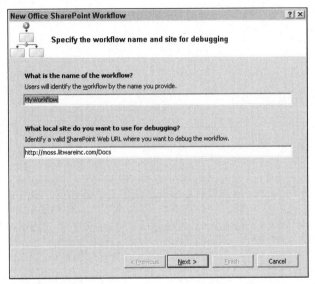

Figure 5-5

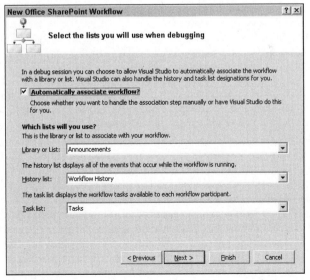

Figure 5-6

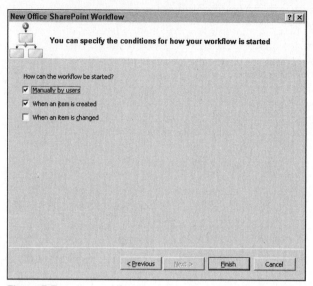

Figure 5-7

The final step in the wizard provides three checkboxes for starting the workflow. Here, your choice depends on how you want your workflow to be initiated. For example, if you only want the workflow to be able to be manually generated by the user, you select the first option. If you want the workflow to start when an item is created (for example, a document is saved to a document library), select the second option. Likewise, you can select the third option if you want to start the workflow when an item is changed (for example, a document is updated). Select the choice that you want, and then click Finish to complete the workflow creation. Clicking Finish will generate a project shell for you, which will include some default files. For example, included in the project is your core workflow code file (for example, `MyWorkflow.cs`) and some other resource files (for example, `feature.xml` and `workflow.xml`). The core workflow code file essentially represents the code-behind file for your custom workflow code. There are two main views within which you'll work when adding your custom code and activities to the workflow solution: code view and designer view. The designer view is where you can drag and drop activities from the Toolbox onto the designer surface. Similar to other designer experiences within Visual Studio 2008, you double-click the activities and then add your events to the activity (see Figure 5-8).

After you've created your new workflow, you can add activities from the Toolbox to the designer surface. An activity is a task that executes a specific action within a workflow; for example, creating a task, sending an email, connecting to Web services, and so on. To create activities, you drag them from the Toolbox onto the designer surface. When added to the designer surface, activities are built as classes, and have properties, events, and methods associated with them. You will notice three different tabs on the Toolbox when creating your workflow projects: Windows Workflow 3.0, Windows Workflow 3.5, and SharePoint Workflow. You can use activities from any one of these tabs, however the SharePoint Workflow tab contains activities that can be used only with your SharePoint workflow project. For example, some of the sample activities in the SharePoint workflow tab are CreateTask, OnTaskCreated, SendEmail, and so on. Once you've added the activities to the designer, you can also double-click the activities to add your own custom code and set breakpoints from the designer (right-click and select Insert Breakpoint).

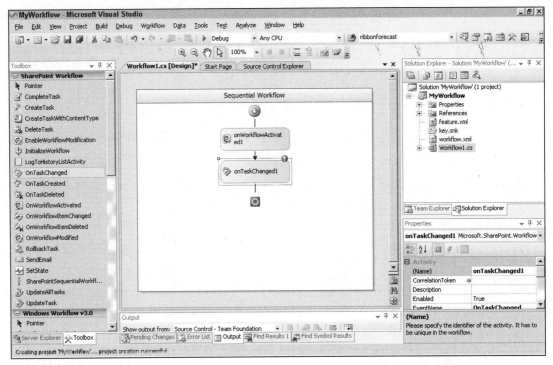

Figure 5-8

Note that one of the tricky elements of creating and deploying workflow is the association of the workflows to events through an object called a correlation token. A correlation token is a unique identifier that maps objects within a workflow. Your workflow uses a correlation token to identify and respond to other objects within the SharePoint workflow project. For example, if you create a Sequential workflow and you add a CreateTask activity and a CompleteTask activity, you need to ensure the correlation of the CompleteTask is set to that of the CreateTask so the two objects are bound together within the project. Further, each activity within the workflow must map back to the initial workflow activity to be mapped to that workflow and execute within that workflow. You set the OwnerActivityName to complete this mapping.

Correlation tokens are integral when creating your workflow because, if you assign them incorrectly, your workflow will not work properly (that is, activities may not execute properly because they are not cross-bound to the objects to which they should be bound). For example, you set the CorrelationToken property of the OnWorkflowActivated activity (that is, the beginning point of your workflow) in your project and call it NewApprovalWorkflow. You want to have a mail with a custom message sent as part of the workflow, so you create a SendMail activity and add it to the designer surface. To map the new activity to the initial workflow, you need to set the CorrelationToken property to NewApprovalWorkflow. Note that all of the available correlation tokens will appear in the drop-down list when you set it. If you do not set the token properly, the SendMail activity will not execute properly, thus your mail will not be sent.

For example, if you add a CreateTask event from the Toolbox to a workflow project, you can create a correlation token within the Properties window of that workflow project and map it to, for example, a SendMail activity. To illustrate this mapping of activities to properties, with the workflow designer, drag a CreateTask activity onto the workflow designer between onWorkflowActivated1 and the end of the workflow in a new workflow project. The new activity is named createTask1 by default, but you can change this, if you want, in the Name property in the Properties window. Figure 5-9 illustrates the new createTask1 activity added to the Sequential workflow. Figure 5-9 also illustrates the correlation token and other properties that have been set in the Properties window to make sure the workflow solution (albeit small) works as designed.

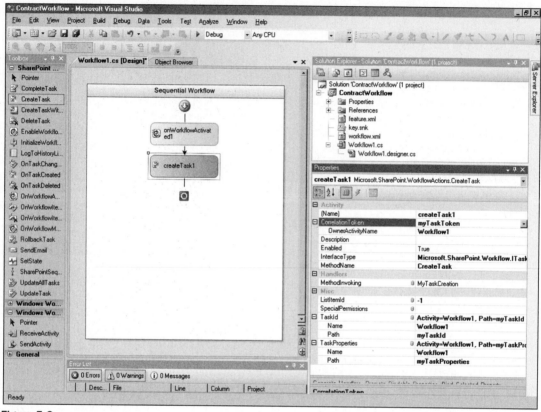

Figure 5-9

Though the workflow solution wouldn't do anything interesting, the key point here is that you use the Properties window to map your activities to your workflow. For the example project in Figure 5-9 you would create a new CorrelationToken called myTaskToken, click the plus sign beside CorrelationToken, and then select an OwnerActivityName, which in this case is the default name for the workflow: Workflow1. Note that there is also an event called MyTaskCreation associated with the MethodInvoking event handler in this project. You double-click the Handler to stub out events in your workflow, within which you can add your custom code. You can also assign other properties such as TaskID properties and TaskProperties in the project as well. To set these properties, you also use the Properties window. The TaskID is a unique ID for the workflow task, and the TaskProperties is an object you will use to set the properties of the task. Note that in Figure 5-9, the Name property of the TaskID is set to the name of the workflow. You set the TaskId and TaskProperties by clicking the ellipsis in either the TaskID or TaskProperties field.

The sales forecast OBA uses the State Machine SharePoint Workflow project template, which is very similar to the Sequential workflow project. We did this because the OBA requires certain events to be triggered based on the state of the sales forecast business process. That is, when the salesperson submits his sales forecast the custom workflow issues a request for the sales manager to review the forecast. This means that the workflow must wait while the manager reviews and responds to the request. As we discussed earlier, the responses can either be an approval, rejection, or amendment. These responses are raised either manually, from within SharePoint, or dynamically, from within the custom Outlook form region (see Figure 5-10).

As mentioned earlier, the State Machine workflow projects are a little different from the Sequential workflows in that you need to add states to your project and then create relationships across the states. After you've done this, however, you add activities to each of the states you add to your project in much the same way you added activities to the Sequential workflow we discussed earlier. The implication here, however, is that you need to think about the design of your workflow in a slightly different way; that is, from the standpoint of states as opposed to step-by-step processes. For example, Figure 5-10 illustrates a simple State Machine project. We've drilled into the one default state that is created as a part of the project. Note that the one activity, which is added by default, called onWorkflowActivated1 has all of its properties set (remember the correlation token) by default. You can also browse back and forth across states within your workflow designer by using the breadcrumb links in the designer. (The breadcrumb links are the links located at the top of the designer that allow you to navigate across the objects within your workflow project.)

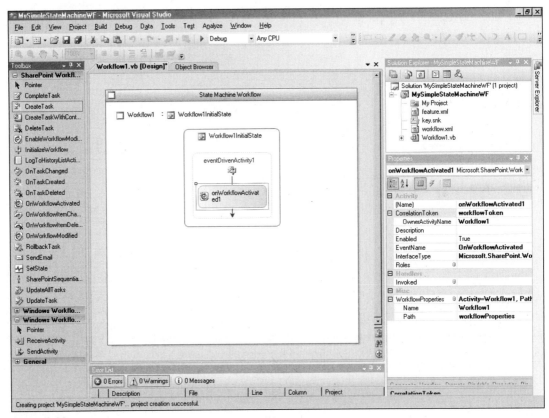

Figure 5-10

The sales forecast OBA contains four workflow states, within which we include a number of processing activities from the Toolbox. The four states in the workflow follow:

1. Initial State: Initializes objects and sets up some document processing for the sales forecast OBA.

2. Request Approval State: Manages the custom options resulting from the manager's response (that is, approve, reject, or amend).

3. Request Review State: Manages the status property of the document.

4. Completed State: Manages the completion of the workflow.

Figure 5-11 illustrates the designer view for the sales forecast OBA workflow.

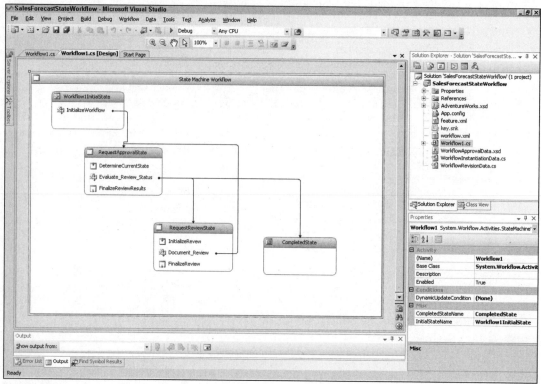

Figure 5-11

If you've downloaded the sample code, you can drill into each of the workflow objects to see additional workflow activities and branching that have been added to the workflow. Figure 5-12 illustrates some of the conditional branching events that are mapped to the Evaluate_Review_Status workflow state, which controls the triggering of custom code given a particular change in the workflow. In Figure 5-12, note that events mapping to the three responses in the workflow are managed. If you continue to drill into each of the activities, you'll see the custom code that is associated with each of the workflow objects.

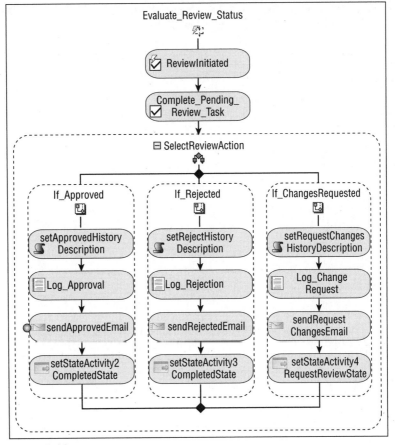

Figure 5-12

Exploring Some Custom SharePoint Workflow Code

Within the sales forecast OBA, there was a modest amount of custom code added to the activities within the workflow. For example, the following code sample shows the onWorkflowActivated1_Invoked event. Because there is custom XML from the custom VSTO Excel 2007 document that is being passed to the custom Outlook form region via the workflow, we must use the XmlSerializer and XmlTextReader objects to manage this XML. For example, in the code sample we create an instance of the XmlSerializer class called serializer, which we use to serialize the data from the Excel spreadsheet into an XML stream that we can pass to the Outlook inspector that will contain the custom Outlook form region. You'll also notice that the use of the ServerDocument object (called serverDocument), which is a class within the VSTO runtime that can be used to perform simple manipulation of Word and Excel documents, is another way of manipulating data within documents and auto-generating documents without having to actually open the document. In the code sample, the serverDocument object enables us to get data out of the Excel document and serialize it using the XmlSerializer and XmlTextReader objects and filtering that data using a LINQ query called salesManager. Lastly, the code snippet illustrates the setting of a number of email properties.

Specifically, we're using sales manager (the approvingUser object) information and the default user (the originatingUser object) of the workflow to set these properties.

```
            private void onWorkflowActivated1_Invoked(object sender,
ExternalDataEventArgs e)
        {
            XmlSerializer serializer = new XmlSerializer(typeof(WorkflowInstantiati
onData));
            XmlTextReader reader = new XmlTextReader(new System.
IO.StringReader(this.workflowProperties.InitiationData));
            WorkflowInstantiationData instantiationData = null;
            try
            {
                instantiationData = (WorkflowInstantiationData)serializer.
Deserialize(reader);
            }
            catch (Exception err)
            {
                string a = err.Message;
            }

            this.instructions = instantiationData.comments;
            SPUser originatingUser = this.workflowProperties.OriginatorUser;

            if (string.Compare(originatingUser.LoginName, "SHAREPOINT\\system",
true, CultureInfo.InvariantCulture) == 0)
            {
                originatingUser = this.workflowProperties.Web.
SiteUsers["litwareinc\\administrator"];
            }
            ServerDocument serverDocument = new ServerDocument(this.
workflowProperties.Item.File.OpenBinary(), ".xlsx");
            CachedDataHostItem hostItem = serverDocument.CachedData.HostItems["Sale
sForecastWorkbook.ThisWorkbook"];
            CachedDataItem salesManagerIdData = hostItem.CachedData["ManagerEmploy
eeID"];
            serializer = new XmlSerializer(Type.GetType(salesManagerIdData.
DataType));
            int salesManagerId = (int)serializer.Deserialize(new
StringReader(salesManagerIdData.Xml));
            AdventureWorksVSTO advwrksDC = new AdventureWorksVSTO(Properties.
Settings.Default.AdventureWorksConnectionString);
            advwrksDC.ObjectTrackingEnabled = false;
            var salesManager = from employee in advwrksDC.HumanResources_Employee
                               where employee.EmployeeID == salesManagerId
                               select employee;
            SPUser approvingUser = this.workflowProperties.Web.
SiteUsers[salesManager.First().LoginID];
            this.originatorAccount = originatingUser.LoginName;
            this.approverAccount = approvingUser.LoginName;
            this.originatorEmail = originatingUser.Email;
            this.approverEmail = approvingUser.Email;
            this.originatorName = originatingUser.Name;
            this.approverName = approvingUser.Name;
```

```
            this.emailTo = this.approverEmail;
            this.emailFrom = this.originatorEmail;
        }
```

One of the interesting connections within the workflow project is with the integration with Outlook. You will see the importance of Outlook and the integration with Outlook as a recurring theme throughout this book, and the sample that follows shows some code that creates an instance of the mail message, formats the message, and then attaches data held in cache (data from the Excel document). The result of this integration is the generation of a custom email that provides richer user interaction with the data that is housed within the custom Outlook form region (see Figure 5-13). The relationship that this sample code has with the sales forecast workflow project is that this is one of the activities that is executed as a part of the workflow. Although the code sample is long, it is essentially creating an instance of a new mail object (called requestAppMessage), setting some properties for the mail message (for example the subject, body, and so on), attaching the data from the Excel spreadsheet (using the ServerDocument and XMLWriter objects), and sending the formatted email with data attached to the sales manager for approval:

```
        private void sendApprovalRequestedEmail_ExecuteCode(object sender,
    EventArgs e)
        {
            MailMessage requestAppMessage = new MailMessage();
            this.emailSubject =
                string.Format(
                    "{0} has requested approval for the document '{1}'",
                    this.originatorName,
                    this.workflowProperties.Item.Name);
            requestAppMessage.Subject = this.emailSubject;
            this.emailBody =
                string.Format(
                    "<html>" +
                    "<head>" +
                    "<meta http-equiv='Content-Type' content='text/html;
    charset=utf-8'/>" +
                    "<style>" +
                    "table.mail" +
                    "{{border-style:none;" +
                    "border-collapse:collapse;" +
                    "font:8pt Tahoma;" +
                    "width:100%}}" +
                    "td.header" +
                    "{{background:#F8F8F9;" +
                    "border:1px solid #E8EAEC;" +
                    "padding:12pt 10px 4pt 10px}}" +
                    "td.body" +
                    "{{padding:12pt 10px 24pt 10px}}" +
                    "td.footer" +
                    "{{border-width:1px;" +
                    "border-style:solid none none none;" +
                    "border-color:#9CA3AD;" +
                    "padding:4pt 10px 4pt 10px}}" +
                    "a" +
                    "{{text-decoration:none}}" +
                    "div.title" +
                    "{{font:16pt Verdana}}" +
                    "div.headertext" +
                    "{{margin:5px 0px 0px 0px}}" +
```

```
                                "div.error" +
                                "{{font-weight:bold}}" +
                                "div.comment" +
                                "{{color:#9CA3AD}}" +
                                "span.wfname" +
                                "{{font:bold italic}}" +
                                "</style>" +
                                "</head>" +
                                "<body>" +
                                "<table cellpadding='2' cellspacing='0' class='mail'
        dir='none'>" +

                                "<tbody>" +
                                "<tr class='header'>" +
                                "<td class='header'>" +
                                "<div class='title'>{0}</div>" +
                                "<br/>" +
                                "<div class='error'>Due by {1}</div>" +
                                "</td>" +
                                "</tr>" +
                                "<tr class='body'>" +
                                "<td class='body' valign='top'>" +
                                "<div>{2}</div>" +
                                "</td>" +
                                "</tr>" +
                                "<tr class='footer'>" +
                                "<td class='footer'>" +
                                "<div class='comment'>" +
                                "To complete this task:" +
                                "<br/>" +
                                "<ol>" +
                                "<li>" +
                                "Review <a href='{3}' target='_blank'>" +
                                "{4}" +
                                "</a>." +
                                "</li>" +
                                "<li>Perform the specific activities required for this task.</
        li>" +

                                "<li>" +
                                "<a href='{5}' target='_blank'>Edit this task</a> to resubmit
        the document for approval." +
                                "</li>" +
                                "</ol>" +
                                "</div>" +
                                "</td>" +
                                "</tr>" +
                                "</tbody>" +
                                "</table>" +
                                "</body>" +
                                "</html>",
                                this.emailSubject,
                                this.taskDueBy.ToShortDateString(),
                                this.instructions,
                                string.Format(
                                    "{0}/{1}",
                                    this.workflowProperties.Web.Url,
```

```
                    this.workflowProperties.Item.Url),
                this.workflowProperties.Item.Name,
                string.Format(
                    "{0}/_layouts/WrkStat.aspx?List={1}&WorkflowInstanceID={2}",
                    this.workflowProperties.Web.Url,
                    this.workflowProperties.ListId.ToString("B"),
                    this.workflowProperties.WorkflowId.ToString("B")));
            requestAppMessage.Body = this.emailBody;

            ServerDocument serverDocument = new ServerDocument(this.
workflowProperties.Item.File.OpenBinary(), ".xlsx");
            CachedDataHostItem hostItem = serverDocument.CachedData.HostItems["Sale
sForecastWorkbook.ThisWorkbook"];
            CachedDataItem intData = hostItem.CachedData["SalesEmployeeID"];

            XmlSerializer serializer = new XmlSerializer(Type.GetType(intData.
DataType));
            int salesEmployeeID = (int)serializer.Deserialize(new
StringReader(intData.Xml));
            intData = hostItem.CachedData["ForecastID"];
            int forecastID = (int)serializer.Deserialize(new StringReader(intData.
Xml));
            intData = hostItem.CachedData["SalesContactID"];
            int salesContactID = (int)serializer.Deserialize(new
StringReader(intData.Xml));
            intData = hostItem.CachedData["ManagerEmployeeID"];
            int managerEmployeeID = (int)serializer.Deserialize(new
StringReader(intData.Xml));
            intData = hostItem.CachedData["TerritoryID"];
            int territoryID = (int)serializer.Deserialize(new StringReader(intData.
Xml));
            CachedDataItem forecastDateData = hostItem.CachedData["ForecastDate"];
            serializer = new XmlSerializer(Type.GetType(forecastDateData.
DataType));
            DateTime forecastDate = (DateTime)serializer.Deserialize(new
StringReader(forecastDateData.Xml));

            requestAppMessage.To.Add(approverEmail);
            requestAppMessage.From = new System.Net.Mail.
MailAddress(originatorEmail);

            MemoryStream attachMe = new MemoryStream();
            XmlWriter XMLAttach = XmlWriter.Create(attachMe);
            XMLAttach.WriteStartDocument();
            XMLAttach.WriteStartElement("CompanyData");

            AdventureWorksVSTO advwrksDC = new AdventureWorksVSTO(Properties.
Settings.Default.AdventureWorksConnectionString);
            advwrksDC.ObjectTrackingEnabled = false;
            PopulateGeneralInfo(XMLAttach, salesContactID, territoryID,
forecastDate, advwrksDC);
            PopulateSalesData(XMLAttach, forecastID, salesEmployeeID, forecastDate,
advwrksDC);
            XMLAttach.WriteEndElement();
            XMLAttach.WriteEndDocument();
```

```
            XMLAttach.Flush();

            attachMe.Position = 0;
            requestAppMessage.Attachments.Add(new Attachment(attachMe,
    "LitwareForeCastData.xml", "text/xml"));

            requestAppMessage.IsBodyHtml = true;
            SmtpClient smtp = new SmtpClient("localhost");
            smtp.Send(requestAppMessage);
            return;
        }
```

The result of the execution of this workflow code is a custom inspector that contains a custom Outlook form region. The form region code takes the attached data from the email and generates a view of the data (graphs that provide dynamic views of the data) and a view that enables the sales manager to respond to the workflow right within the email. Figure 5-13 displays this custom mail message.

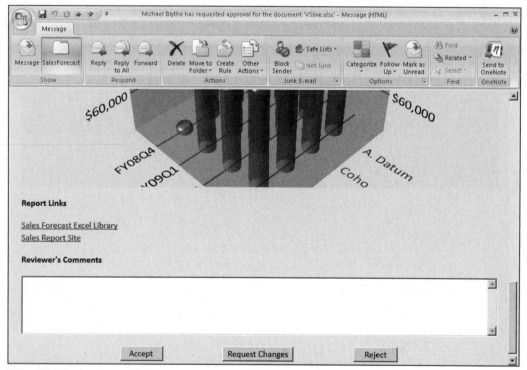

Figure 5-13

Debugging and Deploying SharePoint Workflow

After you complete your SharePoint workflow project, it will be time to debug it. You can do this by simply clicking the Debug button or pressing F5 on your keyboard. The debugging experience is very rich when you use VSTO. For example, the debugger invokes your default browser and instantiates the environment within which your workflow will execute. If your workflow activity defines an activity that invokes when a new document is created, then once you create your document and save it to the SharePoint library to which you've mapped the workflow (remember the wizard that walks you through this process), your workflow will now be active. You can view the workflow in SharePoint by hovering over the document, clicking the down-arrow, and then selecting Workflows. This invokes the Workflows page for that document library and will list your particular workflow. If you have not programmatically started your workflow, you can manually start your custom workflow by clicking it within this view. In the sales forecast OBA, when you open the workflow project and click F5, Visual Studio invokes Internet Explorer and then opens the Sales Forecast document library, the library to which the workflow is attached. If you create a new document (using the custom template we discussed earlier in the book) by clicking New, Edit, and then Save, you can either start the workflow manually from SharePoint or click the Start Sales Forecast Approval Workflow button on the custom ribbon in the Excel 2007 sales forecast document. Figure 5-14 illustrates the invocation of the SharePoint environment. Note that in the SalesForecastApprovalWorkflow column (the status column for the workflow that SharePoint creates for workflows associated with a document library) a document named SalesForecastWorkbook2 is created, edited, and saved to the document library, but the workflow is not yet in progress.

Figure 5-14

Similar to the other documents listed in the Sales Forecasts document library, the status for the workflow will be Completed once the workflow is complete. At this point, if you're debugging your own SharePoint workflow project, the debugger will return you to the Visual Studio IDE, and your workflow debugging session will conclude.

If you remember back to the workflow project wizard (see Figures 4-5, 4-6, and 4-7), Visual Studio prompts you to associate the workflow with a specific SharePoint site. As part of the debugging experience, Visual Studio deploys the SharePoint workflow project files, or workflow template, to the SharePoint site and makes all of the appropriate configurations along the way. The nice thing for you is that a lot of the work is done for you. For example, Visual Studio automatically creates a .wsp package (a deployment package of files that is specific to SharePoint deployment). This package includes a feature.xml file (which treats the workflow template as a feature and provides some information about the workflow feature), a workflow.xml file (which provides some information about the workflow template), and the assembly files (which represent the core managed code assemblies within the SharePoint workflow project).

The following provides an example of the type of information you find within a workflow.xml file:

```xml
<?xml version="1.0" encoding="utf-8" ?>

<Elements xmlns="http://schemas.microsoft.com/sharepoint/">
  <Workflow
      Name="MyWorkflow"
      Description="My SharePoint Workflow"
      Id="b4ffa83c-3a47-4c6e-962e-de7b10a5dff4"
      CodeBesideClass="SharePointWorkflow5.Workflow1"
      CodeBesideAssembly="MyWorkflow, Version=1.0.0.0, Culture=neutral, Public
KeyToken=d833507c5828a45e">

      <Categories/>
      <MetaData>
        <StatusPageUrl>_layouts/WrkStat.aspx</StatusPageUrl>
      </MetaData>
    </Workflow>
</Elements>
```

The following provides an example of the type of information you find within a feature.xml file.

```xml
<?xml version="1.0" encoding="utf-8" ?>

<Feature   Id="519fbf46-5f7b-48e6-b125-ea9d5b15324c"
        Title="SharePointWorkflow5 feature"
        Description="My SharePoint Workflow Feature"
        Version="12.0.0.0"
        Scope="Site"
        ReceiverAssembly="Microsoft.Office.Workflow.Feature, Version=12.0.0.0,
Culture=neutral, PublicKeyToken=71e9bce111e9429c"
        ReceiverClass="Microsoft.Office.Workflow.Feature.
WorkflowFeatureReceiver"
        xmlns="http://schemas.microsoft.com/sharepoint/">
  <ElementManifests>
    <ElementManifest Location="workflow.xml" />
  </ElementManifests>
  <Properties>
    <Property Key="GloballyAvailable" Value="true" />

    <!-- Value for RegisterForms key indicates the path to the forms
relative to feature file location -->
    <!-- if you don't have forms, use *.xsn -->
```

```
        <Property Key="RegisterForms" Value="*.xsn" />
    </Properties>
</Feature>
```

To deploy your own workflow solution, right-click the solution name and select Deploy Solution. If you want to remove the workflow from SharePoint, navigate to the Settings page for the document library, click Workflow Settings, Remove Workflow, and then select the workflow you want to remove.

We encourage you to download the solution files that go along with this book, try the workflow debugging experience by opening the workflow solution files, setting a couple of breakpoints in the workflow project file, and then walking through the debugging experience. You will have to set up a SharePoint site to be able to do this. We cover that later in the book.

Summary

This chapter introduced you to Windows Workflow Foundation (WF) and provided an introduction to SharePoint workflow capabilities within Visual Studio 2008, providing some discussion around how to create a Sequential workflow using VSTO 3.0. This chapter also discussed selected parts of the workflow within the sales forecast OBA, which is a State Machine workflow, and described some of the differences between types of workflow. It also provided some code samples within the sales forecast solution to give you an idea of what is possible when creating your own workflow solutions.

You can find all of the solution files that map to this chapter at `http://wrox.com` or at `http://www.codeplex.com/obasales`. We encourage you to download the files and walk through the source code not only to get a better understanding of SharePoint workflows in general, but also to get a better sense for how you could apply the concepts and code discussed in this chapter to your own production environment.

Further Reading

Here are some additional links to technologies that were discussed throughout this chapter:

- ❑ Information on .NET 3.0: `http://msdn2.microsoft.com/en-us/netframework/aa663309.aspx`

- ❑ VSTO Developer Center: `http://msdn2.microsoft.com/en-us/office/aa905533.aspx`

- ❑ SharePoint Developer Center: `http://msdn.microsoft.com/en-us/sharepoint/default.aspx`

- ❑ VSTO SharePoint MSDN Walkthrough: `http://msevents.microsoft.com/CUI/WebCastEventDetails.aspx?EventID=1032345928&EventCategory=3&culture=en-US&CountryCode=US`

- ❑ SharePoint Workflow Virtual Lab: `http://msevents.microsoft.com/CUI/WebCastEventDetails.aspx?EventID=1032345928&EventCategory=3&culture=en-US&CountryCode=US`

6

Creating A Custom Outlook Form Region

This chapter introduces the Outlook Form Region (OFR) to the list of technologies used in this OBA. The OFR is one of the most powerful tools available to the developer of an OBA because it integrates your custom business logic and data with arguably the most used and liked tool of the Office Suite — Outlook. In the case of the sales forecast OFR, we see the power of that integration within email. Over the years, everyone from the mailroom to the boardroom has used email, and unlike creating a spreadsheet or typing a document, handling email is a task that occurs across all levels of an organization. As a result, as long as your organization is leveraging Outlook as an email client, everyone in the organization from the sales representative to the uber-nerd is familiar with the interface of Outlook.

The result is that if you can go beyond embedding data as an attachment, and instead provide a custom interface that is displayed with the email, you will expose that data to the people who really need to review it. No more unexpected responses that someone couldn't get an attachment to open, or that they lost the "link" to the project site, or any of a dozen other reasons work couldn't be completed. Instead, Outlook will host their work in the one application they all check several times a day, and the convenience of directly updating line of business application data will result in a happier user.

This chapter focuses on the steps and key elements of developing an OFR. The chapter talks about pitfalls based on the type of OFR you select, and walks through the key elements of the OFR that is part of the sales forecast OBA implementation. The sales forecast OFR was designed using WPF as the display engine, allowing you to embed 3D graphics within a custom display hosted inside of Outlook. To do this, you'll walk through the steps to leverage WPF-Windows Forms interoperability, create a custom WPF user control, and populate that control with data retrieved from an XML attachment in your email message. Finally, to make this more than just eye-candy, the OFR will be coded to allow the manager receiving it to connect to the running Sales Forecast Approval Workflow and update the current status of that workflow from within Outlook.

The topics in this chapter include:

❑ OFR types

❑ Filtering when an Adjoining or Separate OFR is visible

❑ Accessing email attachments

❑ Using the `ElementHost` control for your WPF display elements

❑ Parsing the XML attachment to populate the form data

❑ Leveraging 3D graphics in WPF

❑ Making Web-service calls to a running workflow to update the MOSS-hosted workflow state

We start with an overview of VSTO and how it allows you to leverage Outlook Form Regions as a development platform for your business requirements.

Outlook Form Regions

Outlook Form Regions (OFR) provide you with the ability to customize what users see as they open an email message or a contact or any of several other inspectors within Outlook. As you'll see in this chapter, the OFR is a window that can be presented by these inspectors. Based on Windows Forms it will, by its nature, allow you to embed anything you can on a Windows Forms application. From an HTML view to a custom WPF user control, the OFR allows you to incorporate the display of these items within Outlook. Because Outlook is as popular as almost any other Office client application, this feature will have a broad reach.

OFR provides a canvas that isn't simply visible alongside your primary focus; the OFR provides a very configurable UI that allows you to extend or replace the default interface associated with typical inspectors in Outlook. Because email has become the ubiquitous office and home communication tool, the ability to embed and present key business data in a medium leverages a user's home familiarity with the environment in the office, which is powerful and helps reduce training requirements.

Though the sales forecast OBA leverages a message-based OFR, it is possible to create an OFR that is displayed as part of your contacts, appointments, messages, or any of several other content classes within Outlook. One way to build up this illustration is for you to go through the process of creating an OFR from scratch, instead of just pointing you to the existing code base for the sales forecast OFR. Open Visual Studio 2008, and start a new project.

> *Note that though you can, in theory, customize Outlook 2003 and Outlook 2007 using Visual Studio 2005, Visual Studio 2008 and Office 2007 incorporate several enhancements related to Visual Studio Tools for Office v3.0 that provide a significant productivity bonus.*

More importantly, unlike either the Sales Forecast Workbook or the Sales Forecast Approval Workflow project, the OFR is a project that doesn't need to be built in an environment with an actual MOSS server. In fact, it has no knowledge of the overall sales forecast OBA or the involvement of any other servers. It does at some point need to refer to the MOSS Web services so that it can make updates to the workflow; however, from the standpoint of building this project, you can use your local stand-alone developer workstation. Of course this project will require that Outlook 2007 be installed on your local machine — but that's expected because you'll be using Outlook.

Selecting the Correct OFR Template

The first step of doing this from "scratch" is to create a new C# project using the Outlook Add-In template for Office 2007. As part of this, name your project `SalesForecastOFR` as shown in Figure 6-1. At this point, Visual Studio will generate your new Outlook Add-In project. When complete, the project will open showing the `ThisAddIn.cs` source code. You can close this file, because you don't need to make any changes to the core of the default Add-In project.

> *You could and probably would like to create this same project using Visual Basic. The selection of C# for this project wasn't related to language capabilities. Processing the XML for the workflow update would probably be easier with Visual Basic.*

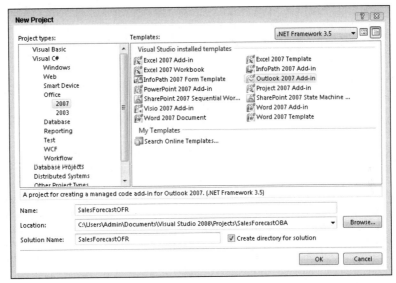

Figure 6-1

Instead, your next step is to add a new item to this project. If you don't have the Solution Explorer open, go to the View menu in Visual Studio and select it from the list of available windows. With the Solution Explorer window open, right-click your SalesForecastOFR project in that window and choose Add ➪ New Item. Within the Add New Item dialog, select the Outlook Form Region template. This template should be located at the top of the right column of the two-column list of installed templates if you are using small icons as pictured (it will be the second icon in the large icons display). Change the name of this class to `SalesForecast.cs` and click the Add button.

On clicking the Add button, instead of being returned to Visual Studio, you'll be presented with the first screen in the New Outlook Form Region wizard. This wizard walks you through several different options related to your OFR. The first choice, shown in Figure 6-2, is whether you would like to generate your form from scratch or would like to import an existing OFS template. Outlook ships with several such templates and you can design additional templates within Outlook and then import them to use as the basis for your business logic.

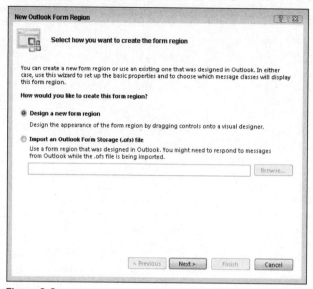

Figure 6-2

The dialog shown in Figure 6-3 lists four different types of potential regions. As you move between the different options, the wizard displays a graphic to better illustrate how each impacts the default display. These four options can actually be placed in two groups. The first two options — Separate and Adjoining — are form types that extend the built-in inspectors of Outlook. At their core, these forms continue to display the underlying inspectors associated with whatever class they are associated with. For example, in the sales forecast OBA this is the IPM.Note class used by email messages. The second group consists of the Replacement and Replace-all regions. These OFR types completely replace the underlying class that would normally display within Outlook and instead define a custom interface for that object.

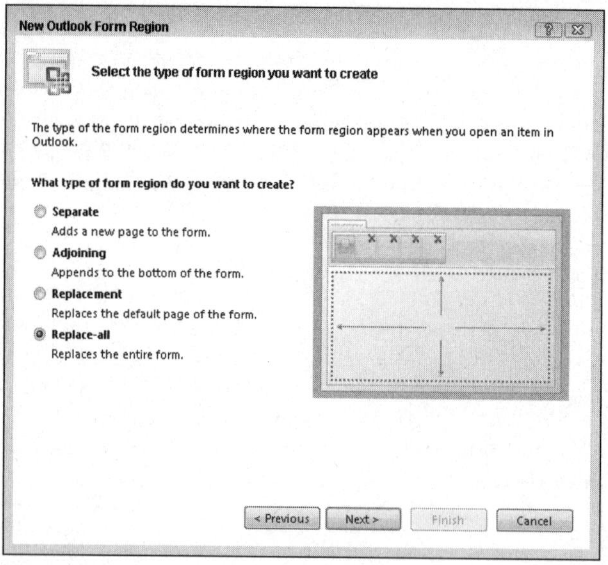

Figure 6-3

The current sales forecast OBA uses a Separate OFR, but it wasn't always this way. In the original design we planned to use a Replace-all OFR. In working with MOSS, however, we learned an important lesson. It turned out that MOSS won't transmit a Replace-all OFR because the Replace-all uses a custom class. Because during discussions with Microsoft it was agreed that there didn't appear to be a way to tell the MOSS server and the standard email handling classes provided by ASP.NET that your custom class is a valid class for SMTP transmission, you are required to use Exchange Server.

Integrating Exchange Server for the purposes of hosting demonstration code was seen as performance cost prohibitive. For demonstration purposes you are looking at having a single machine instance where possible, and in fact when a Replace-all region was tested, attempting to host an Exchange Server as part of the demonstration prevented a successful demonstration. We bring this up because, in a production environment where you most likely have an Exchange Server in place to handle your email requirements, our decision might not be appropriate for you.

Several considerations are related to the choice of form region. For example, an Adjoining region has an advantage in that it is immediately visible to the end user. When the user opens the message, your customization is automatically accessed and run at the same time, and the user doesn't have to search to find the appropriate tab. A Separate region is still accessed and filtered when the message is opened, but only a button to take the user to the separate display area is visible on the inspector window ribbon. Similarly, a Replace or Replace-all region is opened by default when the user opens the email; however, in these cases the body of the original message isn't seen.

Finally, in the case of the Replace-all OFR, the entire form provided by Outlook is replaced for the user. This means that the indicators associated with attachments as well as the original message body are concealed. Using an OFR that completely hides the message data, including attachments, can be useful in the sales forecast example. As we build this OFR you'll see that the data used in the OFR is cached in the message as an XML file. Because the sample does not hide the underlying message data, the user can open that XML file manually. This isn't significant because the user is going to see the data within the context of the OFR, but using a Replace-all OFR does hide what we might consider to be the application infrastructure from the end user.

If you are interested in changing from the default you would select the Replace-all form as shown in Figure 6-3. To re-create the sample code, select a Separate OFR and click the Next button.

Selecting a Separate OFR and clicking Next should bring you to the screen shown in Figure 6-4. In this screen you have the option to provide a display name for your OFR. For the purposes of the sales forecast code, the default values can be left alone, or for your own benefit you can alter this value. Note that the inactive Title and Description fields are available for editing when creating a custom Replace or Replace-all OFR.

Below the Name, Title, and Description text fields shown in Figure 6-4, you'll note that there are three checkboxes in this dialog. These represent times when this OFR will by default be available in Outlook. For most OFR types, all three are checked by default. For the purposes of the sales forecast you might not want to accept the default selections. The first checkbox, Inspectors That Are in Compose Mode, allows you to determine whether someone who is creating a new message or contact should also see your OFR region by default.

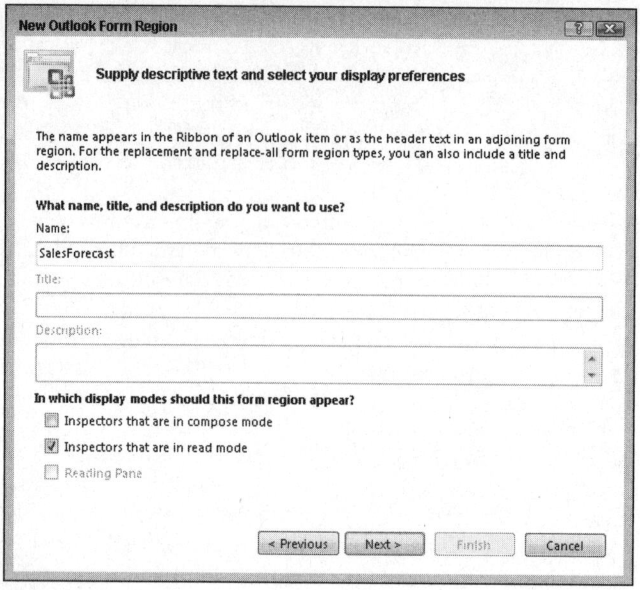

Figure 6-4

The focus of this OFR is reviewing the sales forecast data. For Separate and Adjoining forms, Outlook will, if you leave this checked, automatically add your custom region to the standard new message, contact, or appointment window. It will also do this for OFRs created to target other inspectors, such as contacts or appointments. This could get quite annoying if your users aren't going to be placing data into that OFR, and it is for display only. Having the OFR displayed when creating a message is both counterintuitive to the review process and creates additional screening challenges. Knowing which messages should include the OFR as part of the composition process and which shouldn't is a screening challenge beyond the coverage of this chapter, which focuses on recognizing when to display a Separate OFR.

For Replacement and Replace-all OFR types, because they are based on a custom class definition, Outlook doesn't automatically offer these as an option for creating a new message. Instead, users will need to access the File menu and select the Forms option to tell Outlook that they are attempting to send messages defined by the custom type.

Additionally, if you are creating a Separate OFR similar to the sample, you will find that only the first two checkboxes are active, as shown in Figure 6-4. This is because the Separate OFR leverages a separate tab that is accessible only from within the message display window. The Reading Pane, which is hosted within Outlook's main display, does not provide a means to switch from the message pane to a custom separate pane.

Once you have clicked the Next button, you'll be in the dialog shown in Figure 6-5. This time this dialog allows you to select from any of the standard classes that are used within Outlook. The goal is to allow you to create a custom OFR for one or more of these classes, although typically you'll select just one. For now you can select just Mail Message and click the Finish button to complete the creation of your OFR and exit the Outlook Form Region wizard. That is, unless you are creating a Replacement or Replace-all OFR.

Figure 6-5

For a Replacement or Replace-all OFR, the custom message class is one that you will define within your custom Add-In. To better explain what is occurring, let's use a mail message as an example. Typically, when Outlook receives a mail message, the message is assigned to the class IPM.Note. The IPM.Note class is what provides all of the typical display elements that you see in a message within Outlook. If you create a Replacement form, then when that form is emailed, it is flagged not as a typical message, but as an instance of your custom class.

In other words, the sender of the message needs to be aware of the name of the class used for this type of OFR. The good news is that this is, in theory, all that the sender needs to be aware of. As noted earlier, however, the Replacement and Replace-all form types work fine only so long as the initial message is sent to the Microsoft Exchange Server. If you are attempting to trigger a message from, say, SharePoint, there is a problem. Typically, when SharePoint is installed and configured the email options are set up so that SharePoint handles sending its own messages. Nevertheless, SharePoint doesn't allow for sending messages with custom message types. As a result, when your code attempts to trigger this custom message type from within SharePoint, the message will be sent only if, in fact, you have configured your Share-Point server to communicate with an Exchange Server.

Either way, once you have complete this dialog, click Finish to exit the New Outlook Form Region wizard. On your return to Visual Studio you'll be in the designer for your Separate OFR user control. That's right, you are working with a Windows Forms user control that has been customized by the wizard to reflect the logic you'll need. The VSTO team worked to ensure that the characteristics you defined going through the preceding wizard are automatically defined in the resulting code.

Customizing Your OFR Display

At this point you can open the Toolbox and drag and drop controls onto the form. Because the goal is to host a WPF-based display within this OFR, you need to leverage the WPF Interop library and ElementHost control. Drag a single ElementHost control onto your display. Use the Dock property visible in the lower-right corner of Figure 6-6 to fill up the area in the display.

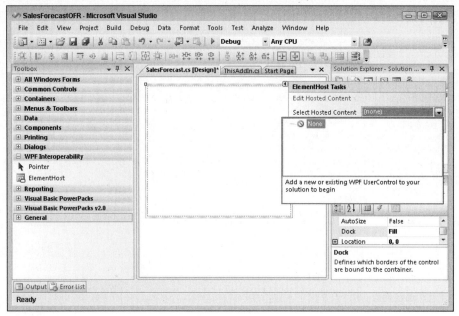

Figure 6-6

The base OFR is automatically set to fill the message window's display area. As such there is no reason to set a display size for the Sales Forecast Windows Forms user control.

Note how the Figure 6-6 shows the docking state in the partially concealed Properties pane. The pane is currently set to display/edit the properties for `ElementHost1`. Additionally, the context menu in the upper-right corner of the control is expanded, and the display for selecting the associated WPF user control is open. Currently, however, there are no controls to add to this display. You need to add the WPF user control to the solution.

Right-click the project heading and again select Add ⇨ New Item. From the Add New Item dialog select User Control (WPF) and name your user control `EmailControl.xaml`. Visual Studio will then generate a default XAML control for you. For now, the only change that you are going to make to the default code shown in the following listing is to add a background color of PaleGoldenrod to your user control:

```
<UserControl x:Class="SalesForecastOFR.EmailControl"
    xmlns="http://schemas.microsoft.com/winfx/2006/xaml/presentation"
    xmlns:x="http://schemas.microsoft.com/winfx/2006/xaml"
    Height="300" Width="300" Background="PaleGoldenrod">
    <Grid>
    </Grid>
</UserControl>
```

This provides a simple colored background that you'll use in the final version of this control. You should, at this point, build your application so that the new `EmailControl` is registered as an available control within your project. Then, returning to the `SalesForecast` user control, assign the newly available `EmailControl` as the hosted control for your `ElementHost1` control seen in Figure 6-6. Once you have assigned this control, the display of your user control should match the display of your XAML control.

Test Run, Remove, and Sample Data

At this point you still haven't written any actual code, so this is a great time to test your application. Use F5 to build and run your application. Once the build is complete, Outlook will automatically open. Your view will not be completely unlike the one shown in Figure 6-7. It doesn't appear that there is anything different about your Outlook display; however, this chapter is focusing on a Separate OFR, and that is visible only when a message is actually opened, so you need to open a message in its display window.

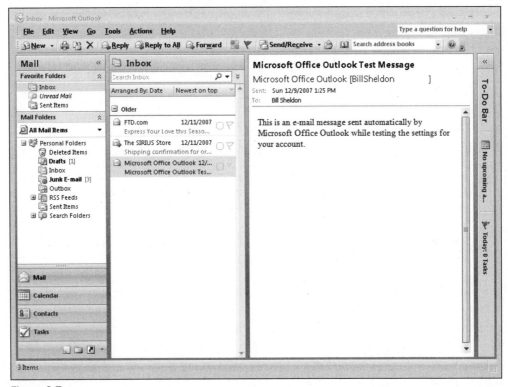

Figure 6-7

When you open a message, you'll note that, even though the original message was received prior to the creation of your OFR, its display, shown in Figure 6-8, now includes your custom OFR. In fact, you'll find that every single message you open includes the OFR — which could easily become annoying, given that in a real application your OFR would probably be targeting a single message type. Similarly, if you receive a new message, there it is again — an OFR that has only display information. Once you have satisfied yourself with the impact of this region on Outlook, close Outlook and return to Visual Studio.

Now that you've seen your OFR in action, your next question should probably be, "How do I get rid of it?" Seriously, if you are developing on the same machine that you use for email, you've just installed something that, for you as a developer, can become somewhat annoying. The answer is that after you have returned from the debugger you can access the Build menu and select Clean Solution. This menu option uninstalls your Add-In assembly, which includes your OFR, so that the next time that you open Outlook you won't see your custom OFR displayed with all of your messages.

Figure 6-8

Of course, the complete solution to that is to have your OFR displayed only when it is appropriate. For the sales forecast OBA, that is when the XML attachment containing the actual sales forecast data has been included. Before you code that, you'll add some sample data to your environment. One of the files in the download package is a sample of the XML attachment used by the OFR. This file, LitwareForeCastData .XML, contains sample XML from a test run of the completed application. For the purposes of testing, you could create an empty file called LitwareForeCastData.XML and get the same results in terms of screening that your OFR should display. Instead, using a data file that is populated with sample data allows you to start coding against that data, because by definition this file will contain all of the data displayed in the OFR.

To do this you need to modify the code that was generated as part of your OFR user control. There are two parts to handling the enclosed XML file. The first is to use it to screen the display of your OFR, and the second is to access the file to make it available to your user control. Both require custom code within the SalesForecast.cs file that was generated when you added the OFR to your project.

The first item to note in this file is the Form Region Factory code block, which has been collapsed. There are actually three generated methods, and it is the method hidden inside this code block to which you'll want to apply the custom logic to decide when this OFR should be visible. When expanded, as shown in the following code block, you'll see that not only do you have your SalesForecast class, but within this block is a second partial class definition that defines an implementation to create your OFR as part of a Factory. Factories are a well-known software pattern, wherein the calling application might not know the details the class being created, but only the base-class OFR and the methods and properties exposed at the base-class level.

Software patterns are generally outside the scope of this chapter, but in short, patterns define a concept that is then implemented in any of several languages. In the case of the Factory pattern, the basic principle is that there is some interface that will be exposed by every implementation that matches a standard signature. This interface will define an initialization or construction method that can be called to create a new instance of that object. In this case the OFR has defined a SalesForecastFactory, which implements a standard event handler. The standard event handler FormRegionInitializing is automatically called whenever an instance of the sales forecast OFR is to be created. This method is called prior to actually creating the new class as part of the SalesForecastFactory, which is designed to create that instance.

```
partial class SalesForecast
{
```

```
#region Form Region Factory

[Microsoft.Office.Tools.Outlook.FormRegionMessageClass
        (Microsoft.Office.Tools.Outlook.FormRegionMessageClassAttribute.Note)]
[Microsoft.Office.Tools.Outlook.FormRegionName
                                    ("SalesForecastOFR.SalesForecast")]
public partial class SalesForecastFactory
{
    // Occurs before the form region is initialized.
    // To prevent the form region from appearing, set e.Cancel to true.
    // Use e.OutlookItem to get a reference to the current Outlook item.
    private void SalesForecastFactory_FormRegionInitializing(object sender,
            Microsoft.Office.Tools.Outlook.FormRegionInitializingEventArgs e)
    {
    }
}


#endregion

// Occurs before the form region is displayed.
// Use this.OutlookItem to get a reference to the current Outlook item.
// Use this.OutlookFormRegion to get a reference to the form region.
private void SalesForecast_FormRegionShowing(object sender,
                            System.EventArgs e)

{
}

// Occurs when the form region is closed.
// Use this.OutlookItem to get a reference to the current Outlook item.
// Use this.OutlookFormRegion to get a reference to the form region.
private void SalesForecast_FormRegionClosed(object sender,
                                        System.EventArgs e)

{
}
}
```

As you can see in the preceding code block, the declaration of the `Factory` class's customization is embedded within your `SalesForecast` class definition. To prevent your OFR from being displayed with every message, you need to add custom code to the `FormRegionInitializing` event handler. This code should of course do the minimum amount required to determine whether adding the OFR to the current message is appropriate. In this case you simply want to determine whether the message has a copy of the `SalesForeCastData.xml` attachment. If it doesn't have this attachment, you want to bypass creating your OFR. In a production environment it is likely you would more fully qualify the naming of your attachment and possibly open the associated file to validate the XML Schema, but for the purposes of this code, validating the name of the attachment is sufficient.

```
private void SalesForecastFactory_FormRegionInitializing(object sender,
            Microsoft.Office.Tools.Outlook.FormRegionInitializingEventArgs e)
{
    try
    {
        Outlook.MailItem mail = (Outlook.MailItem) e.OutlookItem;
```

```
                    if (mail.Attachments.Count != 1)
                    {
                        e.Cancel = true;
                        return;
                    }
                    foreach (Outlook.Attachment att in mail.Attachments)
                    {
                        if (att.DisplayName != "LitwareForeCastData.xml")
                        {
                            e.Cancel = true;
                        }
                    }
                }
                catch
                {
                    e.Cancel = true;
                }
            }
```

The preceding code handles the task of screening your messages for the OFR. In addition to handling this task, the preceding code illustrates some of the key elements to screening your OFR. The first thing to note is that you can access the inbound email message by retrieving the `OutlookItem` object from the parameter `e`. Of course you need to cast this item, because it is passed as type Object. Once you have done this, you have full access to the Outlook object model for email messages. Therefore, you can quickly check for the number of attachments, and if there are none, you can set the `Cancel` property to True.

The next step is to cycle through the collection of mail attachments using an iterator. In this case we are expecting only a single attachment named `LitwareForeCastData.xml`. The conditional actually checks for the appropriate casing of that file name; because it will be a machine-generated file name, the condition helps ensure that the enclosed file is the correct file. Additionally, if the logic finds more than a single attachment, it is going to presume that the selected message is not of the correct type for this particular OFR.

Keep in mind when implementing the `FormRegionInitializing` code that the logic is executed for every single message that a user accesses. The code in this section needs to be minimal and focused on performance. This isn't the place for database calls, but rather an opportunity to screen various messages when the user displays them. You can again test your code at this point. To do so, you'll need to send yourself a message containing the `LitwareForeCastData.xml` file as an attachment. Your display is still a blank pale yellow page, but you can see that the screening works correctly.

Running the Sales Forecast OFR with Data

Before you start to implement the code that will display the sales forecast OFR, you should take a look at the final result. It will be a little while before the code is again in a state where you can really test run, so it makes sense to ensure you are up to speed on the capabilities of the OFR. Figures 6-9 through 6-12 show the completed OFR.

Figure 6-9 shows the top section of the OFR, which looks similar to the data elements displayed within the Sales Forecast Excel Spreadsheet, covered in Chapter 4, "Customizing the Office Fluent Ribbon and Task Pane." This data is updated dynamically when the form is loaded based on the contents of an enclosed XML file. Aside from the typical data display, there are two colorful charts displaying the forecast and actual sales. These charts are instances of a custom WPF user control that was originally developed by Kevin Kennedy of InterKnowlogy. Kevin leveraged his knowledge of both WPF and 3D graphics to create these charts. What isn't obvious in looking at Figures 6-10 and 6-11 is that these charts respond to mouse actions.

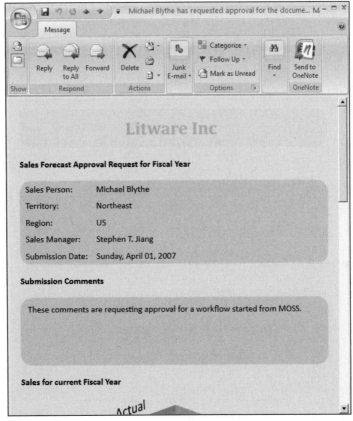

Figure 6-9

Specifically, each chart can be scaled to fit the display area better by using the scroll wheel on the typical mouse. In this way you can focus in on a smaller section of the chart. Additionally, by using the right mouse button, the user can click, hold, and rotate the charts. Thus, if the perspective seems off the user can reorient the selected chart. You'll find that as the mouse hovers over any of the columns, the numeric value associated with that column is displayed in the upper-right section of the chart. These charts make this update message much more engaging and interesting for the manager.

The final image, Figure 6-12, relates to the ability of the manager to update the workflow status of the custom Sales Forecast Approval Workflow on the MOSS server. While the manager has the option of opening and reviewing the Sales Forecast Worksheet directly or reviewing the report document associated with this sales forecast, it allows the manager, as shown in Figure 6-12, to respond to the data that was presented within this approval request message without needing to leave Outlook.

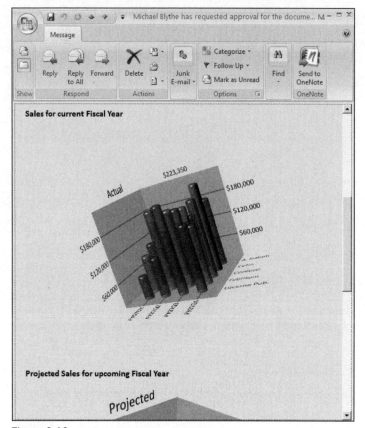

Figure 6-10

Passing the Attachment to the Control

Next up is getting the number of attachments in your message into the OFR. This is a fairly easy task. Unlike the decision on whether to display the OFR, which occurs at the time the code is looking to create that OFR, your ability to influence what is displayed doesn't occur until the `FormRegionShowing` event handler is called. In the code block that follows, you'll see that instead of retrieving the current email object from a parameter, it is one of the member values for your OFR:

```
// Occurs when the form region is being displayed.
// Use this.OutlookItem to get a reference to the current Outlook item.
// Use this.OutlookFormRegion to get a reference to the form region.
private void SalesForecast_FormRegionShowing(object sender, System.EventArgs e)
{
    Outlook.MailItem mail = (Outlook.MailItem) this.OutlookItem;
    string path = "C:\\OFRTemp\\LitwareForeCastData.xml";
    foreach (Outlook.Attachment att in mail.Attachments)
    {
        // In an ideal scenario this goes to a temporary or cache directory...
        // however, for development & demonstration purposes it makes sense to make
```

```
        // this easily accessible so that a developer can review the attachment
        // content. If you need to support more then one attachment then you'll need
        // a unique name for each - standard file management logic.
        att.SaveAsFile(path);
    }
    if (this.elementHost1.Child == null)
        this.elementHost1.Child = new SalesForecastOFR.EmailControl(path);
}
```

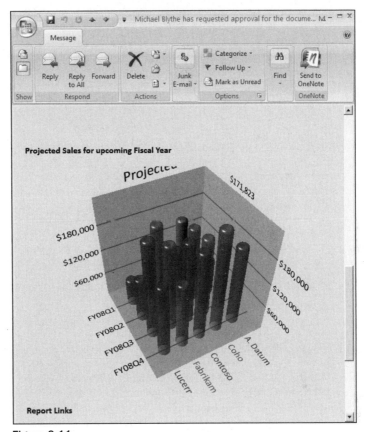

Figure 6-11

Similar to the code used to screen the OFR from unrelated messages, the code for getting the attachment to pass to the custom OFR implementation refers to the Outlook message. Unlike the Factory class where the message was passed as a parameter, at this point your code is running within the context of that message. As such the code in the preceding code block refers to the OutlookItem, which is part of the context of the current object. For demonstration purposes, it declares a path to the local file system. In theory this path would be based on a folder dedicated to temporary files; however, in order to make it easy to find this data as part of the development process, it has been placed on the C: drive in a top-level directory.

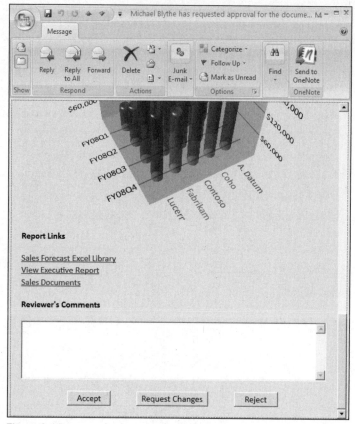

Figure 6-12

You know that this code is executed only if the preceding event handler to initialize the OFR was successful, so you can retrieve the one and only attachment from the message. This attachment is then saved to a temporary directory, and the fully qualified name of that newly created file is passed to the constructor of your WPF control. At this point, the last item in this code will prevent compilation and testing until after you complete several customization steps. If you would like to comment out this line and test run your application prior to the next section of this chapter, you should find that the OFR still functions correctly. When you open the custom OFR that still doesn't display anything, you should find that your XML file is copied to the temporary directory you specified. Note that you will get an error at this point if you haven't created the appropriate directory defined in the path. If you did test to ensure that you take the time to uncomment the associated line, that calls your custom control's constructor passing the data as a parameter.

Setting up the ChartData Class

Now that you have an operational OFR, it's time to customize this framework with actual data. The sales forecast OFR was designed such that all of the custom display elements were created in WPF. Not everything in the user interface requires WPF; for example, the display of text data and the text box, links, and buttons could all just as easily be written to using a Windows Forms UI. In the case of the 3D graphs displays for the current and future sales data, the grids require WPF in order to support things like scaling, rotating, and other advanced graphic features. Accordingly, the entire user interface was built using WPF.

To work with the user interface it should be noted that, as part of the customization you just added for passing the name of the data file to the WPF control, the earlier test case that assigned the control at design time won't work. Once you implement the custom constructor for this class the default constructor will no longer be available. Before moving forward you need to return to the design surface for the `SalesForecast.cs` user control and set the `Child` control for the `ElementHost` to (none). This means that if you run the application, by default you will once again have a blank page, however now you won't even have a pale yellow background. As the code block in the preceding section demonstrated, you will assign an instance of the `EmailControl` to that `Child` property when you are initializing the control with data.

Having done that, it is time work on the `EmailControl` and its supporting classes. The first step in this process is to create two custom classes. The first is a placeholder for the custom display logic of the custom charts that are embedded in this OFR, and the second is a custom class to hold the data used by the `charting` class. Right-click your project name and select Add ➪ Class from the context menu. This opens the Add New Item dialog. Change the name of your new class to `Chart` and click Add to continue. Once the new file is created, add a new reference to the `System.Windows.Controls` namespace. This ensures that your new class is a WPF user control; in other words, its base class is `System.Windows.Controls.UserControl`. Update your class so that it inherits from the class `UserControl`.

Next, change the namespace of this class from `SalesForecastOFR` to `Charting`. You'd like to move the current charting control to a separate assembly that can be linked to from several different applications. The 3D charts shown in Figures 6-10 and 6-11 have a great deal of appeal, and as you go through the code to implement this chart control you'll see that it could easily be used in other applications. The resulting code that follows doesn't do anything yet, but it is a placeholder for the custom control that is used later in this chapter:

```
using System.Windows.Controls

namespace Charting
{
    class Chart : UserControl
    {
    }
}
```

Again, right-click your project and select the Add ➪ Class context menu item to open the Add New Item dialog. Rename this class to `ChartData` and click the Add button to add it to your solution. This class will hold the data used by the graphical elements of your chart class. Obviously, this class was developed over several weeks; however, for the purposes of this walkthrough, we will take you through the resulting properties and methods of this class, and talk about the steps to create your own instance of this class.

The first step is to add a reference to the `System.Windows.Media` namespace with a using statement at the top of your file. For brevity we have omitted the default namespace declarations from the code block that follows. Next, you'll need to identify your namespace, which, just like the `Chart`, class should be the `Charting`. Finally, add four list properties. The first is the list of column names, and the second is the list of rows. Each of these is typed as a `List(Of String)` in VB speak. These lists are defined as strings because the control doesn't care if the rows and columns are identified by numeric position or by name. The chart will later use the combination of a row name and a column name from these lists to define the items in a grid, where each item in the grid is then displayed as a column, or in the wording of the project class, a tube on the chart.

Next, add a dictionary that will accept a string as the key and a double (or this code could be enhanced to use the Decimal type) as the data item. This dictionary will hold the actual sales and forecast values, keyed based on the combination of row and column. Finally, add a list to contain the colors used in the display, List(Of System.Windows.Media.Color):

```
using System.Windows.Media;

namespace Charting
{
    public class ChartData
    {
        List<string> columns = new List<string>();
        List<string> rows = new List<string>();
        Dictionary<string, double> dataDictionary = new
                                      Dictionary<string, double>();
        List<Color> colors;
```

After adding some of the properties of your class, the next step is to create your constructor, which will initialize the list of colors. For demonstration purposes, this code uses hard-coded color values; one potential enhancement is to make the colors used in each grid dynamic and allow these values to be retrieved from a configuration file.

The list of colors includes one color for each of the expected five companies that will be part of a typical sales forecast in this demonstration code. The sixth color is for the background. The goal is to use colors with visibly different appearances so that they stand out in the display. You can change these colors as you see fit, up to making them all the same for a monochromatic display, although we don't suggest this. You could also add additional colors if you wanted to have unique colors for more than one company, or you could transmit the color associated with each company if you wanted a company to consistently carry the same color.

```
public ChartData()
{
    this.colors = new List<Color>
    {
        Color.FromRgb(83, 84, 138),
        Color.FromRgb(67, 128, 134),
        Color.FromRgb(160, 77, 163),
        Color.FromRgb(196, 101, 45),
        Color.FromRgb(139, 93, 61),
        Color.FromRgb(92, 146, 181)
    };
}
```

Once you have added a constructor, it is time to add some public accessors for the chart data. The first of these is a string property, which allows you to customize the title of your chart. Next is a property that will retrieve the brush to be used when displaying that title; as noted, the colors in this version are hard coded. Next are the accessors that allow you to retrieve the list objects defining the columns and rows. It should be noted that, because these properties don't return copies of the underlying `List` properties, but instead return the object reference, the code that refers to these objects can then directly set the column and row names.

This isn't to say that some thought didn't go into the returns; instead of returning concrete `List<>` classes the interfaces have been coded to leverage the interface definition. If, at some point, you changed internally how the array of columns and rows were stored, so long as the new model could be cast to the `IList` interface, anyone leveraging your interface wouldn't need to know about the change. More importantly, because it's just an interface cast, you wouldn't need to spend time coding up a backward-compatible workaround.

```
public string Title { get; set; }

public Brush TitleBrush { get { return new SolidColorBrush(this.colors[5]);
} }

public IList<string> Columns { get { return this.columns; } }

public IList<string> Rows { get { return this.rows; } }

public int Range { get; set; }

public string RangeFormatString { get; set; }
```

Additionally, the preceding code block defines a range value. The chart uses an implicit start value of zero, another item that you might want to customize from this solution, and an upper limit for the dollar range. Additionally you can format the way that the range is displayed, so if you wanted to use euros or some other currency instead of using U.S. dollars, you could pass in an alternative formatting string.

Once you have the preceding properties in place, it is time to handle getting and setting data in the grid. The `SetValue` method allows you to specify the row and column along with a double value. The code then gets the resulting key based on the row and column. Finally, the new value is added to the data dictionary if it is associated with a previously undefined row and column. If the given key does already exist, the dictionary is updated to contain the new version of this data.

The `GetValue` logic accepts a row and column and returns the double value for that row and column. Similar to the method to set a value it uses a custom method called `GetKey` to compute the key based on the row and column. It then looks to see whether the dictionary contains an entry for that key. If it does not, the code returns a zero; otherwise, it returns the double value associated with that row and column.

```
public void SetValue(string row, string column, double value)
{
    string key = GetKey(row, column);

    if (!this.dataDictionary.ContainsKey(key))
        this.dataDictionary.Add(key, value);
    else
        this.dataDictionary[key] = value;
}

public double GetValue(string row, string column)
{
```

```
       string key = GetKey(row, column);

       return this.dataDictionary.ContainsKey(key) ?
                                  this.dataDictionary[key] : 0;
}
```

Both the `get` and `set` value methods refer to a private static method called `GetKey`. This method simply takes the row and column strings and passes each to a method that uses Base 64 encoding to capture any special characters that might be embedded in these names. Finally, the resulting encoded strings are combined with a vertical bar, and the resulting value represents a unique key for that row and column.

```
static string GetKey(string row, string column)
{
       return Encode(row) + "|" + Encode(column);
}

static string Encode(string value)
{
       byte[] bytes = Encoding.Default.GetBytes(value);
       return Convert.ToBase64String(bytes);
}
```

In theory this provides enough code in the `ChartData` class for you to set and retrieve the necessary data as the OFR is loaded. The actual `Chart` control will need some additional methods to retrieve the characteristics associated with it, consistently. In this case, the methods have been marked internal, or Friend in VB speak. What should also be noted, if it isn't obvious, is that the chart objects are being designed such that you can migrate these classes out of the current project and into a custom WPF user control, which could then be reused in other applications. This was something we hoped to do as part of this project but didn't have an opportunity to accomplish.

The first internal method returns the list of `RangeLabels`. The chart doesn't just display the start and top of the range for the values it contains. It displays a set of four values that increment to represent some of the values between zero and the upper-limit range for that chart. This first method returns those interim range labels:

```
internal IList<string> RangeLabels
{
    get
    {
        var rangeLabels = new List<string>();

        for (int i = 3; i > 0; i--)
        {
            int markerValue = i * this.Range / 4;

            if (this.RangeFormatString != null)
              rangeLabels.Add(markerValue.ToString(this.RangeFormatString));
            else
              rangeLabels.Add(markerValue.ToString());
        }
        return rangeLabels;
    }
```

```
        }

        internal Color GetRowColor(string row)
        {
            return this.colors[Math.Max(0, this.rows.IndexOf(row) % 5)];
        }

        internal IList<Brush> GetRowLabelBrushes()
        {
            var rowColors = new List<Brush>();

            foreach (string row in this.rows)
                rowColors.Add(new SolidColorBrush(this.GetRowColor(row)));

            return rowColors;
        }
    }
}
```

The next method is used to get the appropriate color for a given row in the chart. Because there are only five colors available, the logic takes the modulus operator to determine an index based on the remainder of the row index divided by five. The result is always a number from 0 to 4. This way, if additional rows beyond five are added to the grid, the logic will cycle through the available colors in order. The columns of each row are color coordinated, and each row represents the sales or sales forecast data for a given company. This method is used in two ways. The first is to define the appropriate foreground color for the company associated with a given row. Next, as the GetRowLabelBrushes method illustrates, it's used to define the collection of brushes that will be used to paint that row's columns within the grid. Both the GetRowColor and GetRowLabelBrushes methods will be used by the Chart class as it displays the information associated with the actual sales and forecast sales within the OFR display. Finally, the closing braces at the bottom of the preceding code close the ChartData class and the Charting namespace.

Defining the OFR Display

Finally, it is time to begin work on the actual XAML and C# files for the EmailControl class. Rather than talk about how to drag the various controls onto the display, we're going to refer to the XAML file associated with the main sales forecast OFR. Because this is a rather large file, we will have to break it into chunks so that the discussion can remain in context. Note that because this chapter walks through all of the XAML and then the associated C# methods, the XAML will not compile and run until after the event handlers and related items associated with the OFR have been defined.

The first section of this file represents the definition of the page and the top-level control on the page. The first customization is at the top of the XAML in the attributes of the user control. Remove any references to height and width from the attributes of the UserControl. Notice that the fourth line of the XAML now imports the Charting namespace, which was defined for your Chart and ChartData classes. These classes provide display elements and are referred to as user controls within the XAML. As a result, you need to let the XAML compiler know where to find these classes. In short, the clr-namespace declaration indicates to XAML that these classes are defined in code and provides the namespace wherein the classes are located.

The FlowDocumentScrollViewer has a single customization that disables the discrete selection of sections within the scrolling area. Using the scroll viewer as the panel for this control ensures that when the display goes beyond the current area available on screen, WPF handles providing the scroll-bar and managing the display of the flow document within this code.

```
<UserControl x:Class="SalesForecastOFR.EmailControl"
    xmlns="http://schemas.microsoft.com/winfx/2006/xaml/presentation"
    xmlns:x="http://schemas.microsoft.com/winfx/2006/xaml"
    xmlns:Charting="clr-namespace:Charting">

    <FlowDocumentScrollViewer IsSelectionEnabled="False">
    <FlowDocument FontFamily="Calibri" Background="PaleGoldenrod">
```

Once the flow document has been defined in the preceding code block it is assigned a default font so that the display of text throughout the document will have a uniform look. Additionally, the default background color for the control can be placed into the document definition.

In the following code block you see the definition for the first UI block. Each UI block represents a horizontal slice of the flow document. Thus you can think of each block as being appended to the preceding sections to build up the complete display. The first block uses a simple set of WPF components to build the title you see displayed at the top of the OFR. For now, the name of the company associated with this OFR has been hard coded, but, as with the other labels that will be seen in this source file, it could easily be replaced at runtime by specifying the Name attribute for this label in the XAML at design time and then referring to the control from within your code. The border around the company name acts like a geometric shape providing the underlying background, which has been varied from the default in order to highlight the company name. The code then closes the associated elements and is followed by a stand-alone paragraph.

```
<BlockUIContainer >
    <Grid >
        <Border Background="#FFFFDE93" BorderBrush="#FFF1AF22"
                CornerRadius="20">
            <Label FontFamily="Cambria" FontSize="32" FontWeight="Bold"
                    HorizontalAlignment="Center" VerticalAlignment="Center"
                    Foreground="#FFF1AF22" Margin="0,10,10,10"
                    >Litware Inc</Label>
        </Border>
    </Grid>
</BlockUIContainer>
<Paragraph FontWeight="Bold" Name="paragraphFYTitle"
    >Sales Forecast Approval Request for Fiscal Year</Paragraph>
```

The stand-alone paragraph shown in the preceding code block simply adds a paragraph element to the display. The paragraph element leverages the default background of the form and is directly supported by the FlowDocument panel, which is used as the background for this control. Notice how the paragraph has been given an addressable name; this is because the text in the paragraph will be updated to reflect the actual report dates associated with this sales forecast.

The next block of code provides essentially the same standard information that is presented to the user when they are in the Sales Forecast Excel Spreadsheet (Chapter 7). Again, there is a reference to a custom background with rounded corners to highlight this data. The border contains a stack panel, and the result is that as each label is defined that label is placed vertically below the preceding label. The effect is that the labels are stacked within this panel.

```
<BlockUIContainer >
  <Grid>
    <Border Background="#FFCDCECD" CornerRadius="20">
      <StackPanel Margin="5,0,0,0" >
        <Label Name="labelSalesPerson" VerticalAlignment="Bottom"
          >Sales Person: Michael J. Blythe</Label>
        <Label Name="labelSalesTerritory" VerticalAlignment="Bottom"
          >Territory: Northeast</Label>
        <Label Name="labelSalesRegion" VerticalAlignment="Bottom"
          >Region: USA</Label>
        <Label Name="labelSalesManager" VerticalAlignment="Bottom"
          >Sales Manager: Stephen Jiang</Label>
        <Label Name="labelSubmitDate" VerticalAlignment="Bottom"
          >Submission Date: 2/1/2008</Label>
      </StackPanel>
    </Border>
  </Grid>
</BlockUIContainer>
```

Notice that in the preceding code block each of the label controls has been assigned a name so that it is directly addressable from within the code behind it. Therefore, when the OFR processes the XML data file, it can replace these default values with the actual values associated with the data file that was enclosed in the message.

The next code block displays the comments that were submitted as part of the workflow that triggered this OFR. It follows the same pattern as the other UI blocks, with a container to hold the grid element, which then contain a border that is overlayed with a stack panel. Notice how each of these elements adds to the consistent look and feel of the OFR display. At the core of this section is a TextBox control that has been made read-only. In theory, this section could again use a label control, but we wanted to demonstrate another method for displaying read-only text. The TextBox includes an optional scrollbar that will allow a user to scroll through a large block of comments and protect the display from being overwhelmed with line after line of comments.

```
<BlockUIContainer >
  <Grid>
    <Border Background="#FFCDCECD"  CornerRadius="20">
    <StackPanel Margin="8,8,8,8">
      <TextBox Name="textBoxSubmitComments" MaxLines="10" MinLines="5"
        AcceptsReturn="False"  IsReadOnly="True"
        VerticalScrollBarVisibility="Auto" ToolTip=
                          "Comments regarding the submitted forecast."
        IsUndoEnabled="False" AutoWordSelection="True"
        Background="#FFCDCECD" BorderBrush="Transparent"
        IsHitTestVisible="False"
      >Here are my projections for the coming year.</TextBox>
    </StackPanel>
    </Border></Grid>
</BlockUIContainer>
```

After the comments come the charts showing the actual and forecast data. Each of these charts is defined in its own container and sets the height for the display area of that control. Note that each is also preceded by a simple paragraph that acts as a title for each of the charts.

```
<Paragraph FontWeight="Bold">Sales for current Fiscal Year</Paragraph>
<BlockUIContainer>
  <Grid>
    <Charting:Chart x:Name="ActualChart" Height="400"  />
  </Grid>
</BlockUIContainer>

<Paragraph FontWeight="Bold"
                >Projected Sales for upcoming Fiscal Year</Paragraph>
<BlockUIContainer>
  <Grid>
    <Charting:Chart x:Name="ProjectedChart" Height="400" />
  </Grid>
</BlockUIContainer>
```

Following the charts the OFR adds a set of links to the original data sources. Note that in this case instead of using a block container the individual paragraphs are grouped using a Section control. This allows for the definition of spacing between the different paragraphs. Each of these controls also includes a definition of a click event. When we start showing the code-behind for this XAML, you'll see how each of these events is constructed. For now, just note that while each link includes a default URL, each link is also addressable, and these links will be updated to more specific locations based on the contents of the XML attachment.

```
<Section LineHeight="2">
    <Paragraph><Hyperlink Name="ExcelLink" Click="ExcelLink_Click" NavigateUri=
          "http://moss.litwareinc.com/docs/sales%20reports/Forms/updated.aspx"
       >Sales Forecast Excel Library</Hyperlink></Paragraph>
    <Paragraph><Hyperlink Name="WordLink" Click="WordLink_Click" NavigateUri=
          "http://moss.litwareinc.com/docs/documents/Forms/AllItems.aspx"
       >View Executive Report</Hyperlink></Paragraph>
    <Paragraph><Hyperlink Name="SiteLink" Click="SiteLink_Click" NavigateUri=
          "http://moss.litwareinc.com/docs/sales%20reports/"
       >Sales Report Site</Hyperlink></Paragraph>
</Section>
```

The final two sections of the OFR are used in the approval, rejection, or request changes process. The OFR isn't just about displaying data, it is also designed to allow managers to work within their most comfortable environment — Outlook. Because the manager has already opened the message and reviewed the data, the next logical step is to allow him either to get more detailed information via the preceding links or to allow him to provide feedback immediately.

Thus the next section provides an active text box where the manager can enter his comments regarding the forecast that was submitted. Once he has provided these comments he has the option of clicking any one of three buttons to accept, reject, or request changes in the forecast. The manager can do all of this without needing to open a separate application or access a web site. Of note in the current version are the buttons to make direct Web service calls to update the MOSS workflow; however, this could be enhanced to use an alternative mechanism (for example, an email message) that would be automatically sent after the user was back online.

```
<Paragraph FontWeight="Bold">Reviewer's Comments</Paragraph>
<BlockUIContainer>
    <TextBox Name="textBoxReviewComments" MinLines="5" AcceptsReturn="False"
IsUndoEnabled="True" IsReadOnly="False"
                VerticalScrollBarVisibility="Visible" ToolTip="Comments from the
Review." AutoWordSelection="True"></TextBox>
</BlockUIContainer>
<Section></Section>
        <BlockUIContainer>
            <Grid>
                <Grid.ColumnDefinitions>
                    <ColumnDefinition Width="0.30*" />
                    <ColumnDefinition Width="0.05*" />
                    <ColumnDefinition Width="0.30*" />
                    <ColumnDefinition Width="0.05*" />
                    <ColumnDefinition Width="0.30*" />
                </Grid.ColumnDefinitions>
                <Button Name="buttonAccept" Grid.Column="0" Width="80"
                    Margin="0,0,2.8421709430404E-14,0"
HorizontalAlignment="Right"
                        Click="ButtonAccept_Click">Accept</Button>
    <Button Name="buttonChange" Grid.Column="2" Width="130"
                    Margin="0,0,-5.6843418860808E-14,0" HorizontalAlignment="Center"
                    Click="ButtonChange_Click">Request Changes</Button>
    <Button Name="buttonReject" Grid.Column="4" Width="80"
                    Margin="0,0,-5.6843418860808E-14,0" HorizontalAlignment="Left"
                    Click="ButtonReject_Click">Reject</Button>
        </Grid>
    </BlockUIContainer>
   </FlowDocument>
 </FlowDocumentScrollViewer>
</UserControl>
```

The preceding code block leverages the grid embedded in the BlockUIContainer control to position the buttons. The grid has been divided into five columns and the odd-numbered columns are used for spacing, while the buttons are then positioned within the even-numbered columns. Note that each of these buttons includes a click event that needs to be implemented as the next step in creating this OFR. The preceding code block, in addition to laying out the buttons, also closes out the XAML for the user control. At this point, you are almost ready to test run the application. However, first you need to create a portion of the code to start and load your application data. As previously noted, without the code for the handlers referred to in this XAML, the code will not compile and run.

Implementing OFR Methods

The next step is to create the methods to support this first step in creating your own OFR. You need to create a custom constructor, import the XML data, and generally provide at least stubs related to your event handlers. To do this, open the EmailControl.xaml.cs file. Start by adding a reference to the `Charting` namespace to this file. Next, go within the class and add a new constructor that accepts the path for the attachment as the only parameter.

```
using Charting;

namespace SalesForecastOFR
{
    public partial class EmailControl : UserControl
    {
        public EmailControl(string attachmentPath)
        {
            InitializeComponent();

            //Load Data
            var actualChartData = new ChartData
            {
                Title = "Actual",
                Range = 240000,
                RangeFormatString = "$#,##0"
            };
            var projectedChartData = new ChartData
            {
                Title = "Projected",
                Range = 240000,
                RangeFormatString = "$#,##0"
            };

            LoadXMLData(attachmentPath, actualChartData, projectedChartData);

            //this.ActualChart.SetData(actualChartData);
            //this.ProjectedChart.SetData(projectedChartData);
        }
    }
}
```

The preceding code block shows the constructor for your control. The constructor first initializes the controls that are part of your user control and then creates two instances of the `ChartData` class you defined earlier in this chapter. Each of the two instances is associated with a single chart and the display of sales or forecast data. The code was written to leave these as anonymous types; however, there is no reason for them not to be strongly typed instead of being cast as type `var`. Each `ChartData` instance is initialized with a couple settings, which are currently hard coded. Another potential enhancement in the development of this OFR is to move these static values out into a configuration file or with regard to the range — literally, to determine dynamically the top forecast or sales range and use the appropriate value based on the XML data.

Once the `ChartData` objects have been initialized with the top-level settings, it is time to load the data from the XML attachment. The name of the path to that file along with the `ChartData` objects that will be assigned that data are passed into the method `LoadXMLData`. Finally, the code shows that after the data is loaded it will be passed to the charts that were defined in the XAML for the `EmailControl`. Because we haven't yet implemented this custom control's logic, these two lines are commented out, for now.

Implementing LoadXMLData

The `LoadXMLData` method is used to parse the data in the XML attachment and place this data into both the user interface and the `ChartData` object instances that drive the custom chart controls. This code was written as the XML data was being defined. A schema hadn't been solidly defined, so ideally the next step would be to create a schema based on the final version of the XML that is used not only in this OFR, but also in the Sales Forecast Approval Workflow where it is generated, and in the Sales Forecast Report Document Web services where it is used.

The code that processes this is sample code — it has no exception handling. This was done to keep the sample simple given that we can rely on the XML content in a demonstration application. Realistically, using a schema would be the first step in upgrading this code. This would allow you to validate the XML against a schema first to ensure that the data could be processed by the `LoadXMLData` method.

Defining a schema for this data would also allow you to leverage LINQ for several of the assignments. More importantly, with this sample code you see which data elements are being computed instead of retrieved whole cloth from the XML. Because the XML is generated in the background it would make more sense to update the XML further to include some of the data elements, such as the fiscal year and quarter information.

The code block to process the XML refers to two private methods that should be mentioned prior to getting into the details of loading the XML. The first is the `PopulateZeros` method. This method is used to ensure that each column for a company's row has a value of zero. This is important because in the original design there was no guarantee that each quarter would be included. If a company had no sales for a given quarter, that quarter was just omitted from the XML data. This code is designed to ensure that, as each company is identified, both of the charts are assigned a value of zero for every quarter. This is done prior to retrieving the data for that company so that it isn't necessary to attempt to track which quarters were and weren't represented in the actual data.

Additionally, even though this code is very similar to the code used to determine the fiscal year and quarter column headers, unlike that code, which needs to be run only once, this code needs to be run for each company. The code itself is rather simple in that it determines the quarter, and, based on that determination, assigns a value to each row-column combination for both charts. Rather than show all of the cases, only the first one from the sample code is displayed; the others have been omitted for clarity. You can review the downloaded sample code to see the full implementation of this method.

```
/// <summary>
/// Ensure that each column has a value
/// </summary>
/// <param name="companyName"></param>
/// <param name="actualData"></param>
/// <param name="ForecastData"></param>
/// <param name="pivotYear"></param>
/// <param name="pivotQuarter"></param>
/// <remarks>The XML used to populate the charts does not contain zeros for
/// null values as a result the code needs to ensure that there is at least
/// a starting 0 value for each column so the base of that column will appear
/// in the display. This has to be done on a per company basis.</remarks>
private void PopulateZeros(string companyName, ChartData actualData, ChartData
    forecastData, int pivotYear, int pivotQuarter)
{
```

```
            switch (pivotQuarter)
            {
                case 3:
                    actualData.SetValue(companyName, "FY" + (pivotYear -
                                    1).ToString().Substring(2) + "Q4", 0.0);
                    actualData.SetValue(companyName, "FY" +
                                    pivotYear.ToString().Substring(2) + "Q1", 0.0);
                    actualData.SetValue(companyName, "FY" +
                                    pivotYear.ToString().Substring(2) + "Q2", 0.0);
                    actualData.SetValue(companyName,"FY" +
                                    pivotYear.ToString().Substring(2) + "Q3", 0.0);

                    forecastData.SetValue(companyName, "FY" +
                                    pivotYear.ToString().Substring(2) + "Q4", 0.0);
                    forecastData.SetValue(companyName, "FY" + (pivotYear +
                                    1).ToString().Substring(2) + "Q1", 0.0);
                    forecastData.SetValue(companyName, "FY" + (pivotYear +
                                    1).ToString().Substring(2) + "Q2", 0.0);
                    forecastData.SetValue(companyName, "FY" + (pivotYear +
                                    1).ToString().Substring(2) + "Q3", 0.0);
                    break;
                ... <Code omitted for clarity> ...
                default:
                    break;
            }
    }
```

The other function mentioned as being part of the importation of the data is the IsForecast method. This throwaway method accepts a year and quarter and determines whether those dates fall within the range associated with the actual sales or the forecast sales. The method allows for passing in the year and quarter that represent the start of the forecast data, so, if the year and quarter are less than the start of the forecast date range, then the data in that particular node should be used as actual sales data. This is a throwaway method because the XML should be refined to indicate whether a given node's data is actual sales or forecast sales.

```
    /// <summary>
    /// Determine if a given year and quarter should be for actual or forecast data
    /// </summary>
    /// <param name="pivotYear">The year of the report</param>
    /// <param name="pivotQuarter">The quarter in which the report is being run.</
param>
    /// <param name="year">The year to be checked</param>
    /// <param name="quarter">The quarter to be checked.</param>
    /// <returns></returns>
    private bool IsForecast(int pivotYear, int pivotQuarter, string year, string
quarter)
    {
        // if the pivot year is less then the data then so is the current date
making this a forecast
        if (pivotYear < Convert.ToInt32(year))
            return true;
        // if the pivot year is greater then the data, then the data is in the past
making this an actual
        if (pivotYear > Convert.ToInt32(year))
```

```
            return false;
        // at this point the years are equal... so is the pivot quarter less?
        if (pivotQuarter < Convert.ToInt32(quarter))
            return true;
        return false;
    }
```

Now that we have reviewed the methods referred to in the method that processes the XML, it is time to review the actual LoadXMLData method.

The method starts by defining an XMLNode object that will be used as you traverse the XML and a new XMLDocument, which will hold the sales forecast data. The Load method on the XMLDocument object is then used to load that data into memory. Finally, the code leverages the developer's knowledge of the XML structure to traverse the data and assign each item to the appropriate user interface element.

```
private void LoadXMLData(string attachPath, ChartData actualData,
                    ChartData forecastData)
{
    System.Xml.XmlNode xDocumentNode;
    System.Xml.XmlDocument xDoc = new System.Xml.XmlDocument();
    xDoc.Load(attachPath);
    // Within the document, the first "0" node is the header, 1 is the body.
    // Within this the next node is the common data - "General Info".
    // The final node is the sales and forecast data (combined)
    xDocumentNode = xDoc.ChildNodes[1].ChildNodes[0];
    //<TerritoryName></TerritoryName>
    labelSalesTerritory.Content = "Territory: \t\t" + xDocumentNode.
ChildNodes[1].InnerText;
    //<TerritoryID></TerritoryID>
    //<Region></Region>
    labelSalesRegion.Content = "Region: \t\t" + xDocumentNode.ChildNodes[3].
InnerText;
    //<SalesManager></SalesManager>
    labelSalesManager.Content = "Sales Manager: \t" + xDocumentNode.
ChildNodes[4].InnerText;
    //<SalesPerson></SalesPerson>
    labelSalesPerson.Content = "Sales Person: \t" + xDocumentNode.
ChildNodes[5].InnerText;
    //<SalesPersonID></SalesPersonID>
    //<ReportDate></ReportDate>
    string sDt = xDocumentNode.ChildNodes[7].InnerText;
    DateTime dt = DateTime.Parse(sDt);
    labelSubmitDate.Content = "Submission Date: \t" + dt.ToLongDateString();
    //<SpreadSheetUrl></SpreadSheetUrl>
    ExcelLink.NavigateUri = new System.Uri(xDocumentNode.ChildNodes[8].
InnerText);
    //<ReportUrl></ReportUrl>
    //WordLink.NavigateUri = new System.Uri(xDocumentNode.ChildNodes[9].
InnerText);
    //<Comments />
     textBoxSubmitComments.Text = xDocumentNode.ChildNodes[10].InnerText;
```

The preceding code block simply takes those portions of the non-repeating XML data and assigns them to the appropriate elements within the OFR display. Though some items, such as the submission date, need to be converted, most items are assigned directly. This includes the updates for the Excel and Word documents that are housed on the MOSS server if the user receiving the message wishes to review these items directly.

The next section of this method handles processing the actual and forecast data for the companies contained in the enclosed XML file. To do this it first needs to define the columns that are associated with the dates for both the forecast and actual data. These columns need to be defined only once, and differ from the row names, which are the company names, in that as each row is processed, its name is assigned.

Accordingly, an array of strings for both the forecast and actual chart column names is created. Next, the code uses the report date that was retrieved from the singleton data to determine what the quarters associated with the current estimate should be. It does this by advancing to the next fiscal quarter from the report date similar to the way that the data is retrieved. There is then a simple but lengthy switch statement, which just directs the code to build the appropriate column headers based on the start date. Rather than include the full statement, only the first block referring to the first three months is included here. You can review the full case statement as part of the sample code.

```
string companyName;
string [] forecastColumnNames = new string[4];
string [] actualColumnNames = new string[4];

// But first define the columns
// Within each company is where we'll find the years... the challenge is
that the
// data could span 2 or 3 years. The data is currently coming out with the
most recent first.
// need to add columns based on the year and quarter info provided, so need
to count years
// backward... and quarters forward (projected year(s) 1, quarters from 0
to 3, actual year(s) quarters 0 to 3
// plus I don't want to reset these for each company...

int pivotYear = dt.Year;
int pivotMonth = dt.Month;
int pivotQuarter;
switch (pivotMonth)
{
    case 1:
    case 2:
    case 3:
        pivotQuarter = 3;
        actualData.Columns.Add("FY" + (pivotYear -
                               1).ToString().Substring(2) + "Q4");
        actualData.Columns.Add("FY" + pivotYear.ToString().Substring(2)
                               + "Q1");
        actualData.Columns.Add("FY" + pivotYear.ToString().Substring(2)
                               + "Q2");
        actualData.Columns.Add("FY" + pivotYear.ToString().Substring(2)
                               + "Q3");

        forecastData.Columns.Add("FY" +
```

```
                                      pivotYear.ToString().Substring(2) + "Q4");
            forecastData.Columns.Add("FY" + (pivotYear +
                                      1).ToString().Substring(2) + "Q1");
            forecastData.Columns.Add("FY" + (pivotYear +
                                      1).ToString().Substring(2) + "Q2");
            forecastData.Columns.Add("FY" + (pivotYear +
                                      1).ToString().Substring(2) + "Q3");
            break;
        default:
            pivotQuarter = 0;
            break;
    }
}
```

Now that the columns have been defined, it's time to process the actual forecast data. At this point the code retrieves the node containing all of the customer sales and forecast data from the XML document. It then iterates through this data one company at a time, looking for the actual and forecast data. The first step in this process is to retrieve the name of the company and add that name to the ChartData objects for both the forecast and actual charts. Next, all of the zero values for that company are populated so that the chart will display correctly. Finally, the code sets up some variables and then begins looping through each of the years and quarters that are available for that company.

```
// Get the sales and forecast data...
xDocumentNode = xDoc.ChildNodes[1].ChildNodes[1];

foreach (System.Xml.XmlNode xChild in xDocumentNode)
{
    // In the sales node. It should have 5 children (which can be looped)
    // which represent the customers... get the customer name and data for
each customer.
    companyName = xChild.FirstChild.InnerText;
    actualData.Rows.Add(companyName);
    forecastData.Rows.Add(companyName);
    PopulateZeros(companyName, actualData, forecastData, pivotYear,
pivotQuarter);

    // Now process the data for this company
    // Within each customer need to jump past the name and id and get
       to the years.
```

The process of looping through each year and quarter begins with the third node, which has an index of 2. Thus, the loop in the following code block just starts with that node and then accesses each of the nodes. At the top level these nodes represent years; within each year it is possible to have one or more quarters. Under the original plan it was determined that there would be no guarantee in what order the data would be presented, and because the forecasts might overlap actual sales, the XML structures actually allowed for both an actual sales number and a forecast sales number in the same XML element. For example, if a forecast were being created from the second month of the third quarter, the resulting actual sales data might include values for both ForecastSales in that quarter as well as actual sales in that quarter. The code uses the year and quarter to verify whether a given element is an actual sales number or a forecast.

Once the question of whether the associated value is a forecast or an actual sales data element, the code retrieves that data from the appropriate location. Because the data for actual sales and forecasts could be zero and because forecast numbers are stored in a different location from the data for the actual sales, the determination of the type of data needs to be made first. Then, the code needs to remove any formatting that the code that built the XML added to the XML, because this code just needs the raw numbers. Finally, the number is converted to a double, because that is what the current control logic expects, and then assigned to the appropriate chart with the correct company name for the row and the fiscal year and quarter for the column.

```
string strYear;
string strQuarter;
string rawValue;
double dValue;
for (int i = 2; i < xChild.ChildNodes.Count; i++)
{
    strYear = xChild.ChildNodes[i].FirstChild.InnerText;
    for (int j = 0; j <
            xChild.ChildNodes[i].ChildNodes[1].ChildNodes.Count; j++)
    {
        strQuarter =
  xChild.ChildNodes[i].ChildNodes[1].ChildNodes[j].FirstChild.InnerText;
        // Determine whether this is current or future
        if (IsForecast(pivotYear, pivotQuarter, strYear, strQuarter))
        {
            rawValue =
  xChild.ChildNodes[i].ChildNodes[1].ChildNodes[j].ChildNodes[2].InnerText;
            rawValue = rawValue.Replace("$", "");
            rawValue = rawValue.Replace(",", "");
            if (double.TryParse(rawValue, out dValue))
                forecastData.SetValue(companyName, "FY" +
                        strYear.Substring(2) + "Q" + strQuarter, dValue);
        }
        else
        {
            rawValue =
  xChild.ChildNodes[i].ChildNodes[1].ChildNodes[j].ChildNodes[1].InnerText;
            rawValue = rawValue.Replace("$", "");
            rawValue = rawValue.Replace(",", "");
            if (double.TryParse(rawValue, out dValue))
                actualData.SetValue(companyName, "FY" +
                        strYear.Substring(2) + "Q" + strQuarter, dValue);
        }
    }
}
```

The next step, now that you have implemented the XML processing, is to handle the various events that need to be triggered from your user interface. The first set of events we'll discuss are used by the link elements. The link elements raise a click event and each of these events is shown in the code that follows. Each link overrides the default handler for the click event with a custom method. All of the click event handlers carry out the same action, to start up Internet Explorer by executing that link.

When the Process.Start method is passed a recognizable URL, it will look on the operating system for the default handler, which might be FireFox or another browser, and will use that executable to open the associated link. The user is taken to the page. Of course, because Internet Explorer then recognizes the MIME type for Word and Excel, the links to these documents are then opened in the appropriate application.

```
#region "Link Handlers"
        public void ExcelLink_Click(System.Object sender, System.EventArgs e)
        {
            System.Diagnostics.Process.Start(ExcelLink.NavigateUri.ToString());
        }

        public void WordLink_Click(System.Object sender, System.EventArgs e)
        {
            System.Diagnostics.Process.Start(WordLink.NavigateUri.ToString());
        }

        public void SiteLink_Click(System.Object sender, System.EventArgs e)
        {
            System.Diagnostics.Process.Start(SiteLink.NavigateUri.ToString());
        }
#endregion
```

The other set of events relate to the buttons at the bottom of the form. Because we aren't ready to access the Web service used to update the status of the Sales Forecast Approval Workflow at this point, you should just add the appropriate stubs for these handlers. These will be updated with the necessary code to call MOSS and update the workflow status later in this chapter.

```
#region "Button Handlers"
        public void ButtonAccept_Click(System.Object sender, System.EventArgs e)
        {
        }
        public void ButtonChange_Click(System.Object sender, System.EventArgs e)
        {
        }
        public void ButtonReject_Click(System.Object sender, System.EventArgs e)
        {
        }
#endregion
```

At this point, you are ready to test your updates. You should attempt to build your code and resolve any errors that occur. Once you have a clean build you can start your Outlook Add-In and then go to your test message that contains the appropriate XML attachment. What you should find is that the message opens, and when you select the OFR display, the OFR displays the sample data you provided, with the exception of the chart data. Your results should look similar to what is shown in Figure 6-13 and Figure 6-14. Your links should work, assuming you updated the URLs in the sample data to a locally recognized web site, but, as you would expect, the buttons should do nothing.

Creating the Custom Chart Control

The creation of a custom WPF user control isn't the focus of this book or this chapter. Nevertheless, as part of the OFR used in the sales forecast OBA, a custom control was created. Therefore, we will briefly review the code. Earlier in this chapter you created a class called Chart. The Chart class was set up but not really implemented. This section implements this class and adds two additional support classes used by the Chart object. The Tube class will encapsulate the logic associated with drawing the tubes, which are the core of the custom chart display. The `BoundingPlanes` class is used to manage the positioning of the grid within a three-dimensional area. It is this class that adjusts the basis for the axes when the chart is rotated.

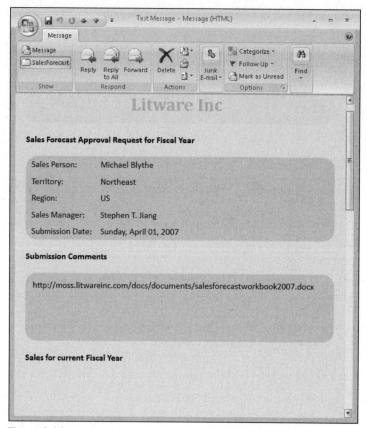

Figure 6-13

The place to start is with the `Chart` class. The first step is to update the current definition with the following code. The class definition begins by defining a series of private fields that will be used when drawing the chart. Most of these are standard .NET controls. The `viewport` represents the surface upon which the chart graphics are rendered. When working with complex 3D graphics, a defined viewport represents the surface that is shown in the display. The `modelGroup` represents the chart in 3D space. The location of the columns is defined within the X, Y, and Z axes.

The `scaleTransform` is used to take the baseline for the placement of the viewport and move it closer to or further from the 3D structure of the model. By manipulating the default location of the viewport in relation to the model, it is possible to make the model seem larger or smaller. Similarly, the `rotateTransform` field is used to take the original orientation of the model and twist the model in 3D space. Having this separate from scaling allows for the model to get larger or smaller in the display independently of the orientation of the model.

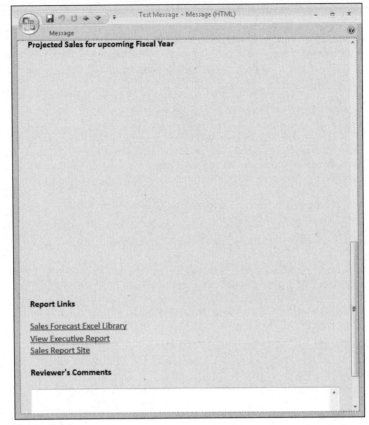

Figure 6-14

The `previousMouseVector` is used when comparing the location of the mouse to indicate whether the column being hovered over has changed. In this way, the logic associated with changing the look of the hovered-over column needs to be called only when there is a change to the column.

Two of the final three fields are exceptions to the standard .NET controls definition. The `BoundingPlanes` object is the other non-standard object that you will need to implement in your project. The `Tube` class is a custom class that defines each of the tubes that are used within the display of the chart. Both of these classes should be created within the `Charting` namespaces as other classes associated with the `Chart` user control. The `List` is a collection of all of the columns in the current chart, and the `hoverTube` field represents the column that is currently being hovered over and is having its display manipulated.

```
public class Chart : UserControl
{
    Viewport3D viewport;
    Model3DGroup modelGroup;
    ScaleTransform3D scaleTransform;
    RotateTransform3D rotateTransform;
    Vector3D previousMouseVector;
    BoundingPlanes boundingPlanes;
    List<Tube> tubes = new List<Tube>();
    Tube hoverTube;
```

Following the declaration of the class fields the code moves to the constructor. The constructor of this class begins by adding a series of event handlers associated with the various mouse actions. The code then creates a viewport. A viewport is the basis of the 3D behaviors, which you see as the object is rotated and scaled. The mouse actions are essentially changes to the viewport, which is why, as the mouse is dragged, the chart will seem to rotate. It is outside the scope of this chapter to go heavily into the details of these 3D objects.

```
public Chart()
{
    this.MouseLeftButtonDown += this.ChartMouseLeftButtonDown;
    this.MouseLeftButtonUp += this.ChartMouseLeftButtonUp;
    this.MouseMove += this.ChartMouseMove;
    this.MouseWheel += this.ChartMouseWheel;

    this.viewport = new Viewport3D { ClipToBounds = true };
    this.Content = viewport;

    viewport.Camera = new PerspectiveCamera { Position = new Point3D(0, 0, 6) };

    var lightingVisual = new ModelVisual3D();
    viewport.Children.Add(lightingVisual);

    var lightingGroup = new Model3DGroup();
    lightingVisual.Content = lightingGroup;

    lightingGroup.Children.Add(
        new AmbientLight(Color.FromRgb(64, 64, 64)));
    lightingGroup.Children.Add(
        new DirectionalLight(Colors.White, new Vector3D(3, -1, -3)));

    var modelVisual = new ModelVisual3D();
    viewport.Children.Add(modelVisual);

    this.modelGroup = new Model3DGroup { Transform =
                                    this.CreateTransformGroup() };
    modelVisual.Content = this.modelGroup;
}
```

The SetData method is the public interface used by your OFR to pass the actual and forecast sales data into a chart. The set data method grabs a bounding plane, and to the bounding plane it adds the rows and columns. The code then cycles through the ChartData object and retrieves the appropriate color for each row. Within each row the code then gets the columns, and a new tube is associated with each column on that row. The tube object is initialized with a height value that is computed by referring to the value associated with that row and column from the ChartData object. The list of tubes is updated with the newly created tube.

```
public void SetData(ChartData chartData)
{
    this.boundingPlanes = new BoundingPlanes(chartData);
    this.modelGroup.Children.Add(this.boundingPlanes.Model);

    double rowSpacing = 2D / (chartData.Rows.Count + 1);
    double columnSpacing = 2D / (chartData.Columns.Count + 1);

    foreach (string row in chartData.Rows)
```

```
        {
            Color color = chartData.GetRowColor(row);
            double offsetZ = (chartData.Rows.IndexOf(row) + 1) * rowSpacing - 1;

            foreach (string column in chartData.Columns)
            {
                string tip =
                    chartData.GetValue(row,
                        column).ToString(chartData.RangeFormatString);

                double offsetX = (chartData.Columns.IndexOf(column) + 1) *
                                            columnSpacing - 1;
                double height = 2 * chartData.GetValue(row, column) /
                                            chartData.Range;

                var tube = new Tube(new Vector3D(offsetX, -1, offsetZ), height,
                                            color, tip);
                this.tubes.Add(tube);
                this.modelGroup.Children.Add(tube.Model);
            }
        }
    }
}
```

The following methods represent the event handlers for the mouse actions. The ChartMouseLeftButtonDown method is called when the mouse button is used while the mouse is over the grid. This method captures the mouse's movement so that events related to its movement can be tracked. As the mouse moves ChartMouseMove looks to see whether the mouse is in a captured state, and if so, it computes an update to the display of the 3D graphic in the user interface. Finally, the ChartMouseLeftButtonUp method handles the release of the mouse button. If the mouse is currently captured, this method releases the mouse.

```
void ChartMouseLeftButtonDown(object sender, MouseButtonEventArgs e)
{
    Point currentMousePoint = e.GetPosition(this);
    this.previousMouseVector = this.ProjectToTrackball(currentMousePoint);
    this.CaptureMouse();
}

void ChartMouseLeftButtonUp(object sender, MouseButtonEventArgs e)
{
    if (this.IsMouseCaptured) this.ReleaseMouseCapture();
}

void ChartMouseMove(object sender, MouseEventArgs e)
{
    Point currentMousePoint = e.GetPosition(this);

    if (this.IsMouseCaptured)
    {
        var currentMouseVector3D = this.ProjectToTrackball(currentMousePoint);

        Vector3D changeAxis = Vector3D.CrossProduct(
            this.previousMouseVector, currentMouseVector3D);
        double changeAngle = Vector3D.AngleBetween(
```

```
                    this.previousMouseVector, currentMouseVector3D);

            if (changeAxis.LengthSquared > 0)
            {
                var rotation = this.rotateTransform.Rotation as
                                                    AxisAngleRotation3D;

                if (rotation != null)
                {
                    Quaternion quaternion = new Quaternion(changeAxis, changeAngle)
                            * new Quaternion(rotation.Axis, rotation.Angle);

                    rotation.Axis = quaternion.Axis;
                    rotation.Angle = Math.Max(-40, Math.Min(40, quaternion.Angle));
                }
            }

            this.previousMouseVector = currentMouseVector3D;
        }

        this.HoverHitTest(currentMousePoint);
    }
```

The preceding code also refers to a Media3D structure called a Quaternion. Getting into the details of 3D programming is outside the scope of OBA development, but a Quaternion defines a 3D model. By manipulating this model, we can rotate the structure. The `System.Windows.Media.Media3D` `.Quaternion` class is the basis for the rotation of the charts in the user interface.

The `ChartMouseWheel` method is called when the user is hovering over the `Chart` control and the user moves the mouse wheel. The code takes the delta, or change, that is part of the `MouseWheelEventArgs` and uses this in an equation to determine the change to the scale of the displayed chart. If the delta is a positive number, the chart increases in size; if it is negative, the chart's display shrinks or pulls out.

The final statement in this method, `e.Handled`, is specific to WPF. It tells the XAML that this event has been handled. XAML introduced the concept of routed events, and a given event might be handled by a series of event handlers that might be defined by containing controls or even those of contained controls. When a given event has been handled and the developer does not want the event to be routed further, the `e.Handled` property is set to true.

```
        void ChartMouseWheel(object sender, MouseWheelEventArgs e)
        {
            double multiplier = Math.Exp((double)e.Delta / -1000);
            double scale = Math.Max(0.4, Math.Min(4,
                this.scaleTransform.ScaleX * multiplier));

            this.scaleTransform.ScaleX = scale;
            this.scaleTransform.ScaleY = scale;
            this.scaleTransform.ScaleZ = scale;

            this.HoverHitTest(e.GetPosition(this));

            e.Handled = true;
        }
```

The `HoverHitTest` method is called to take the height of the tube and display this value as part of the chart header. The code leverages a series of 3D conversions to verify that, given the current location and position of the tubes, the mouse is, in fact, hovering over one of these tubes, and if so, the discrete value of the tube is then displayed as part of the chart's display. This is done using the `RayMeshGeometry3DHitTestResult` class, which is part of the `System.Windows.Media.Media3D` namespace. This class represents an intersection between a ray (the location of the mouse) and Mesh Geometry, one of the columns of the chart.

```
void HoverHitTest(Point currentMousePoint)
{
    HitTestResult hitTestResult =
        VisualTreeHelper.HitTest(this.viewport, currentMousePoint);
    RayMeshGeometry3DHitTestResult rayHitTestResult =
        hitTestResult as RayMeshGeometry3DHitTestResult;

    Tube newHoverTube = null;

    if (rayHitTestResult != null)
    {
        foreach (Tube tube in this.tubes)
        {
            if (rayHitTestResult.ModelHit == tube.Model)
            {
                newHoverTube = tube;
                break;
            }
        }
    }

    if (newHoverTube != this.hoverTube)
    {
        if (this.hoverTube != null) this.hoverTube.IsHovered = false;
        this.hoverTube = newHoverTube;
        this.boundingPlanes.Tip = this.hoverTube != null ?
                                        this.hoverTube.Tip : "";

        if (this.hoverTube != null) this.hoverTube.IsHovered = true;
    }
}
```

The remaining methods in this class are used to support the three-dimensional graphics that are part of this control. The exploration of building 3D graphics is beyond the scope of this chapter, however these methods are presented to ensure a complete picture of this class is included in this chapter. If you intend to create custom WPF 3D graphics, we recommend a book focused on that type of activity, such as *Professional WPF Programming*, Andrade, et. al. (Wrox, 2007) available at: http://www.wrox.com/WileyCDA/WroxTitle/productCd-0470041803.html, or any one of the other graphics-oriented titles available on the market.

```
Transform3DGroup CreateTransformGroup()
{
    var transformGroup = new Transform3DGroup();

    var rotateTransform1 = new RotateTransform3D(
```

```
                new AxisAngleRotation3D(new Vector3D(0, 1, 0), -45));
        transformGroup.Children.Add(rotateTransform1);

        var rotateTransform2 = new RotateTransform3D(
            new AxisAngleRotation3D(new Vector3D(1, 0, 0), 35));
        transformGroup.Children.Add(rotateTransform2);

        var translateTransform = new TranslateTransform3D(0, 0.2, 0);
        transformGroup.Children.Add(translateTransform);

        this.scaleTransform = new ScaleTransform3D(1, 1, 1);
        transformGroup.Children.Add(this.scaleTransform);

        this.rotateTransform = new RotateTransform3D(new AxisAngleRotation3D());
        transformGroup.Children.Add(this.rotateTransform);

        return transformGroup;
    }


    Vector3D ProjectToTrackball(Point point)
    {
        double x = 2 * point.X / this.ActualWidth - 1;
        double y = 1 - 2 * point.Y / this.ActualHeight;
        double zSquared = 1 - x * x - y * y;
        double z = zSquared > 0 ? Math.Sqrt(zSquared) : 0;

        return new Vector3D(x, y, z);
    }
}
```

The code for the `Tube.cs` and `BoundingPlanes.cs` files is available from the sample project. Both of these files are focused on advanced graphics concepts for defining the plane on which the charts exist and the tubes used within the charts. Because these do not directly apply to setting up a WPF user control or to the management of business data, their source code is omitted from this chapter to save space.

Finally, in order to display data within the custom control, you need to return to the `EmailControl` `.xaml.cs` file. Within the constructor for this control, the calls to `SetData` are the last two statements in the constructor. These statements are shown here:

```
            this.ActualChart.SetData(actualChartData);
            this.ProjectedChart.SetData(projectedChartData);
```

These lines were commented out earlier in this chapter. Now that the `SetData` method has been implemented within your `Chart` class, these calls can be uncommented. Once this is done, you are ready to build and test your updated OFR.

Now that the `SetData` method has been implemented within your `Chart` class, these calls can be added as the last two lines of the method explained above. Once this is done, you are ready to build and test your updated OFR.

Using your existing test message, you can bring the OFR up to verify that the data is correct, that the custom charts are now displayed, as shown in Figures 6-10 and 6-11, and that the charts respond as described within this chapter. Rolling your mouse's scroll button should increase or decrease the size of your chart; hovering over a tube should display the actual value which that tube represents. The resulting behavior within the display should be complete, with the exception that you have not connected the buttons at the bottom of the form with the workflow, which needs to be updated.

Implementing the Workflow Update Logic

The final step in implementing the Outlook Form Region is to interface to the MOSS site. The first step in this process involves including the same generated file that is used by the workflow and Excel spreadsheet projects for the workflow approval data. The file is generated by taking the InfoPath form used by the workflow and converting the XML to a C# source file. Typically, this is not the recommended way to interact with InfoPath, because it means that the form is early bound. Early binding allows for strong typing, but limits changes to the forms, because the associated C# file will need to be regenerated and the code recompiled. On the other hand, ensuring that your code refers to the modified version of the data elements will require this same action. (It is also possible to convert the file to Visual Basic if you are working in that language.)

The resulting file in this case is called `WorkflowApprovalData.cs` and you will add it to your project. This file exposes the data elements that have been defined as the parameters for the workflow update. As a result, when users want to update the workflow they need to submit an XML structure that matches the one expected by the Sales Forecast Approval Workflow.

Next open the `EmailControl.xaml.cs` file, and proceed to the button event handlers added earlier in this chapter. Within these handlers you'll create an instance of the `WorkflowApprovalData` class and populate the associated information in this class. Because this process is the same for all three update options, each event handler is modified to update the `WorkflowApprovalData` structure with the appropriate information. Once you have set these properties appropriately you can call another private method called `UpdateWorkflow`, as shown in the methods in the following code block:

```
#region "Button Handlers"
        public void ButtonAccept_Click(System.Object sender, System.EventArgs e)
        {
            WorkflowApprovalData workflowData = new WorkflowApprovalData();
            workflowData.instructions = textBoxReviewComments.Text;
            workflowData.isApproved = "true";
            workflowData.isRejected = "false";
            if (UpdateWorkflow(workflowData))
                System.Windows.Forms.MessageBox.Show("Accepted status submitted.");
        }
        public void ButtonChange_Click(System.Object sender, System.EventArgs e)
        {
            WorkflowApprovalData workflowData = new WorkflowApprovalData();
            workflowData.instructions = textBoxReviewComments.Text;
            workflowData.isApproved = "false";
            workflowData.isRejected = "false";
            if (UpdateWorkflow(workflowData))
                System.Windows.Forms.MessageBox.Show("Change status submitted.");
        }
        public void ButtonReject_Click(System.Object sender, System.EventArgs e)
        {
            WorkflowApprovalData workflowData = new WorkflowApprovalData();
            workflowData.instructions = textBoxReviewComments.Text;
```

```
                        workflowData.isApproved = "false";
                        workflowData.isRejected = "true";
                        if (UpdateWorkflow(workflowData))
                            System.Windows.Forms.MessageBox.Show("Rejected status submitted.");
            }
#endregion
```

The final method for your class is the `UpdateWorkflow` method. This method attaches to the Web service for the appropriate document list — the one associated with the Excel documents. It then makes a series of Web service calls to first retrieve and eventually update the Sales Forecast Approval Workflow. When you refer to your MOSS Web services, you can name the reference `WorkflowSoapProxy`, which then generates the `WorkflowSoapProxy` class. Before making the first call the default credentials of the current user, who will need permission on SharePoint, are associated with the Web service proxy object. Each time a service call is made these credentials will be submitted as part of the request.

The first request to `GetWorkflowDataForItem` returns an XML structure that contains information on the current workflow related to the document in question. Because this spreadsheet's fully qualified URL is already embedded in the OFR, this value is passed to the `GetWorkflowDataForItem` method. This method returns a set of XML nodes that then need to be queried to find whether there is a running instance of the `SalesForecastApprovalWorkflow`. To carry out this query, the returned XML is loaded into a document and wrapped with an XML node: `WorkflowInformation`. The resulting document can then be associated with a namespace. Then the document is queried using this namespace to determine whether there is a node within the XML that matches the name `SalesForecastApprovalWorkflow`. If such a node exists, it is retrieved from the resulting `documentApprovalWorkflowTemplate`. This node is then queried for the template ID, and finally, the template ID is used to find the status of the workflow.

```
        private bool UpdateWorkflow(WorkflowApprovalData workflowData)
        {
            WorkflowSoapProxy workflowWebSvc =
                            new WorkflowSoapProxy(
                                "http://moss.litwareinc.com/docs/sales reports/");
            workflowWebSvc.Credentials =
                            (NetworkCredential)CredentialCache.DefaultCredentials;
            try
            {
                XmlNode itemWorkflowData =
            workflowWebSvc.GetWorkflowDataForItem(ExcelLink.NavigateUri.ToString());
                XmlDocument workflowInfo = new XmlDocument();
                workflowInfo.LoadXml("<WorkflowInformation>" +
                            itemWorkflowData.InnerXml + "</WorkflowInformation>");
                XmlNamespaceManager nsMgr = new XmlNamespaceManager(
                                                        new NameTable());
                nsMgr.AddNamespace("spWf",
                        "http://schemas.microsoft.com/sharepoint/soap/workflow/");
                nsMgr.AddNamespace("z", "#RowsetSchema");
                XmlNode documentApprovalWorkflowTemplate =
                    workflowInfo.SelectSingleNode(
                    "//spWf:TemplateData/spWf:WorkflowTemplates/spWf:WorkflowTemplate
                                    [@Name='SalesForecastApprovalWorkflow']", nsMgr);
                XmlNode documentApprovalWorkflowTemplateIdSet =
                            documentApprovalWorkflowTemplate.SelectSingleNode(
                                        "spWf:WorkflowTemplateIdSet", nsMgr);
                string documentApprovalWorkflowTemplateId =
```

```
documentApprovalWorkflowTemplateIdSet.Attributes["TemplateId"].Value;
XmlNode runningWorkflow = workflowInfo.SelectSingleNode(
"//spWf:ActiveWorkflowsData/spWf:Workflows/spWf:Workflow[@TemplateId='"
+ documentApprovalWorkflowTemplateId + "' and @Status1=2]", nsMgr);
```

If a running workflow that matches the template ID associated with the
`SalesForecastApprovalWorkflow` is found, the code will proceed. If that workflow isn't running,
the code will notify the user that the associated workflow isn't available. One optional change to how
this OFR works is to carry out this check when the OFR is loaded and determine whether the associated buttons should be active or inactive at that time, instead of waiting until the user attempts to
update the workflow.

Knowing that the workflow is running isn't sufficient. The code also looks to see whether there is a task
available for updating. For example, if a manager previously updated a workflow, the workflow might
be awaiting a resubmission and thus wouldn't have a task that is appropriate for the manager to update.
Once a workflow task is identified, however, the next step is to serialize the `WorkflowApprovalData`
object. To do this, you can create an XMLSerializer, which will then transform this object into an XML
structure within a memory stream. The code then creates a new document object that loads the resulting stream. This document is then passed as one of the parameters to the Web service. The `AlterToDo`
method is used to update the Web service with its new status. Once this method executes, you have
updated the status of the workflow. Note that although there is a return value, we don't process the
`AlterToDoResponse` XML node.

```
if (runningWorkflow == null)
{
    MessageBox.Show("Workflow isn't running");
    return false;
}
else
{
    XmlNode todoNode = workflowWebSvc.GetToDosForItem(
                            ExcelLink.NavigateUri.ToString());
    XmlNode workflowTaskNode =
                    todoNode.SelectSingleNode("//z:row", nsMgr);
    if (workflowTaskNode != null)
    {
        int workflowTaskId =
            int.Parse(workflowTaskNode.Attributes["ows_ID"].Value);
        XmlSerializer serializer = new
                    XmlSerializer(typeof(WorkflowApprovalData));
        using (MemoryStream stream = new MemoryStream())
        {
            serializer.Serialize(stream, workflowData);
            stream.Position = 0;
            XmlDocument workflowParametersDocument =
                                            new XmlDocument();
            workflowParametersDocument.Load(stream);
            XmlNode alterInfo = workflowWebSvc.AlterToDo(
                ExcelLink.NavigateUri.ToString(), workflowTaskId, new
                Guid(runningWorkflow.Attributes["TaskListId"].Value),
                (XmlNode)workflowParametersDocument.DocumentElement);
            //MessageBox.Show(alterInfo.OuterXml);
        }
    }
}
```

```
                else
                {
                    MessageBox.Show(
                "You don't have any active Workflow tasks for this document.");
                    return false;
                }
            }
            return true;
        }
        catch (Exception ex)
        {
            MessageBox.Show(ex.Message);
            return false;
        }
    }
}
```

At this point you should be able to run the OFR. Trigger the sending of the OFR from the actual Sales Forecast Approval Workflow. Once the message is received, you should be able to open the associated OFR and accept, reject, or request changes for the workflow associated with creating this OFR. Other enhancements could still be made to this OFR, but at this point you have replicated the basic elements of an OFR that leverages a custom WPF user control.

Summary

This chapter looked at the OFR model for building applications and the Adjoining OFR used in this OBA. An OFR application leverages a rich hosting environment that is natively collaborative. Placing your data and tying your business logic into an OFR allows you to send business data directly into the desktop application that everyone uses. The various OFR models have differing advantages and disadvantages, but each is based on an underlying user control, which allows you to leverage everything that is available via Windows Forms, WPF (via the ElementHost control), traditional Web services, or even Windows Communication Foundation and Windows Workflow.

In particular this chapter looked at:

❑ Types of OFR and the differences between them

❑ Screening an Adjoining or Separate OFR

❑ Accessing email attachments

❑ Using the ElementHost control for your WPF display elements

❑ Parsing the XML data to populate the data

❑ Leveraging 3D graphics in WPF

❑ Making Web-service calls to a running workflow to update the MOSS-hosted workflow state

Though the concept of an OBA is relatively recent, you learned how the OBA model is becoming an increasingly important focus to Microsoft and popular among executives. Outlook is the desktop application your executives use most frequently and has the broadest reach. Whether it is as a tool for displaying business information in a rich context-sensitive display or the ability to send truly actionable business data and logic, an OFR is a savvy interface that your business decision makers will want.

Using OpenXML and Business Data

As part of this book, you expect to see and do a lot of VSTO programming. After all, in building an Office Business Application, you expect to be working with the Office System products. In this chapter, however, you are going to create and work with a project that isn't available under the Office project types. You don't need a VSTO project to work with OpenXML. Instead, you'll leverage a typical application or ASP.NET type project and refer to a Word document and Share-Point library from that custom application.

This chapter focuses on introducing you to the steps and key elements in developing a custom Web service that can create a Word document customized using the OpenXML object model. The Web service will be combined with MOSS and the document will be created in a document library. The topics in this chapter include:

- ❏ Introduction to OpenXML
- ❏ Creating a Web service to generate a Word document
- ❏ Working with the OpenXML data elements
- ❏ Creating a new document on SharePoint

Because this project isn't a VSTO project type, it seems the place to start is with a quick overview of the OpenXML document format. New to Office 2007, this format allows developers much greater direct access to the content of Microsoft Office documents than has been achievable in previous versions of Microsoft Office.

OpenXML

The OpenXML format is based upon the ".*x" file type. Previous versions of Office products, such as Word and Excel, used a `.doc` and `.xls` file extension (respectively). The versions of Word, Excel, and PowerPoint prior to Office 2007 used file types that were based upon binary serialization of the associated document's or spreadsheet's data. Though nothing was encrypted, the fact that a proprietary data structure had been serialized into a binary format made retrieval by outside applications difficult.

In Office 2003, Microsoft started to change this by creating and releasing an XML format for certain document types. This allowed for more open access to the underlying documents. The initial format, while useful, attempted to capture all of the possible attributes that had previously been serialized into a single document. Nevertheless, documents were only saved with this format when a user explicitly made an effort to format them this way.

In Office 2007, Microsoft modified the core not only of the XML format, but of the way that Office approached saving documents. Now, instead of Word, Excel, and PowerPoint saving to binary formats by default, they instead save to an XML format, at least on the inside. If you look at one of the .docx or other document files, and open it with Notepad or a similar application, you'll see something that looks more like a binary format than XML. That's because once the XML has been created, the underlying data is then zipped. By introducing the idea of zipping the contents of a document, Microsoft allowed for a new structure. Instead of all of the files being saved as a single XML file, different special portions of the files could be saved into their own specialized XML structures and this collection of XML files could then represent the document.

The collection of documents that make up the Open Office format were submitted to and approved by the Ecma body. Note that Ecma originally stood for the European Computer Manufacturers Association, but it eventually expanded to international scope and changed its name to Ecma to retain brand identity while removing its past association as a European standards body. Microsoft submitted the Office OpenXML file format to Ecma. This submission was approved in December of 2006 and the result is Ecma 376. This standard has three primary document definitions: WordProcessingML for .docx files, SpreadsheetML for .xlsx files, and PresentationML for .pptx files, where ML stands for Markup Language.

Leveraging a format that uses multiple files that have been compressed to a single file to define a document has several advantages. It simplifies the individual components that may be embedded within a document. For example, a chart embedded in a document will be defined within its own source file, allowing for a simple definition of the base document file, and a more targeted definition of the XML used in the chart. Another advantage is that you can, quite literally, rename .docx, .xlsx, and .pptx files to the .zip extension, and then use Windows Explorer to review the files and directory structure of your document.

Figure 7-1 illustrates what happens when we take the document template used as part of the Sales Forecast Document Service and rename that template with the .zip extension. As you can see, it is now possible to open the file with the standard explorer view, and even to navigate through the directory structure. Figure 7-2 illustrates the contents of the Word directory. You can extract individual XML files from this compressed directory. This allows you, as a developer, to go beyond a description in a standards document and open and review the contents of the individual files that make up your document.

Similarly, it is possible for other tools to reference the contents of the OpenXML document format. For example, both Altova XMLSpy and the Microsoft SDK for OpenXML Formats provide tools designed to help you manipulate, query, and adjust the data in OpenXML documents. For the purposes of the sales forecast OBA the code was written to leverage the standard System.IO.Packaging namespace classes. These classes ship with .NET and allow you to open and manipulate the contents of an OpenXML document. In the time since this code was started, Microsoft released the OpenXML SDK as part of the next set of updates to this service; therefore, making the transition to the OpenXML SDK makes sense.

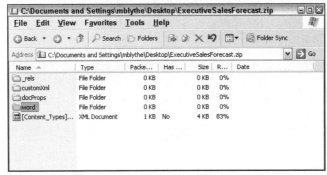

Figure 7-1

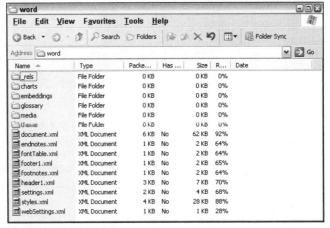

Figure 7-2

Creating the Document Generation Web Service

The generation of Word documents as part of the sales forecast OBA is used to create a report based on the sales forecast. In a real-world scenario, it is likely that the ability to generate documents would be needed for several potential reasons; for example, setting up a printable copy of data or creating a report for external consumption. Regardless of the purpose of the document, the Sales Forecast Document Service illustrates the power of the OpenXML tools.

The first step is to create a new Web service on your development server. As part of installing MOSS in Chapter 3, "Installing and Configuring MOSS," your development environment will support both MOSS (using the fully qualified URL http://moss.litwareinc.com) and the local machine (http://moss) for custom web applications. This means that you are creating your custom Web service on the same server that is hosting MOSS. This isn't required in order to manipulate the OpenXML document object model; however, in order to create the documents and insert them into MOSS, this service refers to the Microsoft.SharePoint and Microsoft.SharePoint.Portal namespaces. These namespaces allow for the creation of the site and document list references used to store the generated document.

To create the project, go to the File ➪ New ➪ Web Site menu item, not the Project menu item. In the New Web Site dialog, select the ASP.NET Web service project type. Ensure that you select a .NET 3.5 targeted solution, and that you mark your solution as targeting HTTP. Because you are building on your MOSS server, this will allow you to change quickly from development to test of your Web service from your Sales Forecast Spreadsheet. For our example, we used the name SalesForecastDocService as shown in Figure 7-3.

Within the project files shown in Figure 7-3 you'll note there are two additions from the default generated project. The first is the mapping to the database. The `AdventureWorks.cs` file is the SQLMetal-generated file used by LINQ to SQL to allow the Web service code to refer to tables and stored procedures from the customized AdventureWorks database.

SQLMetal.exe is a free database-mapping utility that's included in Visual Studio 2008. You can find this command-line tool under Program Files\Microsoft SDKs\Windows V6.0a\bin. SQLMetal generates the necessary DataContext class and Data Entity class definitions for LINQ as either a `.vb` or `.cs` source file. To create source files for a database on your local SQL Server and include stored procedures in them, open the command window, navigate to the installed location (or refer to the SQLMetal tool in that directory), and run the following command:

```
SQLMetal.exe /server:.\OFFICESERVERS /database:AdventureWorksVSTO /sprocs
    /functions /language:cs /code:AdventureWorks.cs
```

Keep in mind that this generation is a snapshot of your current structures. If you make new database changes you will need to regenerate this file in order to see these changes in your application code.

The second file located in the structure is the template for the report. The `ExecutiveSalesForecast.docx` file is a standard Word 2007 document that was created and formatted with the majority of the report format. We look at this file in more detail later in this chapter. Essentially this document is opened by the Web service, the contents are brought into memory, and, when the customization is complete, the resulting file is saved to SharePoint in the appropriate document library.

Figure 7-3

Aside from the files, there are two other project-related changes that aren't shown in Figure 7-3. The first relates to the project references. As shown in Figure 7-4, the project directly refers to two Share-Point assemblies and the System.IO.Log assembly. Given the dependency on the SharePoint namespaces and the fact that this application was developed using Visual Studio 2008, we suggest that you build this application on the server hosting your SharePoint site. As noted, you'll be creating an HTTP Web service. Hosting this on the same server that hosts your site will make the most sense when attempting to access that server and set up security permissions. The second reference is the assembly containing the System.IO.Log namespace. This assembly contains the System.IO.Packaging namespace, which is used for accessing the OpenXML package.

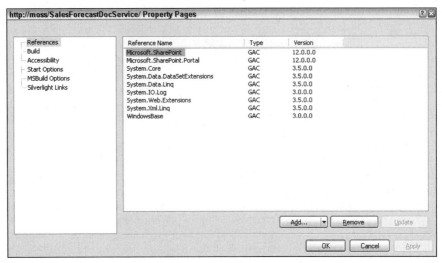

Figure 7-4

The second change to review involves the custom application settings defined in the web.config file. In addition to having the connection string for the AdventureWorks database, this file contains five application settings:

```
<add key="CompanyName" value="Litware Inc."/>
<add key="SharePointSiteUrl" value="http://moss.litwareinc.com"/>
<add key="DocLibSiteName" value="Docs"/>
<add key="SalesReportDocLibName" value="Documents"/>
```

These settings are referred to by the Web service. The first, CompanyName, is relatively obvious and is the company's name, as described by the setting name. The second, SharePointSiteUrl, is the address of the SharePoint site. Third is the sub-site within SharePoint where the document library is located, DocLibSiteName. It is expected that the sales team won't own the entire MOSS application server. Instead the documents associated with sales will be on a sub-site either defined for the sales team or for documents in general.

This example uses a site, Docs, which contains the document libraries used to hold both the sales forecast and forecast documents. There is a temptation to act as if this parameter isn't truly required, because, in theory, it could be combined with the next setting, SalesReportDocLibName, to create a complete path. As you'll see, however, when working with SharePoint, this library makes it possible to retrieve a list of folders associated with that site, as opposed to looking across an entire MOSS server. This is especially important because it is possible that multiple sites within a single installation might use the same library name. The `SalesReportDocLibName` setting contains the name of the document library, and could, with little or no change, be combined with the `DocLibSiteName`.

The Document Template

The document associated with the `SalesForecastDocService` was customized to refer to a custom set of XML nodes. The XML nodes are maintained within the document. In theory, it is possible to associate an Office document with any custom XML Schema, and, as such, it is possible to quickly and easily identify these custom XML nodes when processing the document as an OpenXML document.

> *To modify the custom settings or set up a similar document, you'll need to refer to the XML Schema in Word. To access the XML Schema, you'll need to access the Developer tab in Word's ribbon bar. If you don't have access to this tab on the ribbon bar, you will need to access the Office Button in the upper-left corner of the display to open the Word Options dialog. On the left side of this dialog you'll find a list of sections, and selecting Popular will display the appropriate options page on the right side of the dialog. In this section, select the Show Developer Tab in the Ribbon option and close the dialog.*

Figure 7-5 illustrates how the `ExecutiveSalesForecast.docx` document has embedded XML surrounding key elements, which will be replaced when the final data is merged into this document. This integrated XML allows you to update targeted document content without impacting other existing text portions of the document. These text sections such as "Sales Forecast For" will remain unchanged as the data is integrated, providing a template behavior for this document. Looking at the design view, the heading on the first page of the document will dynamically allow the assignment of a company name. This will be followed by the static "Sales Forecast For" text that is in the document. Next, the date range will be added with a static "-" between the start and end dates. The code knows only which data items to insert; the document carries with it the formatting and support text to tie the data together.

After the heading in the page, the document has a set of formatted elements which are used across several different user interfaces in the Sales Forecast OBA. The labels Sales Person, Territory, Sales Manager, and Current Date are static. Each line has the dynamic data associated with the current Sales Forecast inserted into the embedded XML fields. The same thing occurs in the Sales Revenue and Forecast table that follows. This Word table lists the four quarters of actual sales data and then lists the four quarters of Forecasts with each customer getting one row of data. When the data is processed the Web service simply accesses each of the XML fields by name and updates that node with the appropriate data.

In addition to the XML surrounding the individual table fields in the document, the document also contains a pair of embedded Excel charts. If you look at Figure 7-6, you'll notice that unlike the table data, which has each cell's value encapsulated in XML, the Excel tables are not encapsulated. Instead, the underlying OpenXML model will allow the custom application code to refer to these tables and assign the appropriate labels to each chart, as well as the associated data elements. It should also be noted that whereas the first chart refers to the same data that is used in the table, the second graphic refers to different sales forecast data not shown elsewhere in the document. This was done to illustrate that the tables aren't just mapped to regions within the document, but are, in fact, being populated with data from the Sales Forecast tables in the custom AdventureWorks database.

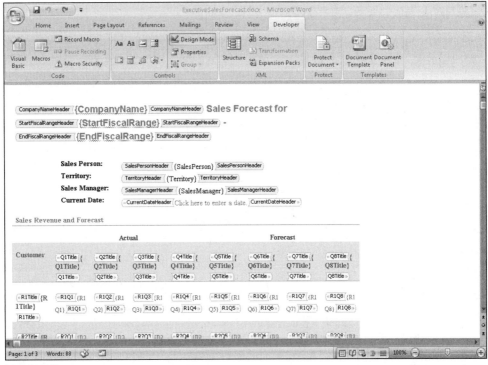

Figure 7-5

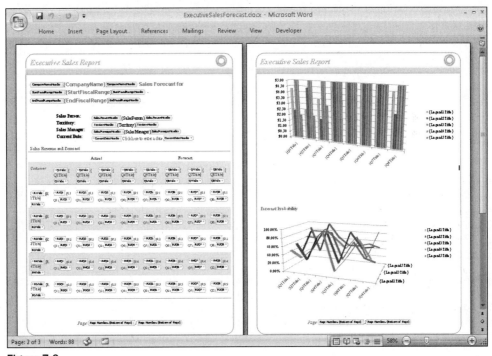

Figure 7-6

Creating the Web Method

Now that you've created the necessary files and the document template, the next step is to create the web method. The `SalesForecastDocService` implements a single web method that can be called to generate a new instance of the document. It accepts the ID of the sales representative in the `Person .Contact` table, the ID of the sales forecast in the `Sales.SalesForecast` table, the ID of the manager in the `HumanResources.Employee` table, and the ID of the sales territory in the `Sales.SalesTerritory` table as its first four parameters:

```
public string CreateSalesForecastWordDocument(int salesContactId, int forecastID,
        int managerID, int salesTerritoryId, DateTime reportDate, int pageSize,
        int pageNumber, string forecastComments, string forecastWorkbookUrl)
         const string TEMPLATE_FILE = @"~/App_Data/ExecutiveSalesForecast.docx";
```

The next three parameters are used to capture the report date, the page or paper size of the document that will be generated, and the page number from which the document should begin. The final two parameters take key data from the spreadsheet first. The comments that have been entered into the spreadsheet are also included at the end of this document.

The preceding code block also includes the project-based reference to the Word document that is the basis of the resulting document.

The following block of code begins the process of creating a custom Word document. It starts by creating a new `MemoryStream`, which will maintain a copy of the original document in memory. The `ReadAllBytes` method call uses the document name defined in the preceding code block to open the local reference to the document used as a template. The entire document is then read into a memory stream, and the file itself isn't locked outside of the time spent reading its contents. By placing the document in memory, the underlying document can be closed and made available to another user who might need to generate a document at the same time. Thus, the code simply uses the file object to copy the contents of the document into an array of bytes. This array is then passed to the `MemoryStream`, before being passed to a `System.IO.Package` object where it is opened as an OpenXML document.

```
using (MemoryStream wordDocumentMemoryStream = new MemoryStream())
{
    byte[] packageBytes = File.ReadAllBytes(Server.MapPath(TEMPLATE_FILE));
    wordDocumentMemoryStream.Write(packageBytes, 0, packageBytes.Length);
    using (Package wordOfficePackage =
       Package.Open(wordDocumentMemoryStream, FileMode.Open, FileAccess.ReadWrite))
    {
```

At this point with a Package object the code is ready to retrieve data from the database and update the in-memory representation of the final document. Note that the code shown in this chapter isn't complete. Key logic is shown, but other items — for example, the top-level error handling — is not shown. Similarly, this was written to prototype standards, in that the error checking and handling is sparse; when working with this code you should expect to enhance error handling and data validation.

Working with OpenXML

To start updating the contents of the Word document, the newly created Package object defined in the preceding code block, needs to be opened and the package parts need to be retrieved. The first of part of the Word document retrieved from the package is the top-level `officeDocument`. The `officeDocument` is the root element, and it indexes the other packages that make up the various XML files that are part of the complete document. In the following code, the first command retrieves the root `officeDocument` element XML file from the package. The next step is to retrieve from the root the various parts of the document that need to be customized. The first part addressed by the code is the collection of custom XML elements that were displayed earlier. These custom XML elements are retrieved, and then this part of the package along with details related to the sales forecast are passed into a method that will update the document and retrieve some of the key data from the database.

```
// Get the word document part
PackagePart wordDocumentPart = GetRootPart(wordOfficePackage
,                       "http://schemas.openxmlformats.org/officeDocument/2006/
relationships/officeDocument");

// Get the custom XML part
PackagePart customXmlPart = GetSinglePart(wordOfficePackage, wordDocumentPart,
"http://schemas.openxmlformats.org/officeDocument/2006/relationships/customXml");

// Generate the XML into the /customXml/item1.xml PackagePart by writing
// the new XML into the PackagePart stream.
GenerateCustomXml(customXmlPart.GetStream(), forecastID, salesContactId,
                   salesTerritoryId, managerID, reportDate,
                   forecastComments, advwrksDC, out salesAccountIds);
```

Of course, all three of these methods are custom code written for this specific assembly. The `GetRootPart` and `GetSinglePart` methods simply encapsulate a series of commands associated with searching for key package elements and returning the appropriate document part. The `GenerateCustomXML` method is a bit more interesting, because, as you'll see, what actually occurs within its implementation is that the `customXmlPart` object that was just received is completely replaced. Because there isn't a concept of editing a file, the contents of the part or file contained within the zip file are just replaced.

Both the `GetRootPart` and `GetSinglePart` methods refer to another custom method called `ResolvePartRelationship`. This method calls the packaging class to retrieve the Uniform Resource Identifier for a given part of the OpenXML package. This is found based on a `PackageRelationship` structure that defines both the source and target URI for a portion of the package defined by an XSL. In the preceding code block you see that the package is passed to each method along with a specific URN. A URN is a Uniform Resource Name (URN). It describes by name a resource, and it is a type of Uniform Resource Identifier (URI). In the case of the `GetSinglePart`, the part to which another portion of the package needs to be related is also passed into the method. Each method transforms these inputs, as you'll see shortly, and a package relationship and the base package memory stream are then passed to the `ResolvePartRelationship` method.

The code for the `ResolvePartRelationship` that follows shows how the relationship's properties for `SourceUri` and `TargetUri` are used in a call to get the necessary URI for the package. This URI is then used to retrieve that portion of the package from the package file, so that it can be updated and replaced in the package.

```
/// <summary>
/// Resolve a PackageRelationship to a PackagePart
/// </summary>
```

```
/// <param name="officePackage">Package (Required)</param>
/// <param name="relationship">PackageRelationship (Required)</param>
/// <returns>PackagePart</returns>
private static PackagePart ResolvePartRelationship(Package officePackage,
                                     PackageRelationship relationship)
{
    // Resolve the relationship
    Uri partUri =
        PackUriHelper.ResolvePartUri(relationship.SourceUri, relationship.
TargetUri);
    PackagePart part = officePackage.GetPart(partUri);

    return part;
}
```

At their core, the two methods used to retrieve package parts end up using the same `GetPart` method from the base `officePackage` memory stream. The first call to this method is in `GetRootPart` that follows:

```
/// <summary>
/// Get a PackagePart from the Package.  This is one of a small number of parts
that
/// have relationships defined at the root package level.
/// </summary>
/// <param name="officePackage">Package (Required)</param>
/// <param name="partUrn">string (Required)</param>
/// <returns>PackagePart</returns>
private static PackagePart GetRootPart(Package officePackage, string partUrn)
{
    PackagePart rootPart = null;

    foreach (PackageRelationship relationship in officePackage.GetRelationships
ByType(partUrn))
    {
        rootPart = ResolvePartRelationship(officePackage, relationship);

        // There should only be one of these types of part in the package
        break;
    }

    return rootPart;
}
```

The method accepts the URN for a given root part; it then iterates the collection of root parts to find that item. Because the collection is returned from the method call `GetRelationshipsByType`, and because that call will only return a single item collection, the code accepts the first relationship found and passes that value to the `ResolvePartRelationship` method to get the root part associated with the URN. The same pattern is repeated in the `GetSinglePart` method code that follows:

```
/// <summary>
/// Get the child PackagePart from the specified parent PackagePart
/// for the specified urn.
/// </summary>
```

```
/// <param name="officePackage">Package (Required)</param>
/// <param name="parentPart">PackagePart (Required)</param>
/// <param name="partUrn">string (Required)</param>
/// <returns>PackagePart</returns>
private static PackagePart GetSinglePart(Package officePackage, PackagePart
parentPart, string partUrn)
{
    // Get the part
    PackagePart part = null;

    foreach (PackageRelationship relationship in parentPart.GetRelationshipsByT
ype(partUrn))
    {
        part = ResolvePartRelationship(officePackage, relationship);

        // Get the first part only
        break;
    }

    return part;
}
```

The GetSinglePart method works almost exactly like the GetRootPart method except that it gets the relationship collection from the parentPart instead of from the root officePackage. To abstract this a little, now that you are seeing a pattern, the root Document object for your .docx package contains references to the various elements of your document — Body, Footnotes, Theming, Styles, CustomXML. The officePackage object has the contents for all of these packages, and the way to retrieve them is to get the URI for each from the root. To get this URI, you need to recognize the relationship from the top of the package to the specific package part you want. That's what the preceding methods handle.

Once you have the custom XML part from the package, you pass this as a stream to the GenerateCustomXML method. This method clears out the original contents and rebuilds the custom XML that will be part of the document, without any concern for other portions of your document table. The first parameter in the call to the GenerateCustomXML method is the stream containing the custom XML part from the template document, the second to last parameter, advwrksDC, which is the data context used for the LINQ queries, and the last parameter, which is actually a returned value indicating the list of customer names. The last parameter is important because the list will always contain five items, even if the sales forecast only includes one or two companies.

```
private static void GenerateCustomXml(Stream stream, int forecastID, int contactID,
                        int territoryID, int managerID, DateTime forecastDate,
                        string forecastComments, AdventureWorksVSTO advwrksDC,
                        out List<int> salesAccountIds)
{
    XmlWriter writerXML = XmlWriter.Create(stream);

    //</GeneralInfo>
    // <?xml version="1.0" ?>
    writerXML.WriteStartDocument();
    //      <CompanyData>
    writerXML.WriteStartElement("CompanyData");
    //          <GeneralInfo>
    writerXML.WriteStartElement("GeneralInfo");
    //              <CompanyName>company name</CompanyName>
```

```
writerXML.WriteElementString("CompanyName",
                              ConfigurationManager.AppSettings["CompanyName"]);
var territory = from terrtbl in advwrksDC.Sales_SalesTerritory
                where terrtbl.TerritoryID == territoryID
                select terrtbl;

//                    <TerritoryName>territory name</TerritoryName>
writerXML.WriteElementString("TerritoryName", territory.First().Name.ToString());
//                    <TerritoryID>territory id</TerritoryID>
writerXML.WriteElementString("TerritoryID", territoryID.ToString());
```

Once this method is called, an XMLWriter is associated with the `MemoryStream` holding the custom XML part from the document package. By default, this writer starts at the beginning of the file, writing the XML in a format that matches what the document is expecting. The first XML written is the company name, which is retrieved from the `web.config` file. After that, the code executes a LINQ to SQL query to retrieve information related to the sales territory associated with this sales forecast. This method continues populating the key individual data values and then builds a section containing each company's actual and forecast sales numbers.

Most of the processing in `GenerateCustomXML` is similar to the processing that is done to create the XML attachment sent from the Sales Forecast Approval Workflow to the Sales Forecast Outlook Form Region. In fact, at their core, they have similar structures. There are a couple reasons for the differences. The custom Sales Forecast OFR can manually process the associated XML file, so it can handle less than the full five companies of data. The document generation logic, on the other hand, expects to replace the underlying XML file from the document's template with one that represents the expected five companies. There isn't an opportunity to process the contents in the same way.

The result is a change in the method `GenerateCustomerXML` to handle the scenario when fewer than five companies are submitted. In this scenario the application has been using a company name of "-" and zeros for all other values. In theory, when this application is rewritten, we will address the idea that there may be one or more companies in a given forecast, handling charts only to display key companies while tables may list all companies. For now, the code is brittle enough that the resulting implementation that keeps placeholders is a better illustration. Ideally, when rewritten, the code will leverage Literal XML, allowing for a much cleaner XML interface to the OpenXML model. The snippet for managing fewer than five companies in a forecast follows:

```
writerXML.WriteEndElement();
if ( customerCount < 5)
{
    //Need placeholder data...
    //  <Customer>
    writerXML.WriteStartElement("Customer");
    //      <Name>customer name</Name>
    writerXML.WriteElementString("Name", "-");
    //      <CustomerID>customer id</CustomerID>
    writerXML.WriteElementString("CustomerID", Convert.ToString(0));
    for (int i = customerCount; i < 5; i++)
    {
        // fill in the remaining customer id's as customer 0 so that
        // customer 0 will be used to fill in the remaining slots in the
        // template.
        salesAccountIds.Add(0);
    }
}
```

The preceding code block runs after the data for all of the submitted customers is retrieved from the database. At this point, if there are fewer than five customers, the XML needs to account for the other customers. On the surface, this would imply creating an empty structure for each of the missing customers. In reality, only a single entry needs to be created. This entry is assigned a company name of "-" and an ID value of zero. The code then updates the list of salesAccountIds to include the necessary entries for five total companies with each company in the list assigned that same zero ID value. In this way, later in the code, when the data in the XML structure is processed via XQuery to populate the Excel charts, each customer above is represented and the queries for the ID zero companies return the same zeroed-out data items. Just as important, when the logic binds the data to the Word table, BindWordSalesTable(), similar logic is used to assign each company name, based on ID, to a row. The logic then uses XQuery to retrieve that company's related sales data, which was just retrieved from the company zero set of nodes that do not need to be repeated.

Once the GenerateCustomXML method has finished, it is, in theory, possible to close the stream and save this part of the document. As noted, instead, the document is kept in memory, and, more important, the now populated custom XML structure is used as input to the Word table and the two Excel chart handling methods.

Updating an Excel Chart from OpenXML

Following the call to the BindWordSalesTable to associate the custom XML with the various cells in the Word table, the code then calls the method BindExcelChartTables to bind the underlying custom XML data to the embedded Excel charts. The input for this call includes the package parts for the customXMLPart and higher-level root wordDocumentPart as well as the top-level wordOfficePackage that contains all of the document files. The calling code then includes the list of sales customers that are represented within the custom XML, so that the logic can query that XML for the data associated with each of these customers, as well as information related to the actual sales versus forecast sales quarters.

Once within the BindExcelChartTables, the code begins the process of identifying and retrieving the embedded Excel files. The comments from the code for identifying each of these items are reasonably self-explanatory as the progression from Excel document to chart to table and shared strings displayed in that chart are retrieved. Eventually these parts, along with the list of companies and the previously customized custom XML data, are passed to the method PopulateChartData.

```
// Get the PackagePart for the embedded Excel document
PackagePart excelPart = GetSinglePart(
                    wordOfficePackage,
                    chartPart,
"http://schemas.openxmlformats.org/officeDocument/2006/relationships/package");

// Load the Excel package
using (Package excelOfficePackage =
        Package.Open(excelPart.GetStream(), FileMode.Open, FileAccess.ReadWrite))
{
    // Get the excel document part
    PackagePart excelDocumentPart = GetRootPart(
                            excelOfficePackage,
"http://schemas.openxmlformats.org/officeDocument/2006/relationships/
officeDocument");
```

```
    // Get the worksheet part
    PackagePart worksheetPart = GetSinglePart(
                            excelOfficePackage,
                            excelDocumentPart,
    "http://schemas.openxmlformats.org/officeDocument/2006/relationships/worksheet");

    // Get the table part
    PackagePart tablePart = GetSinglePart(
                            excelOfficePackage,
                            worksheetPart,
    "http://schemas.openxmlformats.org/officeDocument/2006/relationships/table");

    // Get the shared strings part
    PackagePart sharedStringsPart = GetSinglePart(
                            excelOfficePackage,
                            excelDocumentPart,
    "http://schemas.openxmlformats.org/officeDocument/2006/relationships/
    sharedStrings");

    // Populate the appropriate chart data
    PopulateChartData(chartPart, pageSize, maximumQuarters,
                    worksheetPart, tablePart, sharedStringsPart, customXmlPart,
                    salesAccountIds, fiscalInformation);
```

The `PopulateChartData` method called here takes the various document parts that identify not only the charts, but the components that are displayed in those charts, and processes that XML in order to apply the sales forecast data to the default templated data that is part of the core document.

Populating the Chart Data

As you may recall the document contains two embedded Excel charts. The `PopulateChartData` method updates both charts. XPath is used to query for each node in the chart, and then that node is updated. As a loop traverses the data, an `XPathNavigator` is created and used to retrieve portions of the XML associated with the charts. The charts do not store their entire contents within a single part. The XPathNavigators, which will be used to traverse the OpenXML document structures, are shown in the following code:

```
    // Create the worksheet navigator
    XmlDocument worksheetDocument = new XmlDocument();
    worksheetDocument.Load(worksheetPart.GetStream());
    XPathNavigator worksheetNavigator = worksheetDocument.CreateNavigator();

    // Create the shared strings navigator
    XmlDocument sharedStringsDocument = new XmlDocument();
    sharedStringsDocument.Load(sharedStringsPart.GetStream());
    XPathNavigator sharedStringsNavigator = sharedStringsDocument.CreateNavigator();

    // Create the table navigator
    XmlDocument tableDocument = new XmlDocument();
    tableDocument.Load(tablePart.GetStream());
    XPathNavigator tableNavigator = tableDocument.CreateNavigator();
```

```
// Create the chart navigator
XmlDocument chartDocument = new XmlDocument();
chartDocument.Load(chartPart.GetStream());
XPathNavigator chartNavigator = chartDocument.CreateNavigator();

// Create the custom xml navigator.  Use an XmlTextReader
XmlTextReader reader = new XmlTextReader(customXmlPart.GetStream());
XPathDocument customXmlDocument = new XPathDocument(reader);
XPathNavigator customXmlNavigator = customXmlDocument.CreateNavigator();
```

The preceding code walks through each of the XML parts that were passed into the method and creates for each an XPathNavigator object so that the data can be directly referred to within the XML structures. It is then possible to update a table by simply selecting the appropriate data from the customXmlNavigator instance to populate the appropriate portion of the chart. At this point the method SetCellValue can be invoked. This method does the dirty work of actually updating the individual cells. The code starts by accepting the namespace manager along with both the worksheetNavigator and sharedStringsNavigator. These are the main tools for actually navigating to the individual cells within the charts. The next portion of the equation is the specific cell to update and the new value for that cell. These are the next three parameters to the SetCellValue method: row, col, and value. The following code is then executed to update an individual cell value:

```
/// <summary>
/// Set a cell value.  Only supports simple numeric text strings and shared
/// strings that are simple text strings.  Both row and col number
/// are 1 based not zero based.  In the simple documents in the template
/// all shared strings are row or column headers, all else is numeric so if
/// it's already a shared string then we don't change that or if it isn't
/// a shared string then the value must be numeric.
/// </summary>
/// <param name="nsMgr">XmlNamespaceManager</param>
/// <param name="worksheetNavigator">XPathNavigator</param>
/// <param name="sharedStringsNavigator">XPathNavigator</param>
/// <param name="row">int</param>
/// <param name="col">int</param>
/// <param name="value">string</param>
private static void SetCellValue(XmlNamespaceManager nsMgr,
    XPathNavigator worksheetNavigator, XPathNavigator sharedStringsNavigator,
    int row, int col, string value)
{
    // Navigate to the correct cell.  Use a simple algorithm to get the cell
    // rather than calculate the column designation such as 'A1' or 'F1'.
    XPathNavigator cellNavigator =
        worksheetNavigator.SelectSingleNode(
            string.Format(
                "//ss:sheetData/ss:row[@r={0}]/ss:c[@r='{1}']",
                row.ToString(),
                GetCellAddress(row, col)),
            nsMgr);

    // Check if this cell is using a shared string
    if (cellNavigator.MoveToAttribute("t", string.Empty) &&
        cellNavigator.Value == "s")
    {
```

```
            // Get the share string index
            cellNavigator.MoveToParent();
            cellNavigator.MoveToChild("v",
                        "http://schemas.openxmlformats.org/spreadsheetml/2006/
main");
            int sharedStringIndex = cellNavigator.ValueAsInt;
            // Get the navigator to the shared string value.  We only support
            // simple text strings.  All column headers and row headers will
            // always be unique so we don't check just assume that they are.
            XPathNavigator sharedStringValueNavigator =
                sharedStringsNavigator.SelectSingleNode(
                    string.Format(
                        "//ss:si[position()={0}]/ss:t",
                        (sharedStringIndex + 1).ToString()),
                    nsMgr);
            sharedStringValueNavigator.SetValue(value);
        }
        else
        {
            // Move to the value node
            cellNavigator.MoveToChild("v",
                        "http://schemas.openxmlformats.org/spreadsheetml/2006/
main");
            cellNavigator.SetValue(value);
        }
        return;
    }
```

The first thing the code does is create a `cellNavigator` to get the XML element associated with a specific cell that is used in the chart. Each cell can either contain a numeric value or a reference to a string. In order to manage the size of the file, the OpenXML model leverages a shared strings structure. The code checks to see whether the current node contains a string. If it does, then the processing leverages the `sharedStringNavigator` to update the value of that string inside the string. Of course, it's never that simple; the `sharedStringNavigator` is actually used to retrieve a `sharedStringValueNavigator` in which the end value referred to by the identity of the shared string is stored and updated.

Updating shared strings is relatively complex in comparison to updating actual value cells because the `cellNavigator` that was created at the start of the method allows for a direct update of the values in that cell. This method is called for each value used as part of each chart via the implementation of a loop, which is shown in the following code. The code, extracted from the `PopulateChartData` method, is executed for each row. You should download and examine this method in detail from the materials available on Codeplex at `http://www.codeplex.com/obasales`.

This code will leverage the shared strings along with the other areas that need to be updated. Most, but not all, of the code is repeated for the columns and cells. For the columns, the code was optimized such that, as each column header is updated, the code then goes through each cell associated with that column updating the values in the chart. Updating the charts doesn't involve a solitary call to update the underlying cell value, but also to the related column header information and graphics associated with that chart. As you might imagine, a significant number of updates occur to process the embedded Excel charts.

```
    // Get the customer account number.  The customer will definitely
    // exist so no need to check to make sure we found it.
```

```
string dataPath = string.Format(
                "/CompanyData/Sales/Customer[CustomerID={0}]/Name",
                salesAccountIds[colNumber - 2].ToString());
XPathNavigator dataValueNavigator = customXmlNavigator.SelectSingleNode(dataPath);


// Set the value into the shared strings
SetCellValue(
            nsMgr,
            worksheetNavigator,
            sharedStringsNavigator,
            COL_HEADER_ROW_NUMBER,
            colNumber,
            dataValueNavigator.Value);

// Update the tablePart
XPathNavigator tableColumnNavigator =
                tableNavigator.SelectSingleNode(
                    string.Format(
                        "//ss:tableColumn[position()={0}]",
                        colNumber.ToString()),
                    nsMgr);
tableColumnNavigator.MoveToAttribute("name", string.Empty);
tableColumnNavigator.SetValue(dataValueNavigator.Value);

// Update the chartPart
XPathNavigator chartHeaderNavigator =
                chartNavigator.SelectSingleNode(
                    string.Format(
                        "/c:chartSpace/c:chart/c:plotArea//c:ser[position()=
                        {0}]/c:tx/c:strRef/c:strCache/c:pt/c:v",
                        (colNumber - 1).ToString()),
                    nsMgr);
chartHeaderNavigator.SetValue(dataValueNavigator.Value);
```

The preceding statements simply retrieve information from the data navigator and then update the appropriate object within the OpenXML document objects to use the appropriate value from the data values stored in the custom XML that was built earlier in this process. The process repeats for the data in each of the charts, because the loop is based on the list of sales account IDs populated to exactly five entries. The loop fills in each of the rows for four actual and four forecast quarters. Once this process is complete the OpenXML document elements are closed, but the resulting document continues to live in a `MemoryStream` object until that `MemoryStream` is added to the SharePoint document library.

Adding a Document to SharePoint

At this point, the code has created a new document, and the only remaining step is to add this Web service into SharePoint so that it can be processed. In short, the code is going to take the in-memory stream with all of the custom data and output this stream as a new document. The code will access the MOSS server and make a call to some of the methods exposed on the SharePoint site object to add a new entry into the Sales-ForecastDocuments folder, as shown in Figure 7-7.

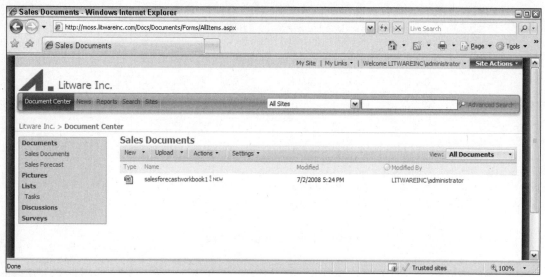

Figure 7-7

The code that was run on your custom Web service creates an in-memory document. In the case of the document shown in Figure 7-7, the original Sales Forecast Workbook was named salesforecastworkbook1. The user creating this test document was signed in with the Administrator account for testing purposes, and after saving a copy of the test spreadsheet to the Sales Forecast folder on MOSS, the user selected the Generate Executive Forecast Report from the custom Sales Forecast Tools tab in the Excel workbook. This calls the Web service executing the preceding code and then a new document, as shown in Figure 7-7, is created within the Sales Documents library on MOSS.

As shown in the following code, the first step in creating a document on MOSS is to create an instance of the MOSS site based on the URL that is provided in the web.config file. This site object then allows for the retrieval of an SPWeb object based on the name of the site that contains the document libraries. Once the web site has been identified, the name of the user associated with the creation of this document is used to create a valid account. This means that a call to this Web service requires Integrated Security on the web server. It should, however, be noted that although the current user's identity will be known the process used will still be the process associated with the web site. This will become important when we discuss installing and configuring the Web service on your server. Once the identity of the user is retrieved, the code moves on to retrieve the appropriate folder from the SPWeb object.

```
using (Microsoft.SharePoint.SPSite site = new SPSite(sharePointUrl))
{
    SPWeb web = site.AllWebs[docLibSiteName];
    web.AllowUnsafeUpdates = true;
    SPUser user = web.SiteUsers[HttpContext.Current.User.Identity.Name];
    SPFolder reportFolder = web.Folders[reportDocLibName];
    // Get the workbook title
    fileUrl = (reportFolder.Url + forecastWorkbookUrl.
Substring(forecastWorkbookUrl.LastIndexOf("/"))).ToLower();
    fileUrl = fileUrl.Replace(".xlsx", ".docx");
    // Get the document bytes to load into SharePoint
```

```
        wordDocumentMemoryStream.Position = 0;
        byte[] documentBytes = new byte[wordDocumentMemoryStream.Length];
        wordDocumentMemoryStream.Read(documentBytes, 0, (int)wordDocumentMemoryStream.
Length);
        // Load the document into SharePoint
        SPFile file =
            reportFolder.Files.Add(
                fileUrl,
                documentBytes,
                user,
                user,
                DateTime.Now,
                DateTime.Now);
        SPListItem item = file.Item;
        item.SystemUpdate();
        fileUrl = web.Url + "/" + item.Url;
    }
```

After the initial objects are retrieved, the code manipulates the name of the Excel spreadsheet associated with the current sales forecast and generates a name for a .docx file based on the original Excel file's name. This generated name could include one or more subdirectories and is generated this way to ensure that in a large organization documents were segmented appropriately. Alternatively, the associated manager's name could be introduced as a sub-folder associated with the document.

In any event, once a name has been defined, the MemoryStream that has been used through the document manipulation process is transformed into a raw byte array. This byte array is then used as part of an Add call on the SharePoint site folder that contains the reports. This call returns a list item, if successful, and it is this list item that eventually provides the name of the newly created document to return to the calling application. Keep in mind that the call to SystemUpdate is required to ensure that all of the data associated with the newly created document is created appropriately.

Once the document has been generated, it is possible to open the document from SharePoint and review the resulting information in Word as shown in Figure 7-8.

Summary

The OpenXML document structure allows you to create rich Office documents on your server without needing to invoke Word, Excel, or PowerPoint. These client applications were never designed for unattended use on a server, and being able to bypass them for the purposes of generating documents is a powerful capability. In the sales forecast OBA, the document is generated based on a user action. A more likely real-world scenario is that each time a user saved a spreadsheet, a background worker thread would be started to generate the associated report automatically. In this way, when the workflow task was started there wouldn't be a question regarding the presence of the associated report; it would always be present. The button option would actually only be used to allow the sales representative creating the forecast a way to review the document that was generated. This chapter is meant to provide you with insight into the power of OpenXML when looking at creating and displaying server data.

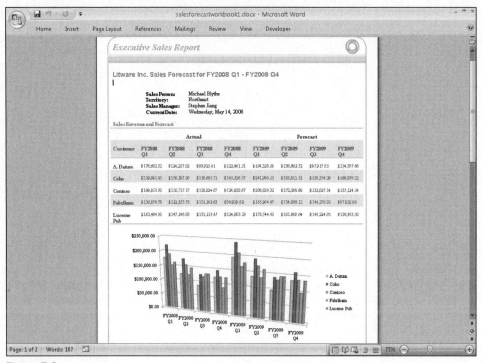

Figure 7-8

This chapter introduced:

❑ The OpenXML document format

❑ A look at leveraging the zip utilities to review an OpenXML document

❑ Creating a template that is used by an XML Web service to generate documents

❑ Writing code to update XML and embedded objects in a Word document

❑ Creating a new document within a SharePoint document library

The OpenXML document format has opened the door to allow independent developers to create custom server solutions that leverage all of the power and formatting of Microsoft Office documents. The ability to open an XML document using the System.IO.Packaging namespace allows a developer to take advantage of embedding application data within an Office document. This capability isn't limited to Word, but is also available for both Excel and PowerPoint, allowing a well formatted presentation to be updated in real time with the latest business data prior to a presentation. Even though the OpenXML document features of Microsoft Office aren't part of Visual Studio Tools for Office, they provide another means for application developers to incorporate custom business data and logic into a solution that leverages the readily available and familiar power of the Microsoft Office client tools.

Further Reading

Take a look at these web sites for more information on OpenXML.

- ❑ Ecma Office OpenXML File Formats Overview

    - ❑ `http://office.microsoft.com/en-us/products/HA102058151033.aspx`

- ❑ The Office OpenXML Formats Resource Center

    - ❑ `http://msdn.microsoft.com/en-us/office/bb265236.aspx`

- ❑ The OpenXML Developer Workshop

    - ❑ `http://msdn.microsoft.com/en-us/office/bb738430.aspx`

- ❑ The OpenXML Format SDK

    - ❑ `http://www.microsoft.com/downloads/details.aspx?FamilyId=AD0B72FB-4A1D-4C52-BDB5-7DD7E816D046&displaylang=en`

- ❑ XML in Office Developer Portal

    - ❑ `http://msdn.microsoft.com/en-us/office/aa905545.aspx`

- ❑ OpenXML Format SDK Forum

    - ❑ `http://forums.microsoft.com/MSDN/ShowForum.aspx?ForumID=1647&SiteID=1`

8

Adding Business Intelligence through Excel Web Services and Key Performance Indicators

Business intelligence (BI) is not something new; as long as business has been around, there has been some degree of data and reporting that provides "intelligence" to help inform the decisions of workers of all types. In the context of Office Business Applications (OBAs), BI takes on a similar meaning. The exciting part for developers, though, is that you have a number of different options available to you to expose important business data within the structure of a report or dashboard to enable information workers to make better business decisions. In some cases, the work of configuring these BI options in SharePoint can be left up to the information worker.

In this chapter, we talk specifically about some of the key features that we used in some capacity in the sales forecast OBA to give you some grounding on these additional features when building your own OBA.

You could summarize the BI features we used in the sales forecast OBA through four main areas:

1. Report Center and BI Dashboards

2. Business Data Catalog (BDC)

3. Key Performance Indicators (KPIs)

4. Excel Services

We discuss each of these in respect to the sales forecast OBA.

Report Center and BI Dashboards

In general, dashboards represent a consolidated view of business intelligence data. In the context of MOSS, the Report Center is one of the major means by which users can create dashboard views of data and more. We used the Report Center dashboard view to provide some business intelligence around sales versus sales forecasts and to provide progress on forecast completion. To create a new Report Center site, navigate to the Home page of your SharePoint site and click Site Actions ⇨ Create Site ⇨ Enterprise ⇨ Report Center. As Figure 8-1 illustrates, you can complete the options in the New SharePoint Site page and then click Create, and your Report Center site will be created. Once created, you can use the Report Center site to store not only your business intelligence reports and Web parts (for example, KPIs), but also store documents through a reports library. (You'll need to store the Excel documents in this document library so you can use them for KPIs and Excel Services.)

We should note that if you absolutely do not want to create a Report Center, you don't need to. For example, you could create a vanilla Team site and then add Web parts that expose BI. Creating a dashboard using the Team site, though, limits you to those SharePoint artifacts that are available to the Team site — such as Web parts, links, and so on. And, creating a Report Center provides you a predefined site template that you can use to build out your BI site. For example, you have some already-deployed Web parts such as the Contact Details, KPIs, Announcements, or Upcoming Events on your page that you can either configure or remove in place of other Web parts that you want to add to the page.

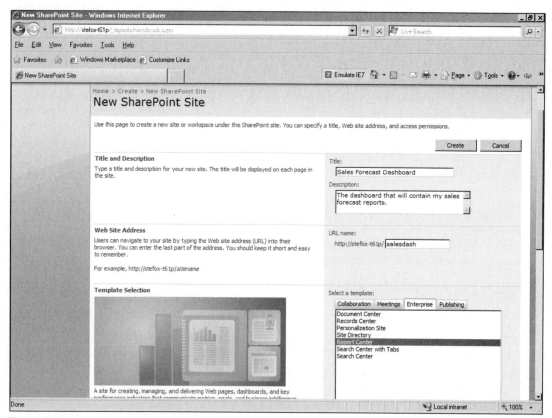

Figure 8-1

To illustrate some of the things that you can create using MOSS, we created a Report Center to manage some of our sales forecast data. Figure 8-2 illustrates the Web parts that can be added to the Report Center. These include some generic Web parts providing information (for example Announcements and Contact Details) and some BI-specific Web parts (for example BDC, KPI, and Excel Services).

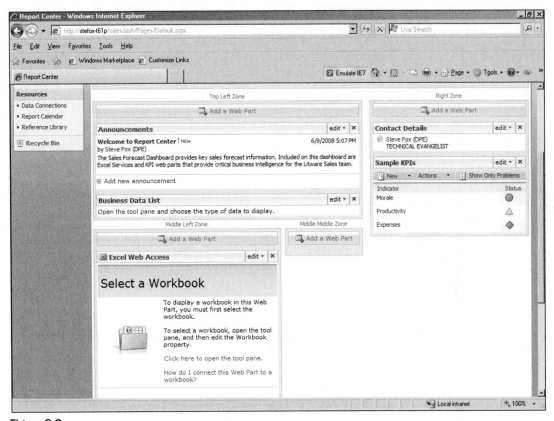

Figure 8-2

After the Web parts are added to the Report Center, you can configure each of them. In some cases, this means manually adding some descriptive content — for example, adding a new announcement in the Announcements Web part — and in other cases it means configuring the Web parts to a specific data source. The type of data source supported varies depending on the Web part within the Report Center. For example, you can integrate the BDC Web part to either a database or Web service, and you can integrate Excel spreadsheet data with Excel Services. We spend some time discussing each of the major Web parts on the sales forecast dashboard to build out the Report Center with some interesting BI data.

Business Data Catalog

The BDC is a set of services (available in the MOSS Enterprise SKU) that enable you to integrate your Web part with an ADO.NET data source or a web method (or data source) via a Web service. To integrate with either of these, you need first to create an application definition file (ADF), an XML file that essentially defines the relationship between the Web part and the data source. Creating the ADF can be challenging, depending on what you're trying to display within the Web part. For example, if you're trying to call a web method to access a business API (BAPI) within an SAP instance, you will need to negotiate not only the call into the Web service (the wrapper around the web method), but also the permissions for the BDC to call into the SAP system. In the sales forecast OBA, we used the BDC to fetch some data from a simple data source that provided some information about the total sales of the salespeople. This data was stored in a SQL Server, so we created a definition that would display this information in a BDC Web part.

Displaying the sales data in a BDC Web part required completing the following steps:

1. Creating an ADF (which has a dependency on an existing database or Web service).

2. Importing the ADF into SharePoint using the SharePoint Shared Services Provider.

3. Adding a BDC Web part (which we've already done).

4. Associating the ADF with the Web part.

After you've completed these steps, your BDC will display whatever data or service call is defined in the ADF. In our case, this was the sales data from the SQL Server database.

To create the ADF, you can use one of two methods:

1. Hand-code the ADF.

2. Use a tool to create it.

The first of these two methods is not recommended because the ADFs can get pretty long (although it is a useful exercise to hand-code a very simple one to become familiar with all of the XML elements in the file, or at least spend some time reviewing the core elements of the ADF). You can use any number of available tools to create the ADF (for example, the BDC Definition Editor or MetaMan). We walk you through a simple example using the BDC Definition Editor, which ships with the MOSS 2007 SDK.

Open the BDC Definition Editor and click Add LOB System. This opens the Add LOB System dialog, in which you can click either Connect to Database or Connect to Web Service. If you want to connect to a data source, you'll need to add a connection string (for example, `Data Source=<server name>;Initial Catalog=<database name>;Integrated Security=True`) or the Web service URL (for example, `http://MyServer/WebService.asmx`). If the connection is successful, a design window opens and you can add the tables or methods to the designer and then click OK and give your entity definition (that is, ADF) a name. After this is complete, the BDC Definition Editor adds a root node in the Metadata Objects view. Depending on whether you're trying to create a connection to a database or Web service, you'll need to configure the entity. For example, take the following definition file that makes a call into a SQL Server database and executes a `SELECT *` against a table called `TotalSales`. This is a very simple definition, so you can imagine what a complex ADF would look like!

```
<?xml version="1.0" encoding="utf-8" standalone="yes"?>
<LobSystem xmlns:xsi="http://www.w3.org/2001/XMLSchema-instance"
xsi:schemaLocation="http://schemas.microsoft.com/office/2006/03/BusinessDataCatalog
BDCMetadata.xsd" Type="Database" Version="1.0.0.0" Name="TotalSales" xmlns="http://
schemas.microsoft.com/office/2006/03/BusinessDataCatalog">
  <LobSystemInstances>
```

```
      <LobSystemInstance Name="TotalSales_Instance">
        <Properties>
          <Property Name="rdbconnection Data Source" Type="System.String">.\BDC</
Property>
          <Property Name="rdbconnection Initial Catalog" Type="System.
String">TotalSales</Property>
          <Property Name="rdbconnection Integrated Security" Type="System.
String">True</Property>
          <Property Name="DatabaseAccessProvider" Type="Microsoft.Office.Server.
ApplicationRegistry.SystemSpecific.Db.DbAccessProvider">SqlServer</Property>
          <Property Name="AuthenticationMode" Type="Microsoft.Office.Server.
ApplicationRegistry.SystemSpecific.Db.DbAuthenticationMode">PassThrough</Property>
        </Properties>
      </LobSystemInstance>
    </LobSystemInstances>
    <Entities>
      <Entity EstimatedInstanceCount="10000" Name="ActualSales">
        <Identifiers>
          <Identifier TypeName="System.Int32" Name="SalesPersonID" />
        </Identifiers>
        <Methods>
          <Method Name="Find_ActualSales">
            <Properties>
              <Property Name="RdbCommandType" Type="System.Data.CommandType, System.
Data, Version=2.0.0.0, Culture=neutral, PublicKeyToken=b77a5c561934e089">Text</
Property>
              <Property Name="RdbCommandText" Type="System.String">Select "Sale
sPersonID","SalesPerName","SalesQuota","Bonus","CommisionPct","SalesYTD" from
ActualSales</Property>
            </Properties>
            <Parameters>
              <Parameter Direction="Return" Name="@ActualSales">
                <TypeDescriptor TypeName="System.Data.IDataReader, System.
Data, Version=2.0.0.0, Culture=neutral, PublicKeyToken=b77a5c561934e089"
IsCollection="true" Name="Reader">
                  <TypeDescriptors>
                    <TypeDescriptor TypeName="System.Data.IDataRecord, System.Data,
Version=2.0.0.0, Culture=neutral, PublicKeyToken=b77a5c561934e089" Name="Record">
                      <TypeDescriptors>
                        <TypeDescriptor TypeName="System.Int32, mscorlib,
Version=2.0.0.0, Culture=neutral, PublicKeyToken=b77a5c561934e089"
IdentifierName="SalesPersonID" Name="SalesPersonID" />
                        <TypeDescriptor TypeName="System.String, mscorlib,
Version=2.0.0.0, Culture=neutral, PublicKeyToken=b77a5c561934e089"
Name="SalesPerName" />
                        <TypeDescriptor TypeName="System.Decimal, mscorlib,
Version=2.0.0.0, Culture=neutral, PublicKeyToken=b77a5c561934e089"
Name="SalesQuota" />
                        <TypeDescriptor TypeName="System.Decimal, mscorlib,
Version=2.0.0.0, Culture=neutral, PublicKeyToken=b77a5c561934e089" Name="Bonus" />
                        <TypeDescriptor TypeName="System.Decimal, mscorlib,
Version=2.0.0.0, Culture=neutral, PublicKeyToken=b77a5c561934e089"
Name="CommisionPct" />
```

```
                        <TypeDescriptor TypeName="System.Decimal, mscorlib,
    Version=2.0.0.0, Culture=neutral, PublicKeyToken=b77a5c561934e089" Name="SalesYTD"
    />
                            </TypeDescriptors>
                        </TypeDescriptor>
                    </TypeDescriptors>
                </TypeDescriptor>
            </Parameter>
        </Parameters>
        <MethodInstances>
            <MethodInstance Type="Finder" ReturnParameterName="@ActualSales" Retur
    nTypeDescriptorName="Reader" ReturnTypeDescriptorLevel="0" Name="Find_ActualSales_
    Instance" />
        </MethodInstances>
    </Method>
    <Method Name="FindAll_ActualSales">
        <Properties>
            <Property Name="RdbCommandType" Type="System.Data.CommandType, System.
    Data, Version=2.0.0.0, Culture=neutral, PublicKeyToken=b77a5c561934e089">Text</
    Property>
            <Property Name="RdbCommandText" Type="System.String">Select
    "SalesPersonID" from  ActualSales</Property>
        </Properties>
        <Parameters>
            <Parameter Direction="Return" Name="@ActualSales">
                <TypeDescriptor TypeName="System.Data.IDataReader, System.
    Data, Version=2.0.0.0, Culture=neutral, PublicKeyToken=b77a5c561934e089"
    IsCollection="true" Name="Reader">
                    <TypeDescriptors>
                        <TypeDescriptor TypeName="System.Data.IDataRecord, System.Data,
    Version=2.0.0.0, Culture=neutral, PublicKeyToken=b77a5c561934e089" Name="Record">
                            <TypeDescriptors>
                                <TypeDescriptor TypeName="System.Int32, mscorlib,
    Version=2.0.0.0, Culture=neutral, PublicKeyToken=b77a5c561934e089"
    IdentifierName="SalesPersonID" Name="SalesPersonID" />
                            </TypeDescriptors>
                        </TypeDescriptor>
                    </TypeDescriptors>
                </TypeDescriptor>
            </Parameter>
        </Parameters>
        <MethodInstances>
            <MethodInstance Type="IdEnumerator" ReturnParameterName="@ActualSales"
    ReturnTypeDescriptorName="Reader" ReturnTypeDescriptorLevel="0" Name="FindAll_
    ActualSales_Instance" />
        </MethodInstances>
    </Method>
    </Methods>
    </Entity>
    </Entities>
```

In the preceding ADF are a number of elements that are common across all ADFs. For example, the LobSystem element provides information about which XML Schema to use (including the type and the version) and the location for the schema. Also, the LobInstances element provides information about the Web service or database you're trying to connect to the Web part. In the following example, you'll see the instance name (TotalSales_Instance), along with the properties that map to that instance, such as connection properties (rdbconnection), server location (.\BDC), database name (TotalSales), and so on. The ADF also defines the entities with which you'll interact in your connection with the database or Web service. For example, in the following ADF, you'll note that the Entities element contains a definition for the Entity (ActualSales) along with the query against the database which is defined in the Property elements. The ADF will also define all of the individual fields within the table that we're querying through the Web part. These are defined through the TypeDescriptor elements. The ADF file also defines any parameters, command text (that is, the SQL command), and any other elements that are required to issue the SELECT * against the TotalSales table.

Creating this ADF using the BDC was very straightforward, but a couple of tweaks were required to make it work properly.

Essentially, you need to do three things when trying to configure this specific entity definition to issue a SELECT * statement without any parameters or clauses:

1. First, remove any WHERE clauses that were added by default to the entity definition in the RdbCommandText. To do this, edit the RdbCommandText field of the root method that was created (see Figure 8-3). This would leave the SQL statement to look like the following:

```
Select "SalesPersonID", "SalesPerName", "SalesQuota", "Bonus", "CommisionPct",
"SalesYTD" from  ActualSales
```

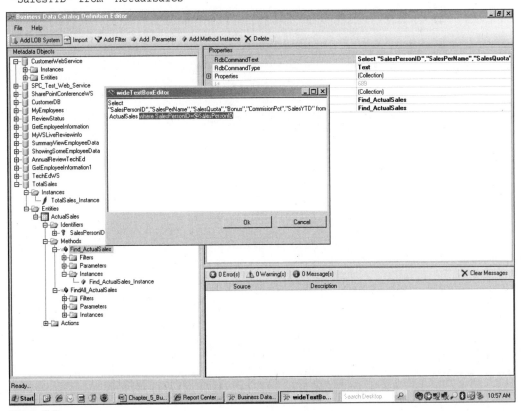

Figure 8-3

185

2. Within the method instance, remove the input parameters from the Parameters node. In our example, we removed the @SalesPersonID parameter.

3. Change the instance MethodInstanceType to be Finder instead of the default SpecificFinder.

After you've completed these steps, you can right-click the entity instance and select Execute. If the ADF works correctly, the query (or Web service call) should work correctly (see Figure 8-4). Assuming it does work correctly, you can then click the root node of the entity definition and select Export, which creates the ADF XML file for you.

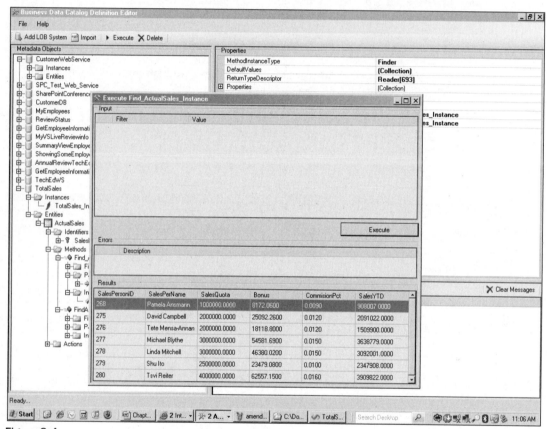

Figure 8-4

After you've created the ADF file, you are now ready to import the file into SharePoint. As mentioned earlier, you do this through the Shared Services Provider in the SharePoint Central Administration site.

To import the ADF into SharePoint, open your SharePoint Central Administration site. Click the Shared Services Provider (for example, SharedServices1) and select Import Application Definition. Click Browse, select the ADF XML file you just created and exported using the BDC Definition Editor, and click Import. This validates and imports the file into SharePoint. If there are any errors, SharePoint will display an error message along with the specific line number on which the error occurred.

At this point, you're ready to create a Web part on your Report Center dashboard, so navigate to your Report Center and select Site Actions ➪ Edit Page. Click Add a Web Part, select the Business Data List from the gallery, and click Add. After SharePoint adds the Web part to the page, click Open the tool pane, and click the Browse icon to find the ADF you just added to SharePoint. Click Apply. This will associate the ADF with your Web part and execute any instructions embedded within the ADF (for example, the SELECT * statement you saw earlier). When done, click OK. This will load the data into your BDC Web part. The resulting Web part will look similar to that in Figure 8-5.

ActualSales List

Actions ▾

SalesPersonID	SalesPerName	SalesQuota	Bonus	CommisionPct	SalesYTD
268	Pamela Ansmann	1000000.0000	8172.0600	0.0090	908007.0000
275	David Campbell	2000000.0000	25092.2600	0.0120	2091022.0000
276	Tete Mensa-Annan	2000000.0000	18118.8000	0.0120	1509900.0000
277	Michael Blythe	3000000.0000	54581.6900	0.0150	3638779.0000
278	Linda Mitchell	3000000.0000	46380.0200	0.0150	3092001.0000
279	Shu Ito	2500000.0000	23479.0800	0.0100	2347908.0000
280	Tsvi Reiter	4000000.0000	62557.1500	0.0160	3909822.0000

Figure 8-5

Depending on what you're trying to display on the Web part, you'll need to configure the ADF in slightly different ways. Also, other tools may work slightly differently. That said, it might be good to show you one more example of the BDC Definition Editor, specifically, one that exposes a couple of web methods. Exposing Web services within a BDC Web part is a little trickier than the straight SELECT * statement, so providing some guidance here (even though we didn't use services within the sales forecast OBA) would likely benefit you. We didn't use the BDC to connect to a Web service, so the following is a mock example we created to help illustrate an often challenging connection to build when trying to integrate Web services with the BDC.

The mock Web service we built for this example is called CustWebService, and it includes two main web methods (GetCustomerLikeName and GetCustomerDetails). The web methods do nothing more than retrieve some hard-coded data, specifically, name and title information, in the case of calling GetCustomerLikeName, and then some additional information, in the case of calling GetCustomerDetails. Note that in this sample code, there is no error handling; it's merely a couple of test methods to retrieve data using a Web service architecture. The sample code for the Web service is as follows:

```
using System;
using System.Collections.Generic;
using System.Collections;
using System.ComponentModel;
using System.Data;
using System.Text.RegularExpressions;
using System.Web;
using System.Web.Services;
using System.Web.Services.Protocols;

namespace CustWebService
{
    /// <summary>
    /// Summary description for Service1
    /// </summary>
    [WebService(Namespace = "http://tempuri.org/")]
    [WebServiceBinding(ConformsTo = WsiProfiles.BasicProfile1_1)]
```

187

```
        [ToolboxItem(false)]
// To allow this Web Service to be called from script, using
//ASP.NET AJAX, uncomment the following line.
        // [System.Web.Script.Services.ScriptService]
    public class CustDetails : System.Web.Services.WebService
    {


        [WebMethod]
        public CustomerSummary[] GetCustomerLikeName(string wildCardedName)
        {
            string[] customerArray;
//Fictional names used to represent customers in the form of an
//array.
            customerArray = new string[5]
            {
                "Kelly Johnson",
                "Bob Hoskins",
                "Jimmy Johnsons",
                "Kevin Eubanks",
                "Craig DeGualles"
            };

        List<CustomerSummary> summary = new List<CustomerSummary>();

            foreach (string name in customerArray)
            {
                Regex regex = new Regex(wildCardedName);
                if (regex.IsMatch(name))
                {
                    CustomerSummary cs = new CustomerSummary();
                    cs.Name = name;
                    cs.Title = "Program Manager";
                    summary.Add(cs);
                }
            }

            return summary.ToArray();
        }

        [WebMethod]
        public CustomerDetails GetCustomerDetails(string name)
        {
            CustomerDetails c = new CustomerDetails();
            c.Name = name;
            c.Salary = name.Length * 10000;
            c.Title = "Program Manager";
            c.Address = "One Microsoft Way, Redmond, WA 98052";
            return c;
        }
    }

    ...


    }
}
```

As you might imagine, configuring the ADF for this, or a similar, Web service is more involved than the SQL connection string. The steps are similar. For example, to create the ADF you follow the same steps as discussed earlier, except where you provided the connection string for the database you'd provide the URL for the Web service, add the web methods to the designer, click OK, and provide a name for your entity definition. Note that when you're adding the web methods, you can add them to the same entity to reduce the number of entity child nodes in your project.

After creating the entity for this specific Web service, you must do a number of things before exporting the ADF file, which are listed as follows:

1. Add an Identifier (of String value) and called it Name (it represents the one input parameter that the web methods can accept).

2. Add a filter called NameFilter and set the FilterType to Equals.

3. Add the NameFilter as the FilterDescriptor for the wildCardedName in the Parameters node.

4. Set the Identifier to Name for the Name in the Return node for both web methods.

5. Add two method instances, one for each of the web methods. The first will be of type Finder, and the second of type Specific Finder.

Also, to make the project easier to read the default root nodes were changed to read more descriptively (for example, Customer for the root entity node, GetCustomerLikeName for the method name, and so on). The resulting ADF looks like the following:

```xml
<?xml version="1.0" encoding="utf-8" standalone="yes"?>
<LobSystem xmlns:xsi="http://www.w3.org/2001/XMLSchema-instance"
xsi:schemaLocation="http://schemas.microsoft.com/office/2006/03/BusinessDataCatalog
BDCMetadata.xsd" Type="WebService" Version="1.0.0.0" Name="CustomerWebService"
xmlns="http://schemas.microsoft.com/office/2006/03/BusinessDataCatalog">
  <Properties>
    <Property Name="WsdlFetchUrl" Type="System.String">http://litwareinc/
CustDetails.asmx</Property>
    <Property Name="WebServiceProxyNamespace" Type="System.String">BDC</Property>
  </Properties>
  <LobSystemInstances>
    <LobSystemInstance Name="CustomerWebService_Instance">
      <Properties>
        <Property Name="LobSystemName" Type="System.String">CustomerWebService</
Property>
        <Property Name="WebServiceAuthenticationMode" Type="Microsoft.Office.
Server.ApplicationRegistry.SystemSpecific.WebService.HttpAuthenticationMode">PassTh
rough</Property>
      </Properties>
    </LobSystemInstance>
  </LobSystemInstances>
  <Entities>
    <Entity EstimatedInstanceCount="10000" Name="Customer">
      <Identifiers>
        <Identifier TypeName="System.String" Name="Name" />
      </Identifiers>
      <Methods>
        <Method Name="GetCustomerLikeName">
```

```xml
            <FilterDescriptors>
              <FilterDescriptor Type="Comparison" Name="NameFilter">
                <Properties>
                  <Property Name="Comparator" Type="System.String">Equals</Property>
                </Properties>
              </FilterDescriptor>
            </FilterDescriptors>
            <Parameters>
              <Parameter Direction="In" Name="wildCardedName">
                <TypeDescriptor TypeName="System.String, mscorlib, Version=2.0.0.0,
Culture=neutral, PublicKeyToken=b77a5c561934e089" AssociatedFilter="NameFilter"
Name="wildCardedName" />
              </Parameter>
              <Parameter Direction="Return" Name="Return">
                <TypeDescriptor TypeName="BDC.CustomerSummary[],CustomerWebService"
IsCollection="true" Name="Return">
                  <TypeDescriptors>
                    <TypeDescriptor TypeName="BDC.CustomerSummary,CustomerWebService"
Name="Item">
                      <TypeDescriptors>
                        <TypeDescriptor TypeName="System.String, mscorlib,
Version=2.0.0.0, Culture=neutral, PublicKeyToken=b77a5c561934e089"
IdentifierName="Name" Name="Name" />
                        <TypeDescriptor TypeName="System.String, mscorlib,
Version=2.0.0.0, Culture=neutral, PublicKeyToken=b77a5c561934e089" Name="Title" />
                      </TypeDescriptors>
                    </TypeDescriptor>
                  </TypeDescriptors>
                </TypeDescriptor>
              </Parameter>
            </Parameters>
            <MethodInstances>
              <MethodInstance Type="Finder" ReturnParameterName="Return" ReturnTypeDe
scriptorName="Return" ReturnTypeDescriptorLevel="0" Name="CustomerSearch" />
            </MethodInstances>
          </Method>
          <Method Name="GetCustomerDetails">
            <Parameters>
              <Parameter Direction="In" Name="name">
                <TypeDescriptor TypeName="System.String, mscorlib, Version=2.0.0.0,
Culture=neutral, PublicKeyToken=b77a5c561934e089" IdentifierName="Name" Name="name"
/>
              </Parameter>
              <Parameter Direction="Return" Name="Return">
                <TypeDescriptor TypeName="BDC.CustomerDetails,CustomerWebService"
Name="Return">
                  <TypeDescriptors>
                    <TypeDescriptor TypeName="System.String, mscorlib,
Version=2.0.0.0, Culture=neutral, PublicKeyToken=b77a5c561934e089"
IdentifierName="Name" Name="Name" />
```

```
                    <TypeDescriptor TypeName="System.Int32, mscorlib,
Version=2.0.0.0, Culture=neutral, PublicKeyToken=b77a5c561934e089" Name="Salary" />
                    <TypeDescriptor TypeName="System.String, mscorlib,
Version=2.0.0.0, Culture=neutral, PublicKeyToken=b77a5c561934e089" Name="Title" />
                    <TypeDescriptor TypeName="System.String, mscorlib,
Version=2.0.0.0, Culture=neutral, PublicKeyToken=b77a5c561934e089" Name="Address"
/>
                </TypeDescriptors>
              </TypeDescriptor>
            </Parameter>
          </Parameters>
          <MethodInstances>
            <MethodInstance Type="SpecificFinder" ReturnParameterName="Return"
ReturnTypeDescriptorName="Return" ReturnTypeDescriptorLevel="0"
Name="GetCustomerByName" />
          </MethodInstances>
        </Method>
      </Methods>
    </Entity>
  </Entities>
</LobSystem>
```

In the same way the SQL connection was tested, you can test the ADF for the Web service; that is, right-click the method instance and click Execute. In either case (whether it's a database call or Web service call), you should successfully execute before you export as an ADF XML file. Once you've saved the XML file, you can now import the resulting ADF file in much the same way you imported the earlier ADF file by using the Shared Services Provider.

In the preceding example, we want to create two Web parts; one would represent the summary view and the other would represent the details view. To do this, you add two Web parts to your page. You configure your first Web part (a Business Data List Web part) to the new Web service ADF file. This should load the first of the two web methods. The second Web part, however, should be the Business Data Item Web part (there are five Web parts in total that map to the BDC services available in Share-Point), and the configuration of the Web part will not only entail adding the Web service ADF, but also establishing a connection with the first Web part. (To do this, select Site Actions ⇨ Edit Page, click the Edit arrow in the Web part, select Connections, select Get Item From, and select the parent Web part name.) This way, when you click a particular name in the list of customers that is displayed, the second Web part will provide details (accepting the name as a string parameter) for that particular customer. What results should be something similar to Figure 8-6, where you click one of the customers and the profile data is displayed.

The BDC is a little tricky and deserves more coverage than we've provided here, but it is pretty powerful in terms of showing data within a Report Center, dashboard, or other site, so you'll definitely want to spend some time exploring it. For additional references on the BDC, see the "Further Reading" section at the end of the chapter.

Now that we've provided some background on the BDC, as you build out the sales forecast OBA we hope that you can apply some of the lessons learned to build some of your own BI Web parts based on the BDC. We turn now to discussing KPIs as another form of BI within MOSS.

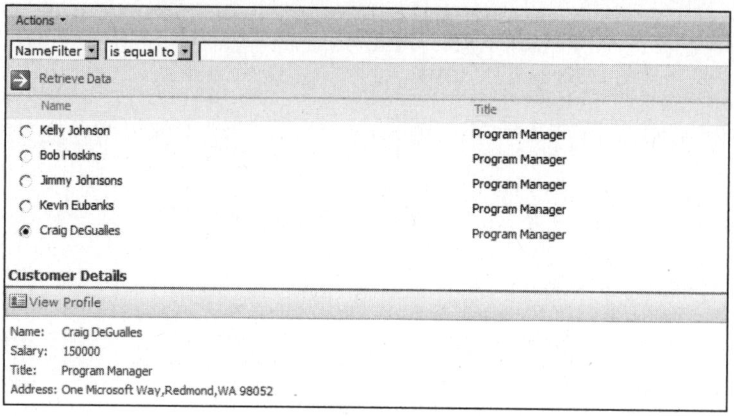

Figure 8-6

Key Performance Indicators (KPIs)

Every company requires a set of metrics to run their business. KPIs are a general term for metrics used in the organization, such as project status, people performance, bugs, and so on. KPIs are also a feature of SharePoint that you can use to measure progress and performance against different types of data. For example, you can use the following data sources when creating SharePoint KPIs:

- ❑ Microsoft Excel worksheets
- ❑ SharePoint lists
- ❑ SQL Server Analysis Services
- ❑ Manually created KPIs

In this chapter, we cover the KPIs that were created as a part of the sales forecast OBA, KPIs that use Excel as the data source. We won't cover the other data sources for KPIs in this book, but we include some references in the "Further Reading" section of the chapter, where these topics are covered in significant detail, so, if you'd like to read up on how these KPIs integrate with other types of data sources, you'll know where to go to find additional information. For the rest of this chapter we discuss KPIs at a high level and then discuss the application of the KPIs to the specific requirements within the sales forecast OBA.

General Introduction to SharePoint KPIs

KPIs can be quite significant in terms of their use and practicality; they represent the measurement of completion or success for specific elements of a project or business. For example, we'll often use KPIs to indicate how far along actual completed work is as compared to the forecasted delivery date when managing our projects. In the sales forecast OBA, we use KPIs to measure two things:

1. Whether the salesperson has completed his or her sales forecast for the fiscal quarter
2. Whether the total forecasts fall within the acceptable projections at the aggregate level (for a given manager)

Each of these is an important element of not only the process of closing down on all quarterly and yearly forecasts, but also of measuring the progress of actual against those forecasts.

That said, before we talk about the specific sales forecast OBA KPIs, it's worth mentioning that Share-Point ships with a Sample KPIs Web part that you can add to your page. Also, when you create a Report Center dashboard, a Sample KPIs Web part is added, by default, to the page. You can use this default KPIs Web part to configure the KPIs to point to a specific data source, which makes the process of connecting the KPIs to that data source very easy. Figure 8-7 illustrates the Sample KPIs Web part and the fact that when you click New, you can select from four options that will invoke a KPI creation page that is specific to the data sources listed in the KPI options list.

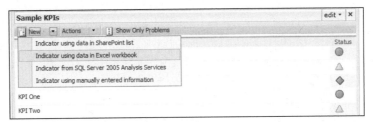

Figure 8-7

One of the key features that we'll show you how to use in this chapter is the Indicator Using Data in Excel Workbook KPI. This KPI links values in an Excel spreadsheet to the KPI values. In the example in Figure 8-8, the Excel spreadsheet contains three fictional items along with the Value of the items, the Goal for that item, and then the Warning for the item. In this example, you might think of the item as being sales of a widget, for example, and the Value being the amount of sales for that widget in a given day. The Goal value will be a number based on the target sales for the widget, and then the Warning value will be a number that provides the threshold below which non-product sales result in profit loss to the company.

Item	Value	Goal	Warning
One	120	100	90
Two	90	100	90
Three	50	100	90

Figure 8-8

When the KPI view is created, the items from the spreadsheet provide a quick view on status using the KPI indicators. In this case, KPI One has a green status because its value is greater than the goal, KPI Two has a yellow status because its value is the same as the warning value, and KPI Three shows a red status because its value is less than the warning value (see Figure 8-9).

Irrespective of the data source, the KPIs in SharePoint work in much the same way; that is, using some value to surface an indicator that maps to the value. In some cases, the indicator values may not always make sense or be entirely clear from the status indicator. In these cases, you can also provide a details view of the particular indicator. This is a very useful way to provide detail on a specific metric and add a second level of detail to your KPI list.

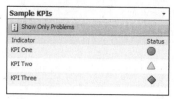

Figure 8-9

KPIs and the Sales Forecast OBA

SharePoint KPIs were used in the sales forecast OBA to provide some indication of whether the sales-people (under a specific manager) had completed their sales forecasts, and how the actual sales that each salesperson achieved mapped against the targets that they created for themselves. In both cases, we used Excel as the source of data (although you could just as easily use the manual KPI or the KPI that maps to SharePoint lists). For example, Figure 8-10 illustrates an excerpt from an Excel spread-sheet that enumerates a set of salespeople that report to a specific manager. It also lists the sales they achieved versus the targets they forecast, and the level that causes a red flag to appear should sales for that salesperson fall below it. The goal of this spreadsheet is to house the necessary data that can then feed the KPIs and display a quick report on the overall performance of not only each of the salespeople, but also the aggregate sales for the specific manager who manages the group of salespeople. Because this is a part of the sales forecast OBA that you will need to build (as a part of creating the MOSS web site), we walk through how you can create a KPI to surface these data points.

	A	B	C	D
1	SalesPerson	FY 08 Sales	Target	Below Target
2	Pamela Ansmann	$ 908,007.00	$ 1,000,000.00	$ 950,000.00
3	David Campbell	$ 2,091,022.00	$ 2,000,000.00	$ 1,800,000.00
4	Tete Mensa-Annan	$ 1,509,900.00	$ 2,000,000.00	$ 1,800,000.00
5	Michael Blythe	$ 3,638,779.00	$ 3,000,000.00	$ 2,700,000.00
6	Linda Mitchell	$ 3,092,001.00	$ 3,000,000.00	$ 2,700,000.00
7	Shu Ito	$ 2,347,908.00	$ 2,500,000.00	$ 2,250,000.00
8	Tsvi Reiter	$ 3,909,822.00	$ 4,000,000.00	$ 3,750,000.00
9	Totals	$ 17,497,439.00	$ 17,500,000.00	$ 15,950,000.00

Figure 8-10

The first step in the process is to make sure you that have a source for the data. Excel, for many people, represents a common way of entering and presenting data in a document that involves calculations and that you can share. Many of you know how to create a spreadsheet, so we'll assume that you've created the spreadsheet and next want to add some values. In Figure 8-10, you'll note that there exist three columns of values; that is, sales, targets, and below target values. These three values are required when building the KPI because you require a value for the indicator value (the value representing the quantitative state of whatever you're measuring), a value for what defines the success of the metric, a value for what represents the line of caution, and then a value for what defines a poorly performing metric. In SharePoint, when you're creating the KPI and mapping it to a value that lives in Excel you need to provide the indicator value and then the success and warning values. All other values are assumed to be defined as the poorly per-forming value.

After you've created your spreadsheet, and you've entered your indicator values, success values, and threshold values, save the document in a document library you've created in SharePoint. The document needs to be accessible from the calling KPI list. At this point, you are now ready to create the KPI list.

To create the KPI list, open your SharePoint site, navigate to the Document Library and click Site Actions ⇨ View All Site Content. Once on this page, click Create and then KPI List in the Custom Lists section (see Figure 8-11). Enter the Title and Description for the KPI and click Create. This creates your KPI list for you. If you click New and select Indicator Using Data in Excel, you can create a KPI that uses data that resides in the Excel spreadsheet you just created and saved to the SharePoint site.

Figure 8-12 illustrates the options menu that displays when you click the New button in your new KPI list.

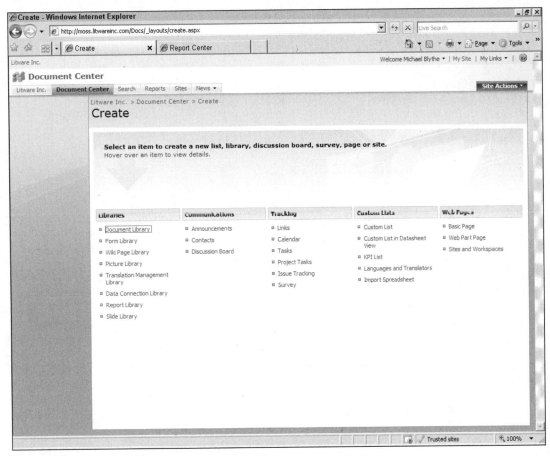

Figure 8-11

Figure 8-12

This invokes the "Indicator using data in Excel workbook" SharePoint page, where you configure the KPI list to use specific values within the Excel workbook. For example, when creating the sales forecast OBA, we specified the values we wanted to use for each KPI by explicitly referring to them in the properties page. Figure 8-13 illustrates the cell address we used to demarcate the indicator value (Sheet1!B2). We specified the met or exceeded goal (or the success metric) with the Sheet1!B3 value and the caution value with Sheet1!B4 value (to see how these values mapped back to the actual workbook cells).

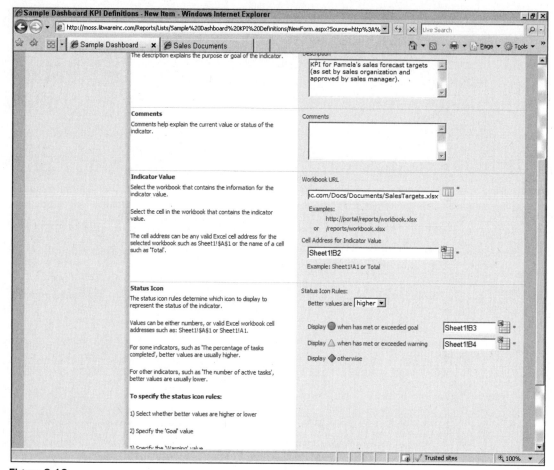

Figure 8-13

After you've set the values for the KPI, click OK, and SharePoint loads the new KPI in your KPI list.

> *You don't have to pull all of the values from one data source in a given KPI list; moreover, you can combine KPI data sources within one list.*

You then repeat the same process for each new KPI that you want to add to your new KPI list. For the sales forecast OBA, what resulted from this process was a KPI list that we could use to track the performance of each of the salespeople and the aggregate team. Figure 8-14 illustrates this final KPI list.

Figure 8-14

As mentioned earlier, we also created a KPI for the status on whether the salespeople had completed their forecasts as a way of measuring progress toward quarterly forecast completion dates. We created these in much the same way as the sales KPI. There was one key difference: the data we used in the Excel spreadsheet was expressed in percentage complete (see Figure 8-15).

The resulting KPI, which we called the Submission Status KPI, looked like the image in Figure 8-16.

	A	B	C	D
	SalesPerson	**Completion**	**Target**	**Below Target**
1				
2	Pamela Ansmann	50%	100%	85%
3	David Campbell	100%	100%	85%
4	Tete Mensa-Annan	90%	100%	85%
5	Michael Blythe	75%	100%	85%
6	Linda Mitchell	80%	100%	85%
7	Shu Ito	30%	100%	85%
8	Tsvi Reiter	50%	100%	85%
9	**Average**	**68%**	**100%**	**85%**

Figure 8-15

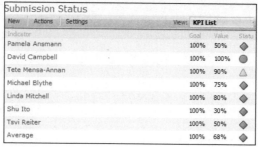

Figure 8-16

One other business intelligence function was used within the sales forecast OBA, and that was the use of Excel Services to display some sales and charting functionality. We cover this in the next, and last, section of the chapter.

Excel Services

Excel Services are a way to reuse your Excel spreadsheets within your SharePoint assets without having to do any special conversions to SharePoint objects (such as lists or Web parts). For example, if you have created a spreadsheet that details a number of budgetary expenses, and you want either to expose an entire worksheet, or charts or graphs on the worksheet, you can use Excel Services to do this on Share-Point. You must have MOSS Enterprise edition to get the Excel Services Web parts functionality. The functionality that you get with Excel Services is listed as follows:

❑ Publishing of entire worksheet

❑ Publishing of objects such as graphs or charts from a specific worksheet

❑ Extension of external data sources to SharePoint

❑ Reuse of user-defined functions within SharePoint

❑ Read/write of data within the worksheet through specially designated cells

❑ Programmatic access to Excel Services

In the sales forecast OBA, we used Excel Services to publish various charts and tables to the main sales forecast SharePoint site. In this section, we walk you through one of the examples we created, the actual sales chart view. This view was a chart that represented the earlier table we created and used in the KPI example (see Figure 8-10). In the updated view, we've added a chart (called Chart 1) that we'll publish using Excel Services and then expose as a Web part in our sales forecast dashboard. This provides a quick view into how salespeople are performing against their targets. Figure 8-17 illustrates the new chart added to the sales table.

Creating the Excel Services–based chart is straightforward. The first step is to create the spreadsheet that you'll be using when exposing data to Excel Services. Because we're reusing the existing spreadsheet, our work is already done. You may choose to reuse an existing Excel spreadsheet or create a new one. Either way, the spreadsheet must be saved to SharePoint.

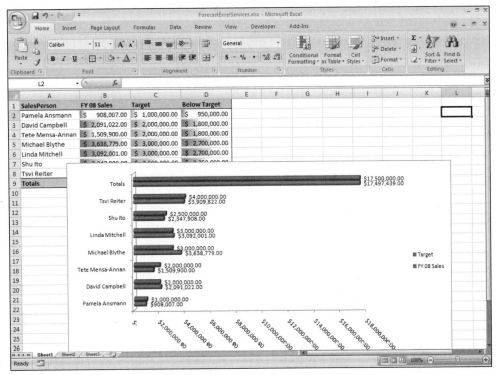

Figure 8-17

After you've added the spreadsheet to SharePoint, you now need to publish the elements of the spreadsheet to Excel Services; you cannot expose what is not published. To do this, open the spreadsheet and click the Office button, click Publish, and then choose Excel Services (see Figure 8-18). This opens the Excel Services Options dialog (see Figure 8-19). In the Excel Services Options dialog, you can select the objects that you want to publish to Excel Services; you can also select parameters that you want to expose as editable fields (or cells) within SharePoint. This latter functionality provides read/write capabilities, as compared to the BDC, which we discussed earlier in this chapter, which has read-only capabilities.

In the Excel Services Options, select the object you want to publish to SharePoint (we selected Chart 1 as the item within the workbook to publish). Once this is done, return to the dashboard where you want to expose the selected chart. You add the chart using an Excel Services Web part, so to do this click Site Actions ➪ Edit Page ➪ Add a Web Part. Select the Excel Web Access Web part and click Add (see Figure 8-20).

This adds a Web part to the dashboard, which needs configuring to the object in the workbook you selected to publish. To do this, select Click here to open the tool pane, and copy and paste the URL into the Workbook URL field, and add the name of the item in the Named Item field (for example, Chart 1). Click Apply and OK, and the chart is exposed in the Web part on the SharePoint dashboard (see Figure 8-21). You may also want to adjust the appearance of the chart within the Web part. Click Site Actions ➪ Edit Page, click Edit (in the top right-hand corner of the Web part), and then select Modify Shared Web Part. If you expand the Appearance section within the tool pane, you can either select the height and width to auto-adjust or provide a fixed height and width for the Web part. The latter enables you to provide a width and height to fit the dimensions of your specific chart.

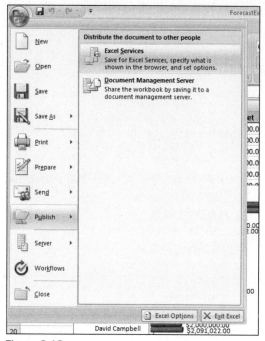

Figure 8-18

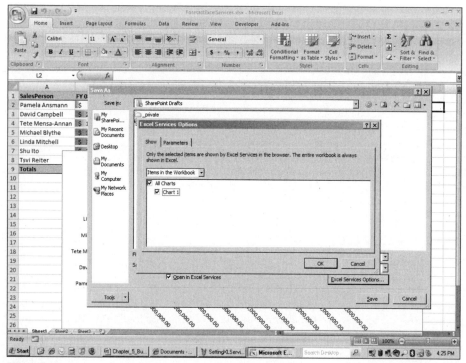

Figure 8-19

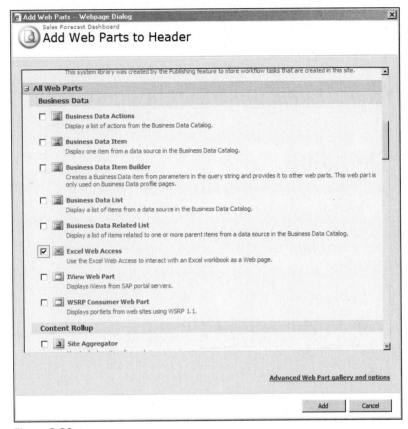

Figure 8-20

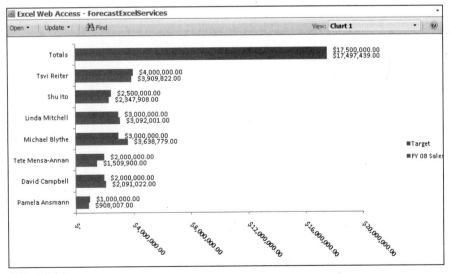

Figure 8-21

Summary

Many options are available to you for different types of business intelligence in SharePoint. In this chapter, we discussed the BDC, KPIs, and Excel Services. In reality, we barely explored the depths that you could go with using these business intelligence options for your solutions. We could devote an entire book to describe how to use them. That said, we've included some additional reading for you to take a look at if you're interested in finding more out about the areas we discussed in this chapter.

Further Reading

Leon, Tynes, and Cathey. *Microsoft SharePoint Server 2007 Bible* (Wiley)

Holloway, Kyselica, and Caravajal. *SharePoint 2007 and Office Development Expert Solutions* (Wrox)

Hillier et al. *Real World SharePoint 2007: Indispensable Experiences From 16 MOSS and WSS MVPs* (Wrox)

Holliday et al. *Professional SharePoint 2007 Development.* (Wrox)

Fox et al. *Programming Office Business Applications* (MS Press)

Prish. *Professional Excel Services* (Wrox)

BDC on MSDN: http://msdn.microsoft.com/en-us/library/ms563661.aspx

Integrating the LOB System using the Business Data Catalog, and Extending Search into your LOB System

One of the ways that the Microsoft Office System has evolved is to integrate new server-based capabilities with what originally was a collection of client components. Over the past several years, however, the Office System has expanded to include collaborative capabilities that are, for the most part, centered on Microsoft Office SharePoint Server (MOSS). In particular, the sales forecast OBA is also centered around a central MOSS server that can act as a collaborative hub.

We shouldn't stop with collaboration as the only service hosted by the central server. Instead, we need to consider how to leverage this architecture for additional services. Microsoft, long a proponent of the concept of Service Oriented Architecture (SOA), has built the BDC around the basic concepts of SOA. The BDC allows you to treat your business applications as services and then consume those services from your MOSS site, or potentially from a client application. In fact, this later model is one type of SOA architecture that Microsoft has chosen to focus on, calling it Software plus Services (S+S).

The idea is that you can leverage certain key capabilities as hosted solutions; in many ways the Web itself is a giant hosted application. To a limited extent, the entire sales forecast OBA leverages this concept; the key business logic is centered on a custom MOSS site. However, we want to demonstrate exposing your line of business in an environment that is not a dedicated Line of Business (LOB) application. One of the more explicit examples of this is the use of the Business Data Catalog (BDC) as a service on your MOSS implementation.

The Business Data Catalog provides an infrastructure to allow you to incorporate your LOB data into your MOSS site. This chapter focuses on introducing the BDC and illustrating a couple of the ways that you can leverage your LOB data. The topics include:

❑ Overview of the BDC

❑ The Application Definition File

❑ Shared Services on MOSS

❑ Working with SharePoint Search

❑ Integrating BDC data with Search

❑ Exposing BDC data through Web parts

The BDC was introduced as a new element with MOSS 2007, and, though the tools to make developing the metadata to define your key business data aren't yet mature, the core capabilities of the BDC allow you to define valuable insight into core operational data. Third-party tools are available that help bridge this initial gap, and, certainly, there is significant potential for future enhancements in this area with future releases of MOSS.

Overview of the BDC

The BDC was introduced as part of MOSS 2007 to allow MOSS to integrate data from several different business applications in a single location. An organization could pull the latest CRM data from its CRM application and then combine that with data from the transactional sales database along with status of the latest product marketing. The idea is that the BDC acts as a generic clearinghouse for business data retrieved across one or more systems. This data is defined using an XML-based metafile that describes both how to connect to the data source and the query, and key data elements available as part of that query.

From an implementation standpoint this means that the BDC needs to provide a framework to handle data queries. In SharePoint 3.0 this capability includes support for ADO.NET, OLEDB, and ODBC. In addition to these "database" protocols, the BDC also provides a framework that will allow you to leverage a Web services connection because this implies that you have data that is exposed as part of a Web service. For our purposes, we'll focus on using ADO.NET to retrieve data from the Adventure-Works database.

To do this, you need to create a connection definition. As noted, part of the BDC's implementation is a metadata file. This file, known as an Application Definition File (ADF), allows you to define your data source, the characteristics of your business data, and the query used to retrieve the data. Once the file is prepared you can upload it to the BDC in order to have the BDC store and process your application's business data.

The BDC is a shared service within your SharePoint infrastructure. When you installed SharePoint, you created three different web applications: the main SharePoint site on Port 80, an Administrative site, and a Shared Services site. The administration of the BDC is handled from the Shared Services site. Similar to administering your Search Settings, you administer the BDC as a service that can be leveraged by one or more applications.

To initiate a new data feed for the BDC, you upload your ADF file to the Shared Services site, which interprets the file and sets up the necessary information to query your data source. Once data has been retrieved by the BDC it is available for other services and uses. For example, you can access that data source from a Web part to display your business data on a web page. SharePoint now views this collection of business data like a list; internally, it can now be indexed for search purposes. Therefore, instead of sending ad-hoc queries against your database, executives can query for business information in the same way that they search the Web. In fact, the list of ways that you can leverage the BDC includes:

❑ **Web parts** — By default SharePoint ships with six Web parts.

❑ **Lists** — The data can be used to create a list or library.

❑ **Actions** — Connectivity to the back-end LOB system can include updates from SharePoint.

❑ **Search** — The data can be indexed and exposed as part of the site search.

❑ **User profiles** — Enterprise data can be transferred into the user profile store.

The result is a very empowering capability with broad reach within your organization. This chapter isn't going to cover everything available to you as part of the BDC. We only explain using a Web part and implementing the BDC. Much more information is available in the SharePoint Server SDK (`http://msdn.microsoft.com/en-us/library/ms563661.aspx`). The SDK documentation is available online, or it can be installed locally as a free download from Microsoft.

The Application Definition File

The ADF is used to define the attributes of data that the BDC is to expose. It consists of several categories of data, including:

❑ **LobSystem** — The LobSystem defines the system associated with a group of data. It is important to note that the name used for the LobSystem can be used only once for the entire MOSS site. If you separate different queries into individual files, you will need to make up a different system name.

❑ **LobSystemInstance** — The instance node is used to define connection information. A given system might support a database connection that is defined based on a set of credentials with permissions similar to a member of the sales team to access data that might otherwise be protected from other departments. However, a view of the data could be exposed in MOSS that would contain only those data elements the sales team wanted to make available to a larger audience. Data access might next be combined with a connection to a Web service as part of the same LobSystem, or another database connection with different credentials. Similar to the LobSystem, the LobSystemInstance value must also be unique.

❑ **Entity** — Within the LobSystemInstance the entity node defines a query, its methods, and result collection. The entity definition includes a primary key for the result collection, called an identifier. Additionally, it is the entity that describes the other columns used for retrieving data, the methods for accessing data, any filters that should be applied when retrieving the data, and other actions that allow for updates and joining of data in the BDC. To keep perspective, an entity might define a query for sales by salesperson or by a product list, whereas the LobSystemInstance defines a collection of entities.

❑ **Methods** — Methods define the operations for retrieving data. A method definition has a great deal in common with a parameterized query or stored procedure definition. There are the in and out parameters, any filters that should be applied to the query, and the query itself. Methods contain three additional object types: Filters, Parameters, and Instances. A given method might actually include more than a single query or instance, but each query within a method uses the same filters and parameters.

Certain Web parts and search indexing may require particular methods. For example, you are required to have both a `Finder` and a `SpecificFinder` method to support indexing. The `Finder` method supports retrieving the list of data. The `SpecificFinder` method finds entries via search.

❑ **Filters** — A filter describes an inbound condition that can be used to screen the result set that will be returned from a method. Filters are type specific and include a default value and can leverage a LobSystem-defined wildcard definition, to allow for partial matching. Filter definitions are primarily used to associate the method parameter with which a filter is associated.

❑ **Parameters** — A parameter defines the data actually passed to a BDC method. The parameters may or may not be directly used within the underlying instance method, because several of the BDC's parameters may be assigned to filters that are then referred to by the query.

❑ **Instances** — An instance is a definition of a query that refers to the inbound request for data and returns a collection of results that match the output parameter(s) for the method. A given method may have several similar instance definitions.

❑ **Properties** — Properties define specific values within the XML structure. Properties exist within each of the preceding element definitions to define discrete values.

These are some of the primary sections of the ADF. We discuss these in some detail, and their relationships to the customized AdventureWorks database, which is part of the sales forecast OBA. For our connection, we'll be using the following definition for the LobSystem. Note that this is just the definition of the LobSystem and LobSystemInstance; it does not include an entity and its associated elements:

```xml
<?xml version="1.0" encoding="utf-8" standalone="yes" ?>
<LobSystem xmlns:xsi="http://www.w3.org/2001/XMLSchema-instance"
xsi:schemaLocation="http://schemas.microsoft.com/office/2006/03/BusinessDataCatalog
BDCMetadata.xsd" Type="Database"
Version="1.0.0.0" Name="AdventureWorksVSTODB"
xmlns="http://schemas.microsoft.com/office/2006/03/BusinessDataCatalog">
  <Properties>
    <Property Name="WildcardCharacter" Type="System.String">%</Property>
  </Properties>
  <LobSystemInstances>
    <LobSystemInstance Name="AdventureWorksVSTO">
      <Properties>
        <Property Name="AuthenticationMode"
Type="System.String">PassThrough</Property>
        <Property Name="DatabaseAccessProvider"
Type="System.String">SqlServer</Property>
        <Property Name="RdbConnection Data Source" Type="System.String">MOSS\
OfficeServers</Property>
        <Property Name="RdbConnection Initial Catalog"
Type="System.String">AdventureWorksVSTO</Property>
        <Property Name="RdbConnection Integrated Security"
Type="System.String">SSPI</Property>
        <Property Name="RdbConnection Pooling"
```

```
Type="System.String">false</Property>
        </Properties>
    </LobSystemInstance>
</LobSystemInstances>
```

To get the preceding XML structure, which does not yet include any entity information, we have two options. The first is to manipulate it manually. Though the fact that it is relatively standard and easily copied make manual editing a possibility, the alternative, generating this XML metadata, is the preferred option.

BDC Metadata Definition Tools

As of the writing of this book, three tools are available that are focused on working with BDC definitions. We should note that these are tools that are specifically targeted at working with BDC metadata. Because the BDC metadata is XML data, any tool that manipulates XML, including XMLSpy and Visual Studio, can be used to manipulate the ADF files. In fact, it is possible to refer to the XSL definition for ADF from Visual Studio and get IntelliSense assistance with ADF development in Visual Studio.

Instead of working with a generic tool, this section introduces three tools that are focused on BDC metadata. BDCMetaMan is the original BDC ADF generation tool. It is a commercially available product with a trial version that you can use to help generate basic ADF definitions. The tool is top of the line in many ways, but we consider it a bit pricey (in excess of $1,000 as of this writing) if you aren't planning to build a lot of ADF files. You can find out more information and download links at www.bdcmetaman.com.

Simego produces the MOSS BDC Design Studio. This product is available for under $200 as of this writing, and, though it may not have all of the features of BDCMetaMan, is a very usable tool. A free trial is available, and is keyed off of your machine's unique identifying information. Once installed, you can use it to generate ADF files for either SQL Server or Web services. It is a very useful tool if you need to do a moderate amount of work with the BDC. You can find out more information and download links at www.simego.com.

There is a free option as part of the Office SharePoint Server 2007 SDK 1.3, the current version of the MOSS SDK. The Application Definition Editor is included as part of the MOSS SDK, but is an unsupported utility.

Because this tool is part of the SDK, it makes sense to use it here for a simple solution to generate an ADF file. The SDK is available for download from MSDN at http://www.microsoft.com/downloads/details.aspx?FamilyId=6D94E307-67D9-41AC-B2D6-0074D6286FA9&displaylang=en.

The SDK requires you to have Visual Studio 2005 installed. If, as we did in the sales forecast OBA, you have installed and used Visual Studio 2008, the SDK will not install unless you also install Visual Studio 2005. Therefore, even though we are only going to access a tool that is embedded within the SDK, we need Visual Studio 2005. Perhaps, by the time you read this, Microsoft will have either updated the SDK to work with Visual Studio 2008 or created a separate download for the BDC Application Definition Editor.

Once you have installed the MOSS SDK, the Application Definition Editor is installed under the default path of C:\Program Files\2007 Office System Developer Resources\Tools\BDC Definition Editor.

During installation, unlike with most Microsoft SDKs, the MOSS SDK path starts with the year 2007, and, as a result, sorts to the top of your Program Files in Windows Explorer.

In this folder, you'll find both an MSI file and a Setup file. As noted later in Chapter 11, "Deploying and Securing Your OBA Server Components," running the Setup file ensures that any prerequisites, for example, the SQL Server Express engine, that the BDC Application Definition Editor uses will be installed. Once you have run the Setup you will have a new icon on your Start menu for the Microsoft Business Data Catalog Definition Editor.

Figure 9-1 illustrates the main window for the BDC Definition Editor. Because you haven't yet defined anything, the display is empty. You have two options at this point: the first is to add a new LOB system definition, and the second is to import an existing LOB system definition. Clicking the Add LOB System button in the upper-left corner of the display opens the Add LOB System dialog shown in Figure 9-2. This dialog gives you the option either to connect to a database or to connect to a Web service. In the case of the sales forecast OBA, you will be connecting to the AdventureWorksVSTO database that is your LOB data source.

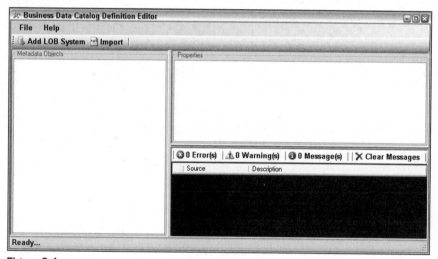

Figure 9-1

Clicking the Connect button opens the popup dialog shown in Figure 9-3. This also introduces the first limitation of using a free tool instead of a third-party tool. Unfortunately, this free tool doesn't allow you to build the connection string using the standard dialog you use everywhere else. Instead, you either need to enter the connection string manually or copy it. One possible solution is to leverage one of the other projects that are part of the sales forecast OBA. For example, the Excel Workbook, Sales Forecast Approval Workflow, and Web service for generating OpenXML documents all refer to the application database and include a copy of the associated connection string. You can open one of the other OBA application projects and access the project settings to retrieve the connection string from the project settings.

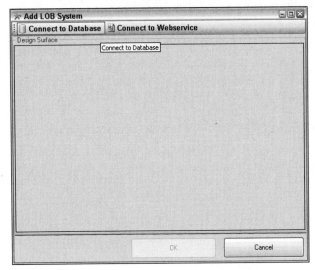

Figure 9-2

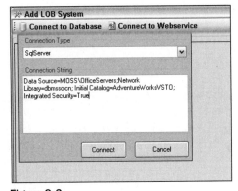

Figure 9-3

Once you've entered your connection string the next step is to select a table. When you click the Connect button you will be greeted with the screen in Figure 9-4. To open the Add Table tab shown in that figure you need to select the Add Table tab shown on the far right border of that display. As you can see, at this point you have a valid database connection, and the tool has retrieved the list of available tables for you to select from.

To add a table to your design surface, you need only drag it and drop it from this list. Drag it to the left side, and drop it on the design surface. In your case, you want to add the SalesPerson table to your LOB definition, however you may note that the list of tables isn't really sorted. Fortunately, there is a Search capability, so you can type in a table name. Note, however, that the search is case sensitive, so if, as in the AdventureWorks database, you have mixed-case table names, you need to match the case. Additionally, or perhaps because of this, the search does not just match the start of the table name, but will match on any table name that contains the searched-for string.

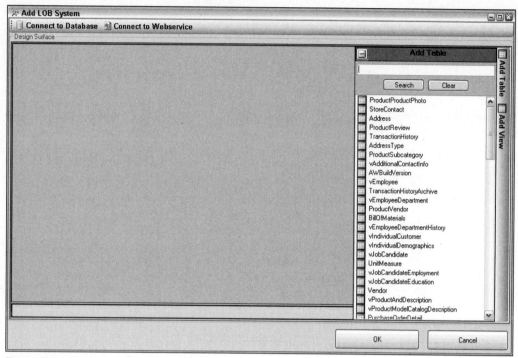

Figure 9-4

At this point if you are connected to the AdventureWorks database, you may see an error similar to that shown in Figure 9-5. Once you clear the error, you'll find that an entry for the table was added, but the various details, such as the key, columns, and foreign keys are in fact empty. This is because the tool attempted to query for details on the table, but failed to successfully find the same table it had listed within the database.

The bad news is that when you now delete this corrupt entry, you'll get an exception from the application. The exception will allow you to continue or quit, and we recommend you continue. Apparently, the fact that there was no data found for the table resulted in an uninitialized collection that the application attempted to empty. If you click Continue, you'll be returned to the screen, and you can gracefully exit. If you click the OK button, you will get a dialog asking you to accept a default name for your LOB system. You should accept the default and return to the editor's main screen. You will see you have a LOB defined but no entities present in the LOB.

If possible, do not exit the editor. The editor does not save your connection string information between sessions, so, if you exit, you will need to reenter your connection string once you return to this screen.

As Bugs Bunny's would say, "Ain't I a stinker?" You see, we've taken you this far only to explain why the error in Figure 9-5 occurs and how to fix it, which requires making a temporary change to the database. The lists of tables shown in Figures 9-4 and 9-5 do not include the schema from the database. In the AdventureWorks database, most of the tables are associated with custom schemas; for example, the SalesPerson table is in the Sales schema. This means that the correct reference to this table is Sales.SalesPerson, not just SalesPerson.

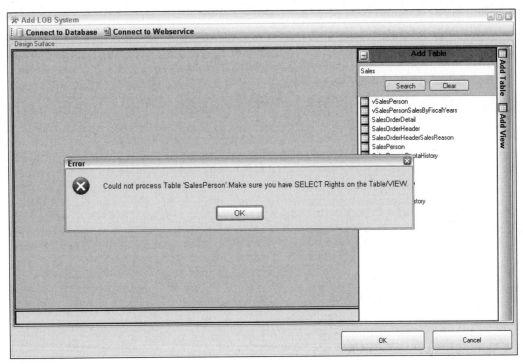

Figure 9-5

Unfortunately, there isn't a setting in this tool to allow you to change the current schema associated with an entry. Therefore, you need to modify the database to create a copy of the structure that is within the default dbo schema. To do this you access the SQL Server Management Studio (or SQL Server Management Studio Express) and open your database. Then, navigate to the SalesPerson table and right-click for the context menu. From the context menu, you want to select Script Table As ⇨ Create To ⇨ New Query Editor Window, as shown in Figure 9-6.

SQL Management Studio will create a new copy of the SQL in the Query Editor. The next step is to edit the first line of this SQL. Figure 9-7 shows a portion of the generated SQL with the schema name highlighted. To resolve the error, you can simply remove this value. You could now run your new SQL statement and a copy of the same structure would be created within the dbo schema; however, this means that the list of tables for your database would include two copies of the SalesPerson table. The table name is now used twice in the database within two different schemas. Since the BDC Definition Editor doesn't differentiate the table names by schema, you would need to guess which entry in the list was the correct instance for the dbo schema.

For the purposes of explaining more of the attributes of the XML within the tool, we're going to assign the SQL with the name SalesPersondbo. This is going to make it possible for us to find this within the tool. The full SQL required is shown in the following code block:

```
CREATE TABLE [SalesPersondbo](
[SalesPersonID] [int] NOT NULL,
[TerritoryID] [int] NULL,
```

211

```
[SalesQuota] [money] NULL,
[Bonus] [money] NOT NULL CONSTRAINT [DF_SalesPerson_Bonus]  DEFAULT ((0.00)),
[CommissionPct] [smallmoney] NOT NULL CONSTRAINT [DF_SalesPerson_CommissionPct]
DEFAULT ((0.00)),
[SalesYTD] [money] NOT NULL CONSTRAINT [DF_SalesPerson_SalesYTD]  DEFAULT ((0.00)),
[SalesLastYear] [money] NOT NULL CONSTRAINT [DF_SalesPerson_SalesLastYear]  DEFAULT
((0.00)),
[rowguid] [uniqueidentifier] ROWGUIDCOL  NOT NULL CONSTRAINT [DF_SalesPerson_
rowguid]  DEFAULT (newid()),
[ModifiedDate] [datetime] NOT NULL CONSTRAINT [DF_SalesPerson_ModifiedDate]
DEFAULT (getdate()),
 CONSTRAINT [PK_SalesPerson_SalesPersonID] PRIMARY KEY CLUSTERED
(
[SalesPersonID] ASC
)WITH (PAD_INDEX  = OFF, STATISTICS_NORECOMPUTE  = OFF, IGNORE_DUP_KEY = OFF,
ALLOW_ROW_LOCKS  = ON, ALLOW_PAGE_LOCKS  = ON) ON [PRIMARY]
) ON [PRIMARY]
```

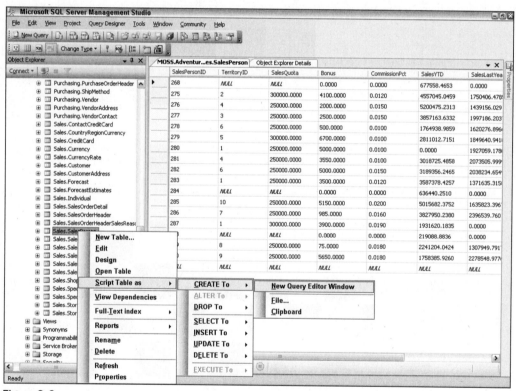

Figure 9-6

By running this script you will create a second table called SalesPerson within your database, but this one will be accessible from within the tool. With that in mind, return to the BDC Definition Editor and again start the process of creating a new LOB system. If you haven't been forced to exit the editor, right-click the Entity node and select Add Entity. You will be asked whether you would like to "design entities using objects from LOB?" and you should select Yes to return to the screen shown in Figure 9-7.

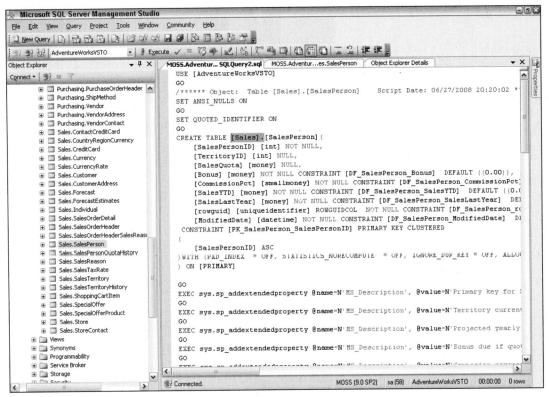

Figure 9-7

Once you are in the Add Entities screen, open the Add Table window again and search for "dbo." Because this isn't a common term, you'll get a direct hit on the new structure, as shown in Figure 9-8. Note that the figure shows the item already dragged onto the display so that you can see the details associated with this table.

Click the OK button in this display to return to the main display. Because we've used a table name that doesn't match the actual table from which the data is to be retrieved, we need to edit the data associated with this definition. Start by accessing the Entity's properties, as shown in Figure 9-9.

Figure 9-9 shows the newly created ADF structure expanded within the Business Data Catalog Definition Editor. Currently, the SalesPersondbo entity is selected, and, in the Properties pane, the Name and DefaultDisplayName values need to be modified to remove the dbo reference and add a Sales.

SalesPerson reference for the correct table. Once this is complete, you'll notice that the information in the tree structure is also updated to reflect this change of table reference.

Figure 9-9 also shows that, as part of the generation of the SalesPersondbo entity, an Identifier, the Sales-PersonID, was recognized, and two methods created. As noted earlier, `Finder` and `SpecificFinder` methods are needed to support Search. `Find_SalesPersondbo` is the `SpecificFinder` method. Unfortunately, `FindAll_SalesPersondbo` is not the `Finder` method. Both need to be edited and a `Finder` method added.

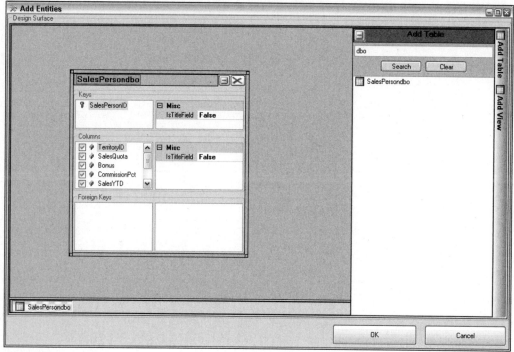

Figure 9-8

Only the changes to the `SpecificFinder` method `Find_SalesPersondbo` are shown. You will need to repeat these edits for the `FindAll_SalesPersondbo` method.

The next step is to open the Methods section, as shown in Figure 9-10. In the properties you will update both the Name and DataDisplayName. Figure 9-10 shows these fields already updated, and also illustrates the updates made to the Entity name earlier in this section. These aren't the only updates needed in the properties for this method.

Figure 9-9

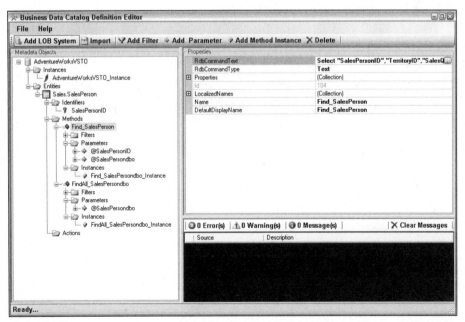

Figure 9-10

Figure 9-10 shows that the top property, the RdbCommandText, is selected. In the far right corner you'll note an ellipsis button. This property contains the text of the query used to retrieve data. As with other Microsoft tools, the Business Data Catalog Definition Editor only generates code for a single table, and, in this case, the code generated isn't even for the table you want. Selecting the ellipsis button will open the wideTextBoxEditor shown in Figure 9-11 containing the default SQL Query.

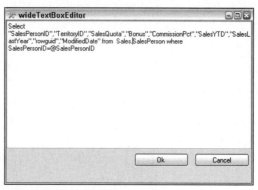

Figure 9-11

This query needs to be modified to replace the SalesPersondbo table name in the `From` clause of the query. The Sales.SalesPerson table should be referred to here as shown in Figure 9-11. The result is a functional query, but more importantly, this change illustrates a key capability of the BDC, which is not directly supported by the BDC Definition Editor. You can edit this query to join multiple tables and return a result set that contains data from multiple tables.

For this to work, of course, you need to update the fields in the query to reflect those that you want returned; however, it isn't that simple. Figure 9-12 shows an expanded MetaData Objects tree that displays the contents of the parameters for this method. The `SpecificFinder` has an inbound parameter for the SalesPersonID for the data to be retrieved. In addition to this inbound parameter there is an outbound parameter, which is a data reader definition. This reader definition describes the columns that are returned by the `SpecificFinder`'s query. If you modify the query to perform one or more joins and instead of displaying, for example, the SalesPersonID, you want to display the first and last name of the salesperson, you need to update this list.

Updating the list of columns is reasonably straightforward. You start by right-clicking the Record node in the tree and selecting Add TypeDescriptor. This will add a new type descriptor to your array of items, and you can then define the properties of this additional data column. The specific property page associated with this parameter is shown in Figure 9-12.

Figure 9-12 also shows that the `Instance` method has been highlighted for the `SpecificFinder` as shown at the top of the Properties display. Right-click the method name and select Execute to run the method and test your changes. Selecting the Execute menu option opens the window shown in Figure 9-13.

When the Execute Find_SalesPerson_Instance dialog opens, the Value 275 shown in the figure will not be present. This is the SalesPersonID of a known entry from the Sales.SalesPerson table and you will need to enter this or a similar value in order to test the method. Once you have entered the parameter you will use the Execute button to execute your query and verify that the results are found as shown in Figure 9-13. If you do not get results when you execute your query in this display, there is a problem with your settings. You will need to go back through and ensure that you have properly updated the table reference to reference the Sales.SalesPerson table.

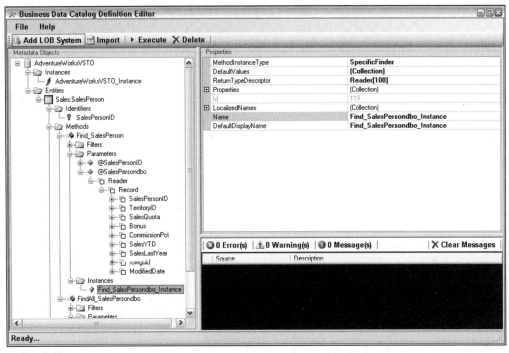

Figure 9-12

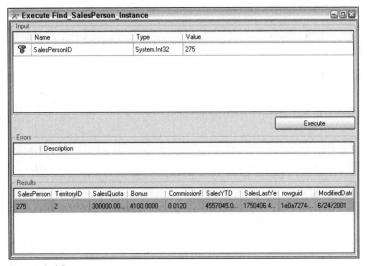

Figure 9-13

As long as your `SpecificFinder` is working, it is time to move to the `Finder` method that returns all of the entries from your query. One item to note here is that the queries for the `Finder` and `SpecificFinder` are related. In fact, they use the same query. Of course, this causes a challenge. How can the same query return a specific item and a list of items? For example, your current query compares the ID values, which are unique. The answer is that the query must be modified such that the where clause can return a range. When a value is passed into the BDC for that parameter, the `SpecificFinder` logic will execute, returning a single record. However, if a parameter isn't passed in, the `Finder` method will be called, and, instead, either a wildcard or minimum and maximum values will be used.

Adding a Finder Method

Unfortunately, a `Finder` method isn't automatically generated. It is needed to support the ability of the BDC to accept a single parameter and use it to replace minimum and maximum values used by the `SpecificFinder`. This is where filters come into play. By default, we don't have any filters as part of the entity definition. As part of the creation of a `Finder` method, however, a filter will be added. In order to modify the existing entity definition to support a `Finder` method, four steps need to be completed:

1. Create the `Finder` method definition.

2. Create the filter.

3. Map the filter to the updated parameter collection.

4. Update the SQL Query to leverage the new parameter collection.

The first step in this process is defining the `Finder` method. To do this, right-click the Interfaces node just above the existing `SpecificFinder` method and select Add Method Instance. This opens the Create Method Instance dialog shown in Figure 9-14.

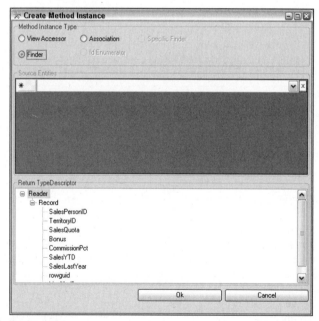

Figure 9-14

Ensure that the `Finder` Method Instance Type is selected, and accept this screen, which will return you to the main display. On the main display you will find that you have a new method instance, as shown in Figure 9-15. This new method has a default name, which you should replace with a more meaningful name, such as `SalesPersonFinder`. Having updated the name of this method, the method is now ready, although you need to add the necessary filter and parameters.

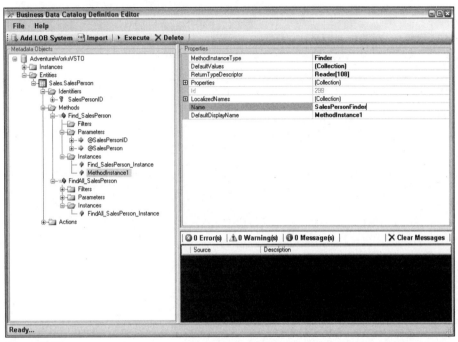

Figure 9-15

To add the filter, right-click the Filters folder shown just under the `Find_SalesPerson` method name and select Add Filter. This will create a new filter with a filter type of WildcardFilter. A wildcard filter is typically used to screen text fields and is tied to the Wildcard character property for your LOB system. In this case, however, the filter is going to be used for a numeric ID range. As a result, instead of using a wildcard filter, change the Filter Type to NotEquals using the drop-down list in the Properties display.

Figure 9-16 shows the newly created filter with the correct filter type selected and the Name value updated from the default to a more meaningful value of SalesPersonKey. Even though there is a plus sign located next to the filter in the display, this is the full list of properties for the filter. Note that, at this point, you haven't really assigned a type to the value associated with your filter.

To do that you need to assign the filter to one or more parameters. In the case of a wildcard filter, only a single parameter is needed, because the wildcard will handle creating an effective range. In the case of a numeric ID, two parameters are needed: a minimum value and a maximum value. The BDC will leverage the mapping of these parameters to create a range from which entries are retrieved. To start this process, select the existing `@SalesPersonID` parameter to display its Properties page, as shown in Figure 9-17. The only thing that is needed on this page is to update the name of the parameter. Because you'll need both a minimum and a maximum, you'll designate the existing parameter as a minimum value.

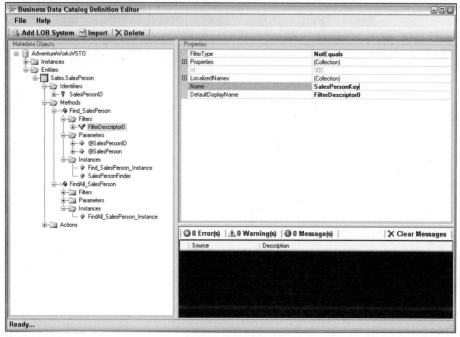

Figure 9-16

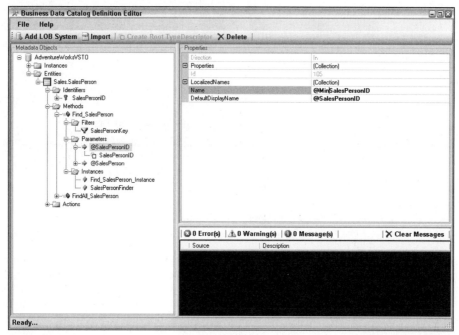

Figure 9-17

Next, you need to access the root type descriptor and ensure that this parameter is associated with your newly created filter. Select the SalesPersonID entry and the screen in Figure 9-18 will be displayed. Within the Properties pane, you'll notice that the second property is the FilterDescriptor. Select this property to open the drop-down box shown in Figure 9-18, and select the newly created SalesPersonKey as the filter.

Finally, before leaving this screen, update the Name and DefaultDisplayName properties to reflect that this is now the minimum parameter. Once you have completed this, the next step is to add a new maximum parameter. To do this, right-click the Parameters node and select Add Parameter from the context menu. You will be presented with a simple dialog to determine whether this parameter is an In, Out, or InOut parameter. It will be an In parameter, because it will only be used as part of the data lookup process.

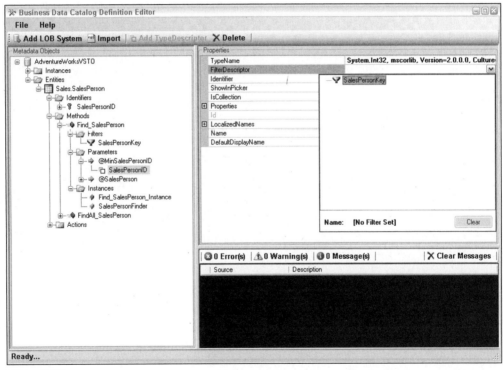

Figure 9-18

Select the newly created parameter, and the Properties pane will be updated as shown in Figure 9-19. Select the Name property and update the name of the parameter to @MaxSalesPersonID. This provides a name that fits the context that this value will represent the maximum value associated with the filter. Once you have updated the name to something meaningful, like @MaxSalesPersonID, you need to add a root definition for this parameter. Right-click the newly created parameter and select Create Root TypeDescriptor. This will generate a new root definition for your @MaxSalesPersonID parameter, as shown in Figure 9-20.

The properties on this page start with a TypeName. The value assigned to the TypeName property needs to be modified from the default of System.String to System.Int32 to match the type of data with which the parameter will be associated. The next property is FilterDescriptor. Just as with the minimum value, you need to associate this second parameter with the same filter.

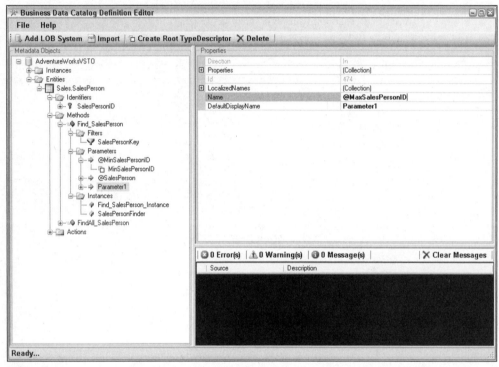

Figure 9-19

Next there is an Identifier property, and this is used if the parameter is associated with one of the identifiers for this entity. In this case, because you are creating a matched pair of parameters for the identity, you also need to associate this value with the identity column for this entity. As with the previous two settings, the drop-down will allow you to select the correct value. Finally, you can update the name of the property to reflect the same naming standard used for your minimum parameter. All of these changes are shown in Figure 9-20.

Because you now have two parameters, you might wonder how the system determines which is the minimum and which is the maximum. More importantly, what are those minimum and maximum values? The answer is that you need to define those values, however they are not defined on either the filter or the parameter. Instead, they are defined on the method instance, allowing you to create multiple method instances that, for whatever reason, might use different minimum and maximum ranges.

Select the SalesPersonFinder method instance, and, in the Properties pane, you'll see that the second property is the Default Values property. Selecting this property displays an ellipsis button, which, when clicked, opens the Edit window shown in Figure 9-21. Here you will define the minimum and maximum default values to be used by your parameters when this method is called.

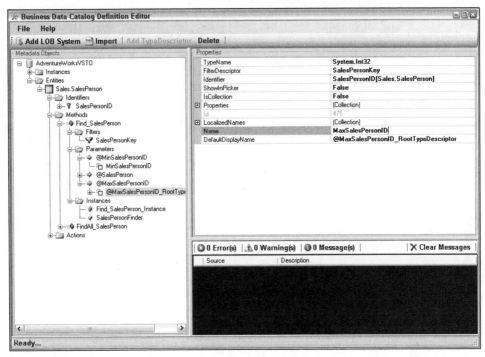

Figure 9-20

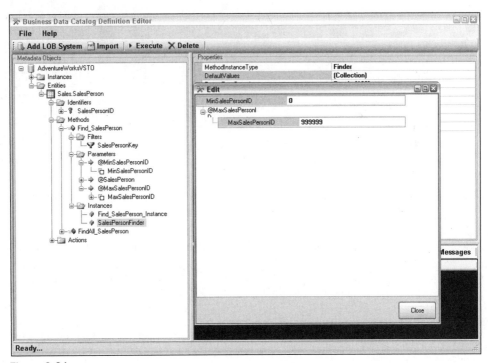

Figure 9-21

This leaves only one last step in integrating the `SalesPersonFinder` method instance. The SQL statement associated with your entity needs to be updated. In this case, the entity needs to support the minimum and maximum values you have provided. Return to the `Find_SalesPerson` method and select the `RdbCommandText` property, which you edited earlier. Open the wideTextBoxEditor and update the SQL statement as shown in Figure 9-22 with the following text:

```
Select "SalesPersonID","TerritoryID","SalesQuota","Bonus","CommissionPct","Sal
esYTD","SalesLastYear","rowguid","ModifiedDate" from  Sales.SalesPerson where
(SalesPersonID >= @MinSalesPersonID) AND (SalesPersonID <= @MaxSalesPersonID)
```

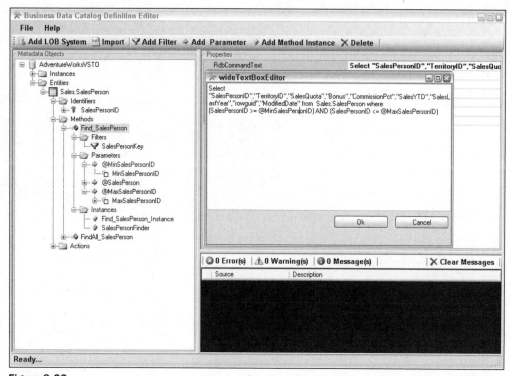

Figure 9-22

At this point, in theory, you are finished. There remains a problem, however, one that you aren't going to correct until after you export this definition. If you return to your instance methods and attempt to execute them, you'll find that they fail. You haven't done anything wrong, rather you've run into another undocumented feature of the tool.

SQL Server requires you to pass query parameters such that all inbound parameters precede outbound parameters. Unfortunately, when you added your new parameter to this structure it was added as the last parameter. SQL Server fails when you attempt to run this query. The solution is fairly simple — export the ADF definition to an XML file. Open the file in Notepad or a similar editor, reorder the parameters, and save your changes. Within the Business Data Catalog Definition Editor, delete your current LOB definition and import your newly edited definition. Now, test your instance methods and they should work.

Rather than walking through all of that in detail, you are going to finish with everything that needs to be done and then export the file. This means you need to edit your second method, `FindAll_SalesPerson`. Figure 9-23 shows how the `FindAll_SalesPerson` method does not accept any input parameters. It has only as single output parameter, which has been expanded.

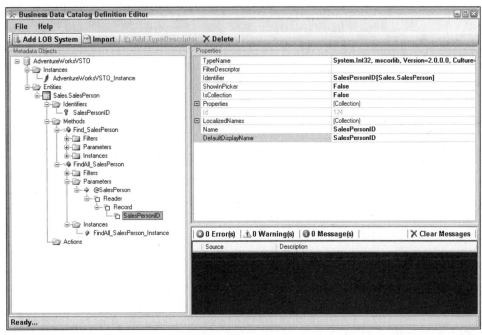

Figure 9-23

The last step in preparing to import your ADF file into MOSS is to test the `Finder` method. When you right-click and select Execute from the context menu, you will see the screen shown in Figure 9-24. You'll note that you bypassed the screen related to defining parameters and that there is a Next button on the screen.

You'll also note that there are no results shown in Figure 9-24, because that is the initial state of this screen, even if your query is working correctly. To see the results, you need to click the Next button, which will execute the `Finder` or `FindAll_SalesPerson_Instance` method to provide a list of results.

When you do review the results, the only thing that will be displayed is a list of the SalesPersonID values from the SalesPerson table. This is because the `Finder` method is returning only that single parameter. At this point, if both of your queries have been tested successfully, you are ready to export your settings as a new ADF file that can be used by MOSS.

To export, you must select the top-level AdventureWorksVSTO LOB definition in the main display. Only when this node of the MetaData Objects tree is selected will the user interface display the Export option on the toolbar. You can also find the Export option by right-clicking the same node. The option is never available from the menu. The Export option will open a standard file save dialog allowing you to save a new ADF file. Unfortunately, it doesn't default to the name of the LOBSystem, because that name needs to be unique within the BDC, but that is our recommendation for how to name the file.

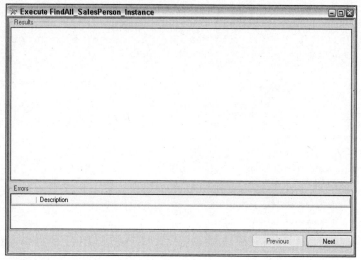

Figure 9-24

Once you have exported the file, remember that the parameters for the `Finder` method need to be reversed in the end. Your XML should look similar to the following XML:

```xml
<?xml version="1.0" encoding="utf-8" standalone="yes"?>
<LobSystem xmlns:xsi="http://www.w3.org/2001/XMLSchema-instance"
xsi:schemaLocation="http://schemas.microsoft.com/office/2006/03/BusinessDataCatalog
BDCMetadata.xsd" Type="Database" Version="1.0.0.0" Name="AdventureWorksVSTO"
xmlns="http://schemas.microsoft.com/office/2006/03/BusinessDataCatalog">
  <Properties>
    <Property Name="WildcardCharacter" Type="System.String">%</Property>
  </Properties>
  <LobSystemInstances>
    <LobSystemInstance Name="AdventureWorksVSTO_Instance">
      <Properties>
        <Property Name="rdbconnection Data Source" Type="System.String">MOSS\
OFFICESERVERS</Property>
        <Property Name="rdbconnection Initial Catalog" Type="System.
String">AdventureWorksVSTO</Property>
        <Property Name="rdbconnection Integrated Security" Type="System.
String">True</Property>
        <Property Name="DatabaseAccessProvider" Type="Microsoft.Office.Server.
ApplicationRegistry.SystemSpecific.Db.DbAccessProvider">SqlServer</Property>
        <Property Name="AuthenticationMode" Type="Microsoft.Office.Server.
ApplicationRegistry.SystemSpecific.Db.DbAuthenticationMode">PassThrough</Property>
      </Properties>
    </LobSystemInstance>
  </LobSystemInstances>
  <Entities>
    <Entity EstimatedInstanceCount="10000" Name="Sales.SalesPerson">
      <Identifiers>
        <Identifier TypeName="System.Int32" Name="SalesPersonID" />
      </Identifiers>
```

```
      <Methods>
        <Method Name="Find_SalesPerson">
          <Properties>
            <Property Name="RdbCommandType" Type="System.Data.CommandType, System.
Data, Version=2.0.0.0, Culture=neutral, PublicKeyToken=b77a5c561934e089">Text</
Property>
            <Property Name="RdbCommandText" Type="System.String">Select "SalesPer
sonID","TerritoryID","SalesQuota","Bonus","CommissionPct","SalesYTD","SalesLastYe
ar","rowguid","ModifiedDate"  from  Sales.SalesPerson where (SalesPersonID &gt;= @
MinSalesPersonID AND SalesPersonID &lt;= @MaxSalesPersonID)</Property>
          </Properties>
          <FilterDescriptors>
            <FilterDescriptor Type="Comparison" Name="SalesPersonKey">
            </FilterDescriptor>
          </FilterDescriptors>
          <Parameters>
            <Parameter Direction="In" Name="@MinSalesPersonID">
              <TypeDescriptor TypeName="System.Int32"
IdentifierName="SalesPersonID" AssociatedFilter="SalesPersonKey"
Name="MinSalesPersonID">
                <DefaultValues>
                  <DefaultValue MethodInstanceName="SalesPersonFinder"
Type="System.Int32">0</DefaultValue>
                </DefaultValues>
              </TypeDescriptor>
            </Parameter>
            <Parameter Direction="In" Name="@MaxSalesPersonID">
              <TypeDescriptor TypeName="System.Int32" IdentifierName="SalesPersonID"
AssociatedFilter="SalesPersonKey" Name="MaxSalesPersonID" />
            </Parameter>
            <Parameter Direction="Return" Name="@SalesPerson">
              <TypeDescriptor TypeName="System.Data.IDataReader, System.
Data, Version=2.0.0.0, Culture=neutral, PublicKeyToken=b77a5c561934e089"
IsCollection="true" Name="Reader">
                <TypeDescriptors>
                  <TypeDescriptor TypeName="System.Data.IDataRecord, System.Data,
Version=2.0.0.0, Culture=neutral, PublicKeyToken=b77a5c561934e089" Name="Record">
                    <TypeDescriptors>
                      <TypeDescriptor TypeName="System.Int32, mscorlib,
Version=2.0.0.0, Culture=neutral, PublicKeyToken=b77a5c561934e089"
IdentifierName="SalesPersonID" Name="SalesPersonID" />
                      <TypeDescriptor TypeName="System.Int32, mscorlib,
Version=2.0.0.0, Culture=neutral, PublicKeyToken=b77a5c561934e089"
Name="TerritoryID">
                        <Properties>
                          <Property Name="ShowInPicker" Type="System.
Boolean">false</Property>
                        </Properties>
                      </TypeDescriptor>
                      <TypeDescriptor TypeName="System.Decimal, mscorlib,
Version=2.0.0.0, Culture=neutral, PublicKeyToken=b77a5c561934e089"
Name="SalesQuota" />
                      <TypeDescriptor TypeName="System.Decimal, mscorlib,
Version=2.0.0.0, Culture=neutral, PublicKeyToken=b77a5c561934e089" Name="Bonus" />
```

```
                        <TypeDescriptor TypeName="System.Decimal, mscorlib,
Version=2.0.0.0, Culture=neutral, PublicKeyToken=b77a5c561934e089"
Name="CommissionPct" />
                        <TypeDescriptor TypeName="System.Decimal, mscorlib,
Version=2.0.0.0, Culture=neutral, PublicKeyToken=b77a5c561934e089" Name="SalesYTD"
/>
                        <TypeDescriptor TypeName="System.Decimal, mscorlib,
Version=2.0.0.0, Culture=neutral, PublicKeyToken=b77a5c561934e089"
Name="SalesLastYear" />
                        <TypeDescriptor TypeName="System.Guid, mscorlib,
Version=2.0.0.0, Culture=neutral, PublicKeyToken=b77a5c561934e089" Name="rowguid"
/>
                        <TypeDescriptor TypeName="System.DateTime, mscorlib,
Version=2.0.0.0, Culture=neutral, PublicKeyToken=b77a5c561934e089"
Name="ModifiedDate" />
                    </TypeDescriptors>
                  </TypeDescriptor>
                </TypeDescriptors>
              </TypeDescriptor>
            </Parameter>
          </Parameters>
          <MethodInstances>
            <MethodInstance Type="SpecificFinder" ReturnParameterName="@
SalesPerson" ReturnTypeDescriptorName="Reader" ReturnTypeDescriptorLevel="0"
Name="Find_SalesPerson_Instance" />
            <MethodInstance Type="Finder" ReturnParameterName="@SalesPerson" Return
TypeDescriptorName="Reader" ReturnTypeDescriptorLevel="0" Name="SalesPersonFinder"
/>
          </MethodInstances>
        </Method>
        <Method Name="FindAll_SalesPerson">
          <Properties>
            <Property Name="RdbCommandType" Type="System.Data.CommandType, System.
Data, Version=2.0.0.0, Culture=neutral, PublicKeyToken=b77a5c561934e089">Text</
Property>
            <Property Name="RdbCommandText" Type="System.String">Select
"SalesPersonID" from  Sales.SalesPerson</Property>
          </Properties>
          <Parameters>
            <Parameter Direction="Return" Name="@SalesPerson">
              <TypeDescriptor TypeName="System.Data.IDataReader, System.
Data, Version=2.0.0.0, Culture=neutral, PublicKeyToken=b77a5c561934e089"
IsCollection="true" Name="Reader">
                <TypeDescriptors>
                  <TypeDescriptor TypeName="System.Data.IDataRecord, System.Data,
Version=2.0.0.0, Culture=neutral, PublicKeyToken=b77a5c561934e089" Name="Record">
                    <TypeDescriptors>
                      <TypeDescriptor TypeName="System.Int32, mscorlib,
Version=2.0.0.0, Culture=neutral, PublicKeyToken=b77a5c561934e089"
IdentifierName="SalesPersonID" Name="SalesPersonID" />
                    </TypeDescriptors>
                  </TypeDescriptor>
                </TypeDescriptors>
              </TypeDescriptor>
```

```
            </Parameter>
          </Parameters>
          <MethodInstances>
            <MethodInstance Type="IdEnumerator" ReturnParameterName="@SalesPerson"
ReturnTypeDescriptorName="Reader" ReturnTypeDescriptorLevel="0" Name="FindAll_
SalesPerson_Instance" />
          </MethodInstances>
        </Method>
      </Methods>
    </Entity>
  </Entities>
</LobSystem>
```

There are a few quick notes on the preceding XML. Prior to the highlighted section, which is the XML node that you need to move manually, is the definition of your RdbCommandText property. Within this property, as you may recall, is your actual T-SQL command. In this case, that command includes a comparison that uses > and <, however, the less than and greater than symbols are reserved characters within XML. As a result, when your ADF file was generated as XML, your T-SQL was modified to replace these characters with lt; and gt; respectively.

Importing the ADF

The BDC is a shared service, and as such it is managed from the Shared Services web site. Note that if you are not signed in as the System Administrator you may be denied access to this site. The permissions for this site are separate from those for the main application site and Central Administration sites. The Shared Services web site is reached from the Central Administration web site. On the left side of the default page for the Central Administration site is a link to the Shared Services site.

> *It is possible to grant accounts other than the local administrator rights to the Shared Services site, however, this was not explicitly covered. The steps are similar to those for adding other users to the Central Administration web site.*

The main display page for the Shared Services site is shown in Figure 9-25. The links for the BDC are on the right side of the page, and the first of those links allows you to import a new application definition. Clicking this link takes you to the Import Application Definition screen shown in Figure 9-26.

The Browse button is used to select the ADF file you exported from the Business Data Catalog Definition Editor. You can leave the existing default values shown in Figure 9-26 and click the Import button to start the import process. It will take a few seconds for your import to complete. If successful, you will be taken to the Application Definition Import Successful screen shown in Figure 9-27. Clicking the OK button on that screen takes you to the View Application screen for the AdventureWorksVSTO application you just imported.

Clicking the link for the Sales.SalesPerson entity takes you to the View Entity screen shown in Figure 9-28. The reason to come to this screen is to verify the third property associated with your entity information. The Crawlable property needs to be set to Yes for you to be able to index your BDC data. For this to be available you need all three of the methods created by the steps in the first portion of this chapter. If any of those methods are missing, the entity will not be able to be indexed.

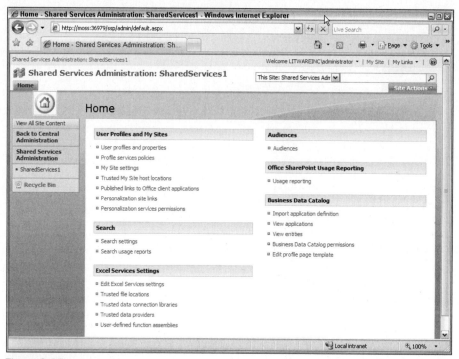

Figure 9-25

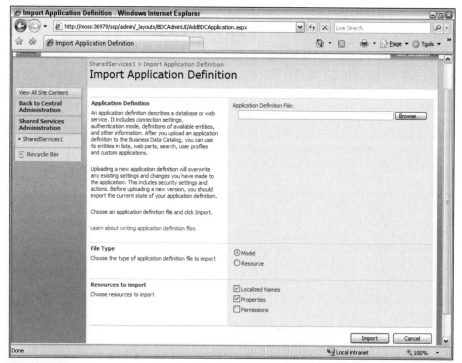

Figure 9-26

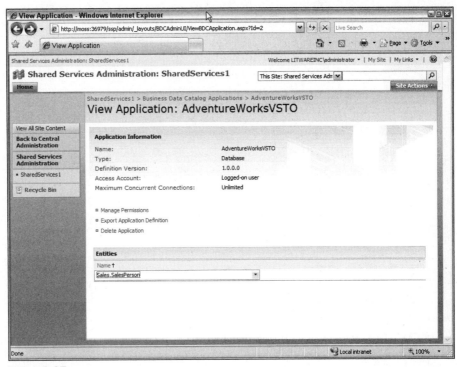

Figure 9-27

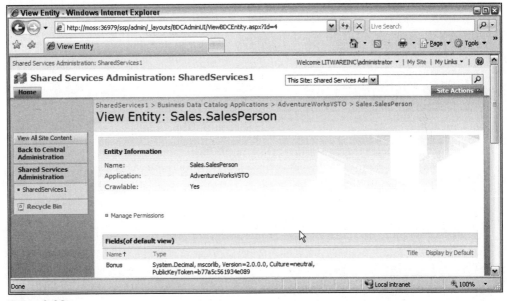

Figure 9-28

Working with Sharepoint Search Settings

Similar to the BDC, searching is a shared service on SharePoint. In reviewing Figure 9-25, you'll find that the Search Settings link is located to the left of the BDC links on the Shared Services default page. Clicking the Search Settings link on this page takes you to the Configure Search Settings page shown in Figure 9-29.

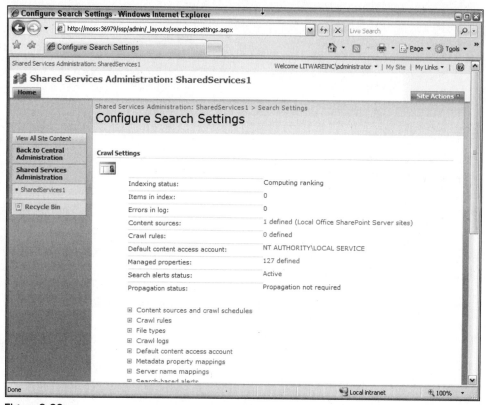

Figure 9-29

This page makes clear that this server doesn't currently have anything indexed. By default when MOSS is installed, the search engine is not given a crawl schedule. To resolve this and prepare to index your BDC data, you need to enable a crawl schedule. Fortunately, the "Content sources and crawl schedules" link allows you to edit both of these items at the same time.

This screen lets you see that there is an existing content source for the SharePoint Server sites, but that it is currently idle, and neither a full nor incremental crawl has been executed on this data source. You can, of course, edit this data source and make it so that the sites are crawled; however, the goal of this chapter is to add a new content source for the BDC. Therefore, click the New Content Source button to open the screen shown in Figure 9-31. Clicking the link for your content sources and crawl schedules will open the Manage Content Sources screen shown in Figure 9-30.

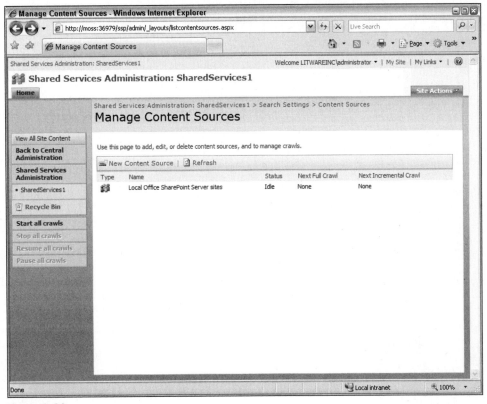

Figure 9-30

The screen allows you to name your crawl source. Use the entity name. Next, select Business Data as your crawl source. When you select this option, SharePoint will adjust the page content. This will take a moment, but as a result, you will have an option either to crawl all of the applications hosted by the BDC or to select one or more applications. In this case there is only one application; however, we have chosen to crawl only that data source.

Optionally, you can set up a full crawl and or an incremental crawl schedule for your new content source. That is outside the scope of what is being covered in this chapter. Instead, you can check the Start Full Crawl of This Content Source checkbox and scroll down to click the OK button.

This will return you to the screen shown in Figure 9-30, and will indicate that your data source is being crawled. There is a potential error here. The crawling is not done using the account of the current user, but, instead, using the Network Service account. For this crawl to succeed, that service account needs permission to access your database. For prototype and development purposes, the easiest solution is to promote that service account to be one of the local system administrators. Once you've given your search a chance to complete, return to the page shown in Figure 9-31 by clicking your content source. Now your page should look similar to what is shown in Figure 9-32, which shows the date of the last crawl and that it completed without error.

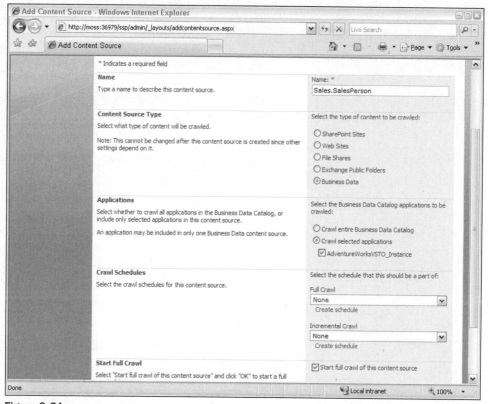

Figure 9-31

The next step, once you have established that your settings are functional, is to define a set of security limits that allow only that access which is necessary. You will create a custom service account that will provide users with access that is as close to what they get through the BDC interface as possible. Then you'll retest using that account so that if an error occurs you know it isn't related to your ADF metadata definition, but rather to the new security settings.

Upon reaching this point, you will recognize that there is another issue with search. The Sales.Sales-Person table doesn't have any text columns. As a result, there isn't any actual text to index, so there isn't anything to retrieve from search with this current BDC application. That doesn't mean you can't use this data source elsewhere.

Exposing BDC Data through a Web Part

Because you can't search your BDC data, try loading it onto your default page. Figure 9-33 shows the current home page with the Site Actions menu open to select Edit Page. Selecting this takes you into edit mode on the current page.

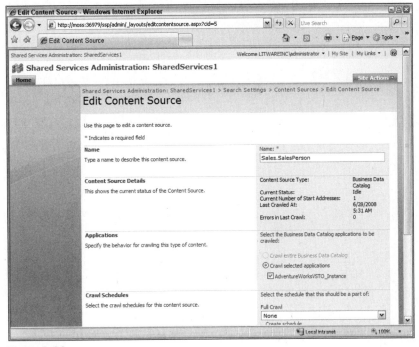

Figure 9-32

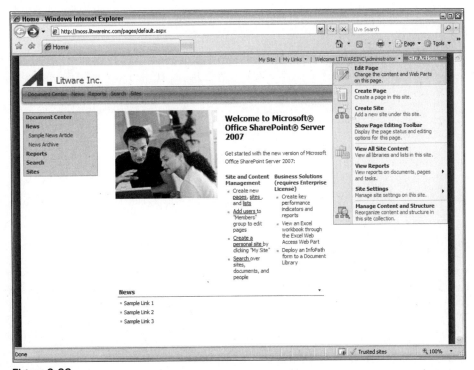

Figure 9-33

Figure 9-34 shows the main page in edit mode. At the bottom of the displayed area is the top content zone where you can add a Web part. Clicking the Add a Web Part button in the Top Zone opens the Add Web Parts to Top Zone dialog shown in Figure 9-35. Expanding the All Web Parts section of this dialog allows you to select the Business Data List. Clicking Add adds this Web part to your Top Zone.

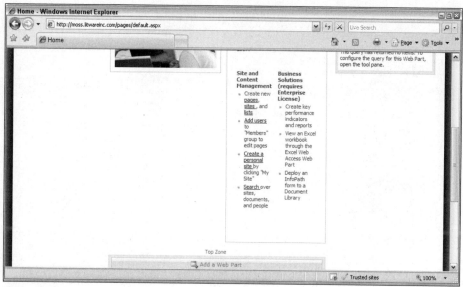

Figure 9-34

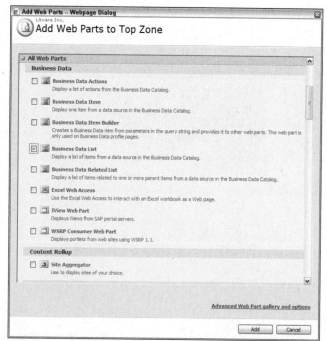

Figure 9-35

Once the Web part is added, you'll need to click the "Open the tool pane" link within the Web part in order to open the tool pane in which you'll configure this Web part. Figure 9-36 illustrates the page after the tool pane has been opened. Note that the first thing you'll need to do is use the Browse button at the top of this tool pane to select your BDC entity. This selection is made from the Business Data Type Picker dialog shown in Figure 9-37.

Figure 9-36

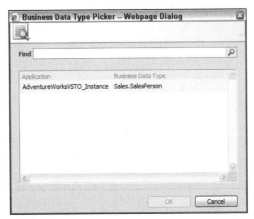

Figure 9-37

Once you have added the definition of your BDC data source to this control, you can click the Apply button at the bottom of the tool pane to assign your data to the Web part. Doing so will populate the Web part with the columns that are part of your Sales.SalesPerson entity. You can even enter a known value in the comparison and test load the data while in design mode, as shown in Figure 9-38.

Figure 9-38

At this point, you can publish your updated page and review and test your new List control. The resulting page, with the data for two different sales representatives, is shown in Figure 9-39. You'll note that none of the data is automatically formatted. Formatting is something that needs to be handled from the tool pane in design mode. The control will allow you to edit the XSL that is applied to the results from the data query, omitting fields and applying, for example, monetary symbols to your data.

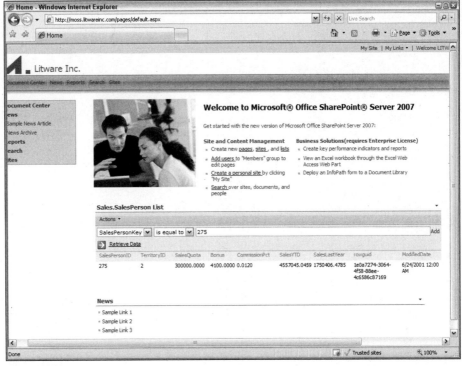

Figure 9-39

Summary

The BDC can be a powerful tool for displaying data from your LOB systems. As you saw in this chapter, however, without a proper tool for designing your ADF files, the ADF creation process can be painful. On the other hand, once you have a valid ADF file, working with the BDC is easy. This chapter walked you through the following:

- ❑ Installing the Microsoft Office Server SDK
- ❑ Working with the Business Data Catalog Definition Editor
- ❑ Defining custom filters, parameters, and method instances
- ❑ Configuring an ADF metadata file so that the data can be used for Search and Web parts
- ❑ Configuring a BDC application as a search content source and starting the crawl of your data
- ❑ Configuring the Business Data List to use your BDC application

Though the freely available tool from Microsoft is limited, the reality is that the BDC is a powerful tool for exposing your LOB data. The ability to make such data available via a web interface has significant implications for long-term service-oriented design. Hopefully, this walk through some of the weeds has helped you understand and appreciate what the BDC is capable of doing with your LOB data.

10

Deploying your Client Components

To create an Office Business Application (OBA), one of the unofficial requirements is that you leverage one or more client Microsoft Office applications. In theory, you could call a SharePoint site an OBA if it weren't for the fact that without some level of custom business logic that extends beyond the web server, calling it a web application based on SharePoint is more accurate and descriptive. The sales forecast OBA includes both an Outlook Form Region and a custom VSTO-enabled Excel Workbook. Installing these on all of the client machines in your organization could be a difficult, time-consuming task. By leveraging SharePoint and Visual Studio 2008's support for ClickOnce installation, the process can be made more manageable. This chapter looks at:

❑ Creating ClickOnce packages

❑ Creating a Sales Tools page

❑ Updating your trusted locations

❑ Setting up the Sales Forecast content type on MOSS

This chapter targets an IT professional who may or may not be a developer, because it is the IT professional who will need to manage the installation process. In the case of ClickOnce deployment, this means that the IT professional needs to be involved in configuring the settings associated with the installation of the package.

Some of these installation settings occur on the server. For example, the packages will be hosted on the SharePoint site. The content type that is assigned to the various document libraries is set on the server; however, even when the settings are based on the server on which the solution will be deployed, some of the settings must be configured as part of the package creation inside Visual Studio. This chapter is all about what the IT professional needs to know, and in some cases, pass to the developer in order to be able to deploy these client-side components successfully. This chapter starts with a need to prepare and set up client components, and this starts within Visual Studio 2008, with the creation of the ClickOnce installation package.

Creating ClickOnce Packages

When developers start working with something like a new OFR implementation, they start on their desktop. Visual Studio 2008, as shown in Chapter 6, "Creating a Custom Outlook Form Region," makes it possible for the developer to create a new OFR and start it up from Visual Studio. Once started the developers have the associated OFR installed on their development box, and that covers their needs.

Therefore, you need set up a real deployment plan. In the cases of both the Sales Forecast OFR and the Sales Forecast Workbook the assemblies involved need to be installed onto each client computer. Additionally, the means of getting your assemblies installed are similar, although, as this chapter demonstrates, the workbook has some additional steps not associated with the OFR. Setting up the ClickOnce installation package is the same for both projects.

Figure 10-1 illustrates the Properties screen for the SalesForecastOFR. The Publish tab allows you to update the settings for publishing your application. The first item on this page is the location from which you will be installing the application. Currently, this page shows the publish location as a new web site on the local machine. Clearly, this setting isn't going to work. The plan, therefore, is to create a host, for example, SharePoint, that will provide an easily discoverable installation link.

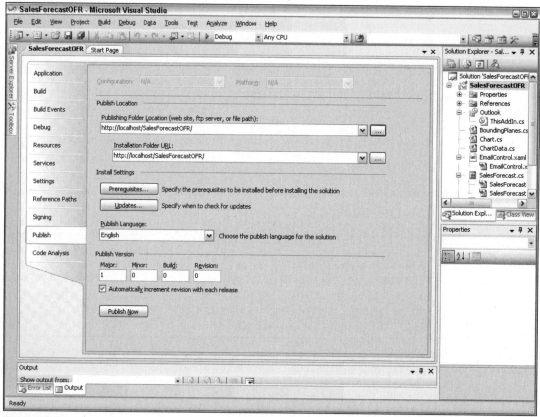

Figure 10-1

The installation files won't be uploaded into SharePoint. Instead, the installation will be linked from a network share by SharePoint. Users will access the installation via a link from SharePoint, but the actual files will reside within a remote network share. In our configuration, the network share will be local to the server hosting SharePoint; however, it might also be a remote network share in a production environment.

To set up your installation you must redefine both the Publishing and Installation folders. These folders should contain the same value. The server in development was called MOSS, and on the server we created a shared folder called OBABinaries. The OBABinaries folder is a top-level share under which we allow the creation of separate installations for multiple projects. Each installation package is placed into its own folder.

Figure 10-2 illustrates the lookup screen, which is opened when the ellipsis (...) button in Figure 10-1 is clicked. You'll need to change the selection in the left column to the file system. You'll then either need to navigate or type the proposed path. Figure 10-2 shows the path for the Sales Forecast OFR. The Sales Forecast Workbook path would be similar except that the final folder name would be SalesForecast-Workbook. Note this must be a shared folder, because both the SharePoint site and clients will refer to this folder when installing and using the workbook assemblies.

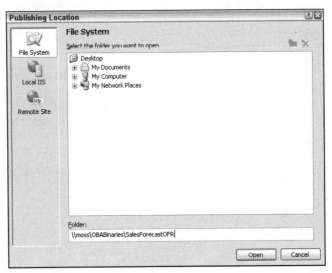

Figure 10-2

Once you have done this for the Publishing folder, you'll need to copy your directory selection to the Installation folder, so that the same path is used to populate both fields. At this point, you should be ready to deploy, but before you do, review the other elements that should have defaulted to the correct settings.

Clicking the Prerequisites button in Figure 10-1 opens the dialog shown in Figure 10-3. By default, the Visual Studio 2008 project templates for Office 2007 client projects automatically include the three prerequisites for the installation. Though you could create a customization that required additional packages, this is not the case for the Sales Forecast OFR and Sales Forecast Workbook.

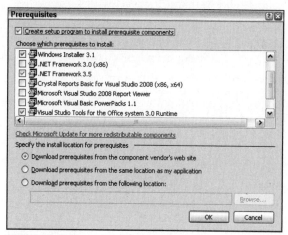

Figure 10-3

The Updates button in Figure 10-1 opens the Customization Updates dialog shown in Figure 10-4. Though the default settings here are acceptable for the OFR, it's necessary to discuss differences in how the OFR and Workbook projects will behave and why these two projects might have different settings for this update value.

The current update settings indicate that the OFR should check for updates only once per week. If you were to check the first option, which is to have the OFR check for updates each time it is started, then, at a minimum, each time Outlook was started, this OFR would need to check for updates and this would slow the startup process for Outlook. Alternatively, it would actually check with each opened message because, as described in Chapter 6, the Separate OFR logic is called for each message to determine whether the separate region should be present.

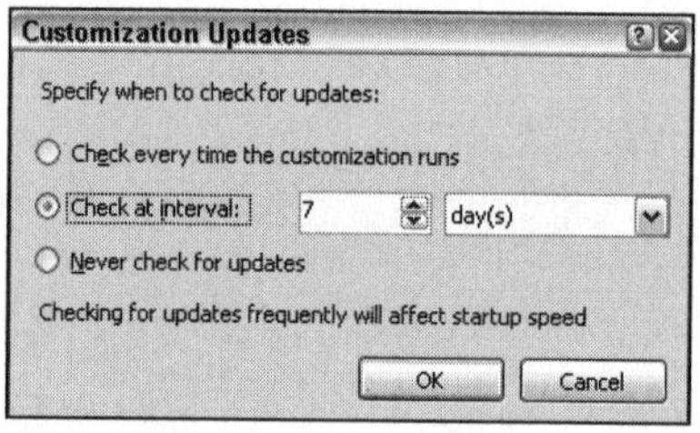

Figure 10-4

Leaving the default setting as shown for the Sales Forecast OFR makes the most sense. This setting will ensure that over time, approximately once each week, the client's computer will check back to see whether, in fact, the binary assemblies associated with this OFR have been updated, and if they have, the computer will update the client's installation. This setting needs to be addressed somewhat differently for the Sales Forecast Workbook.

As we'll show you later in this chapter, not only is the Sales Forecast Workbook installed on the client machines, it is also used as a custom content type in SharePoint. This causes a problem, because the

SharePoint site isn't going to check for updates on a regular basis. Instead, what will occur is that when a new version of the workbook is made available, the site administrator will update the content type.

When the content type is updated, it will be necessary for anyone attempting to use the Sales Forecast Workbook to use the same updated version. If a user is on an older version of the Sales Forecast Workbook than is the SharePoint document library, the user will get an error when attempting to work with the workbook. Therefore, instead of checking only after a seven-day window, we recommend that the Sales Forecast Workbook check for updates either every time the customization runs, as shown in Figure 10-5, or never.

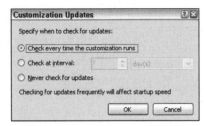

Figure 10-5

Unlike the Sales Forecast OFR, which is an Outlook Add-In that is loaded each time Outlook is loaded, the Sales Forecast Workbook is a document-based customization. As such, it only runs when a user specifically asks to create a new instance of this document, which we would only expect to occur when the user accessed this library. Because in this case the action of creating a sales forecast is relatively infrequent, it makes sense to check on each startup to prevent sending the user an error message related to the versioning of the workbook.

To update the content type, you will first need to remove all documents that refer to it. Unless you have a migration plan for those documents, you may never actually replace the assemblies, and, therefore, would never need to check them.

Signing Your Assemblies

By default, when you create a new VSTO application Visual Studio automatically generates a temporary key that is used to sign your assemblies. If you download the assemblies from Codeplex, even though the default keys are included, in some cases the mapping is lost.

If this has occurred, when you attempt to create a ClickOnce package for your project, you'll get an error related to signing the project. To resolve this error, switch from the Publish tab in the project properties to the Signing tab, as shown in Figure 10-6. When you get to this tab, unlike the image shown in Figure 10-6, you should find that the Certificate data isn't visible on your screen. At this point, people often respond to what Visual Studio is telling them and attempt to sign the assembly. Don't. That isn't the problem, and signing the assembly will not resolve the error message.

Instead, you need to repopulate the certificate information used to sign the ClickOnce manifests. Click the Select from File button that is shown in Figure 10-6. This opens the Select File dialog shown in Figure 10-7. You should see the default certificate in that dialog. Select that certificate, but, when prompted for a password, do not enter one. The certificate was not created with a password. Once accepted your display should look similar to the one shown in Figure 10-6.

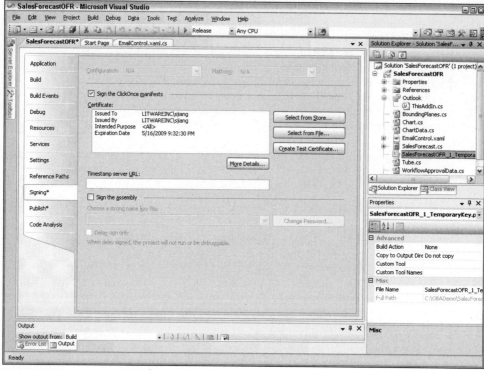

Figure 10-6

Keep in mind that this is a temporary certificate that should only be used during the development process. To deploy your application, you need to purchase or locally generate a valid certificate. You will purchase a certificate if you are intending to have your solution deployed publicly. If you are creating a solution for your internal organization, you can leverage your own custom certificate services to generate a certificate that is valid within your organization.

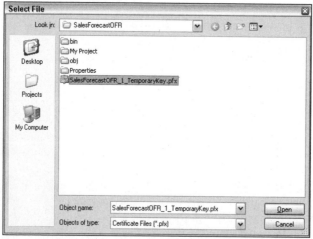

Figure 10-7

Now that any signature issues have been resolved and you have configured your Publish settings, you should be ready to publish your application. The final state of the Publish screen is shown again in Figure 10-8. Although we didn't discuss the publishing language or version, these settings should be self-explanatory. The only item of note is that the automatic incrementing of the version only increments the revision portion of the version. Figure 10-8 illustrates the final paths for the Publishing and Installation folders of the Sales Forecast Workbook, not the Sales Forecast OFR. Clicking the Publish Now button results in Visual Studio building your application and then creating a ClickOnce installation package, which will be placed in that shared folder. The next step is to add a new page to SharePoint so that, instead of having users go directly to that folder, they trust and install the assembly from SharePoint.

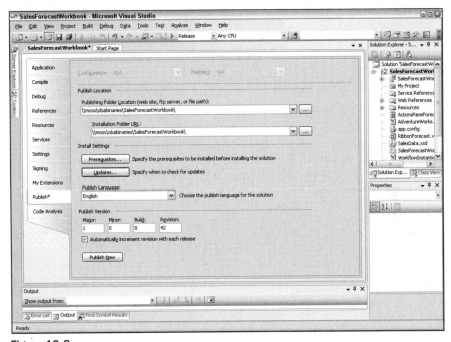

Figure 10-8

Creating a Sales Tools Page

The library site that was created in Chapter 3, "Installing and Configuring MOSS," consisted of two document libraries and one or two other document libraries. At this point you are going to update that default installation and add another list that will provide links to the client installation packages. Because you set up the site, you are familiar with navigating to the Site Settings page for your documents site, as shown in Figure 10-9. One of the challenges with SharePoint is often finding your way to the pages that allow you to complete a task, so we'll start from this easy to locate page.

First, ensure that you have entered the correct level for the site settings, and are in fact within the settings for the Document Center and not at the top corporate level. Notice how the breadcrumb control above the Site Settings header indicates that you are within the Document Center. The breadcrumb header at the top of the page shows that the Document Center is located just one level down from the corporate site, but it is the fact that this Site Settings page is associated with the Document Center that matters.

On the right side of the page in Figure 10-9 you'll see the Site Administration column. The second item in that list is the "Site libraries and lists" link; clicking this link opens the page shown in Figure 10-10. This page lists the current libraries and lists on this site, and at the top includes a link to allow you to create a new list for this site, which is the link you'll click to get to the page shown in Figure 10-11.

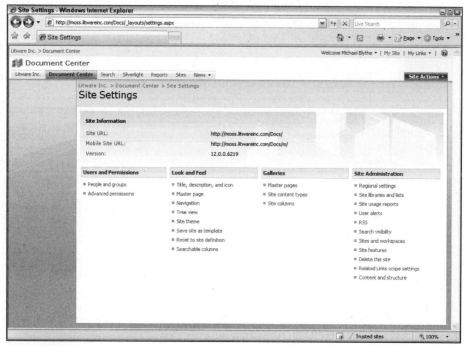

Figure 10-9

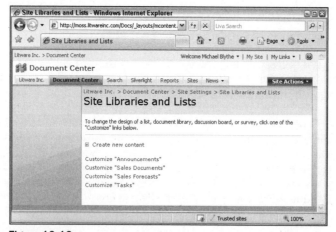

Figure 10-10

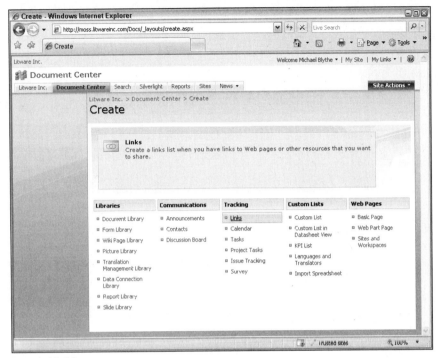

Figure 10-11

Figure 10-11 shows the page to create new content for the Document Center. There are several options here, and obviously Chapter 3 discussed this page in order to create the Sales Forecast Document Library. The Links type is located in the center of the page in the Tracking column. The appropriate link is highlighted in Figure 10-11. A page of this type will allow you to create a list of links to the installation packages that are being created on shared folders. Selecting the Links item takes you to the page shown in Figure 10-12.

Figure 10-12 allows you to provide the name and description and decide whether the newly created list should be part of the Quick Launch bar. Figure 10-12 illustrates the use of the name "Sales Tools" for this page, along with a brief description. Clicking the Create button shown in Figure 10-12 creates your new list and places you within the screen shown in Figure 10-13.

Figure 10-13 illustrates the resulting list. Notice that the list Sales Tools is not only your current page but is also selected from the Site Hierarchy menu on the left-hand side of the screen. It also shows how the New button will allow you to create a new item in the list. Selecting this option opens the New Item page shown in Figure 10-14.

Figure 10-14 allows you to define in SharePoint a link to a file or directory. In this case you'll note that the figure was captured after all of the information associated with creating a link for the Sales Forecast OFR had been entered. The link isn't an HTTP link, but rather a link to the shared folder described at the start of this chapter. You'll note that it not only includes the directory associated with the Sales Forecast OFR, but also specifies the setup.exe file that is produced when the project is published. In this way, a user clicking this link will kick off the installation process.

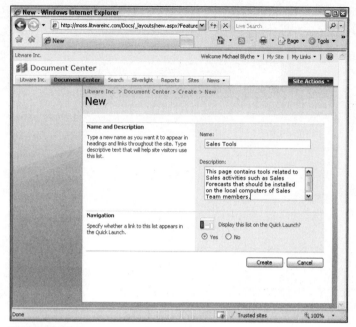

Figure 10-12

The description associated with your hyperlink is the text displayed in your page. Additionally, the information added to the Notes section will be displayed to the user. These fields allow you to provide additional information related to the assembly and explain to the user any specific requirements; for example, requiring Office 2007, which might be associated with the installation packages.

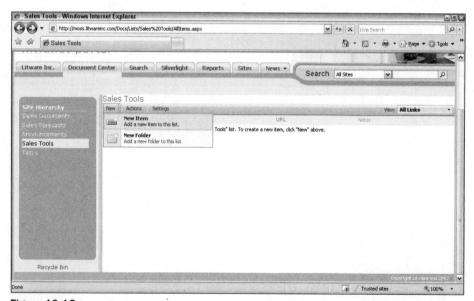

Figure 10-13

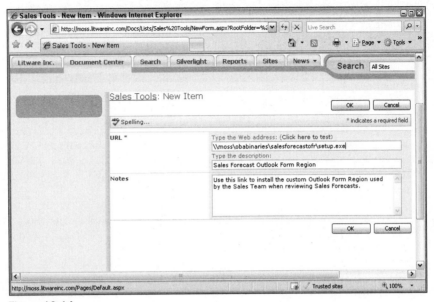

Figure 10-14

When complete your Sales Tools page should look similar to the one shown in Figure 10-15. The two links will be displayed along with any notes. In theory, this same page can be used for any number of related tool installations, including third-party tools that you want to make available to your organization. Now you are ready to go, right?

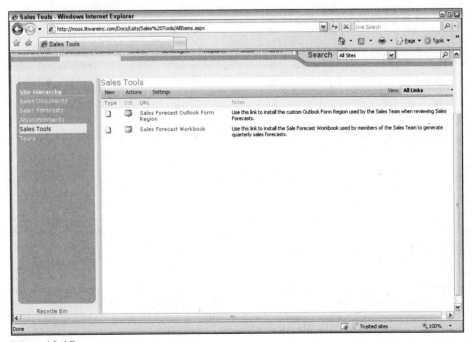

Figure 10-15

Well, almost. Fire up a client machine that doesn't have Visual Studio 2008 installed, and connect to your SharePoint site. Click your Sales Forecast Workbook install and run the installation. You'll get a couple of warnings related to the fact that the certificate you are using isn't trusted. These are expected, and you can continue past them and you'll find that the installation continues without any problem. If it doesn't, you need to review the steps discussed previously to see what happened, because the actual installation should work.

> *In theory, users can attempt to go directly to your Sales Forecast document library and create a new document to trigger the installation of your VSTO package. This is, of course, true only once you have defined the Sales Forecast Workbook as the default content type for your document library. If you are working from a machine that already has all of the prerequisites — VSTO 3.0, .NET 3.5, MSI 3.1 — the VSTO assembly will download and install. If the machine does not have all of these prerequisites, however, you'll get an error message.*

Now navigate to the Sales Forecast document library and click the New button to create a new sales forecast. Excel will start, and you'll see the Sales Forecast spreadsheet load and then — Boom — Figure 10-16 jumps onto your screen and potentially ruins your day.

It turns out that, although you've correctly installed the necessary components, they won't actually run when you attempt to create a spreadsheet from using a custom content type in your Sales Forecast document library. Although setting up that library is actually the next task, the solution actually ties into the installation process and is therefore best resolved here.

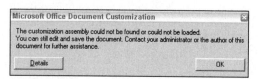

Figure 10-16

There are two steps to resolve this problem, and step one involves the manual changes that you can make related to this issue on your developer machine. During this process, document the steps showing your final location strings, and save this document to your installation directory as part of the installation instructions for the Sales Forecast Workbook. Ensure that you provide a link within the Sales Tools list so that readers will find and open this document and set up their Trusted Locations in Excel appropriately.

Updating Your Trusted Locations

Odds are good that, if you got the message box shown in Figure 10-16, you'll find in the details a relatively cryptic message that equates to, "your computer doesn't trust the location attempting to start this VSTO application." Notice that the customization and all of its prerequisites have been installed; however, the VSTO security model also includes a trusted locations set of protections. Because, as a developer, you'll probably have a development and test area (and who knows what other development-related locations you'll want to trust) that isn't worth developing a repeatable solution for, following are the steps to set up this trust relationship manually.

First open up Excel 2007. You don't need any existing workbook or the project template loaded, just open Excel. In the upper-left corner of Excel is the Office button. Clicking this opens the menu shown in Figure 10-17. You'll notice that the Excel Options button has been highlighted in this figure. Selecting this button opens the Excel Options dialog shown in Figure 10-18.

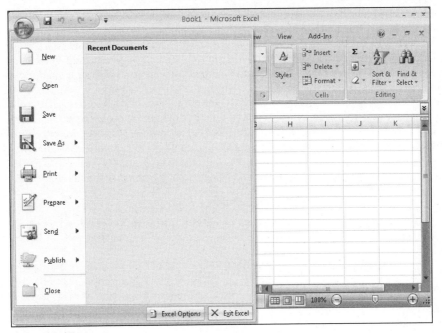

Figure 10-17

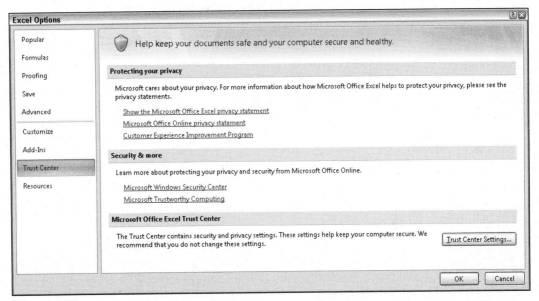

Figure 10-18

Next you'll notice that in the lower-right corner of the Excel Options dialog in Figure 10-18 is the Trust Center Settings button. This screen provides information related to your security and protecting your privacy, however to access your settings for Excel you need to access the Trust Center Settings button in the lower-right corner to open the Trust Center.

Figure 10-19 shows the Trust Center with the Trusted Locations tab selected. This is the source of your problem. The ClickOnce installation package has fully installed your assembly, but it hasn't changed the second element related to VSTO security, when that package can be started.

Essentially, instead of having a local document, your web site is now attempting to download and initiate a VSTO package that is installed, or which it just installed, on your machine. For the Sales Forecast Workbook, the assemblies are being referred to by a web site. This is different from the Sales Forecast OFR. Although a message is sent from the Sales Forecast Approval Workflow running on your SharePoint server, that customization is being activated by your locally running instance of Outlook.

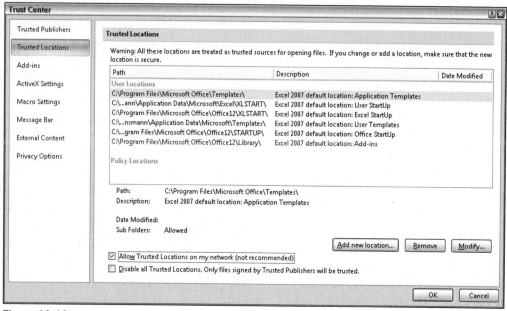

Figure 10-19

When you first open the Trust Center you'll need to update the checkbox shown near the bottom center of the display. By default, the Allow Trusted Locations on My Network (Not Recommended) checkbox is not checked. If you want to run customizations that are part of your local SharePoint site, this checkbox needs to be checked. It has already been checked in Figure 10-19.

The next step is to use the Add New Location button that is highlighted in Figure 10-19 to open the Microsoft Office Trusted Location dialog shown in Figure 10-20. In this dialog, you'll replace the default path (this dialog will open with the path currently selected in the Trust Center dialog) with the Share-Point URL. We're told this is by design; your reaction shouldn't be that you are in edit mode, but that you have been given a valid default from which to start. Figure 10-20 shows that we chose to trust our docs site collection; the idea was to minimize the number of trusted locations within our organization. Make certain that you choose to trust subfolders of this location. That's important because your Excel Workbook will in fact be in a subfolder of the top-level site collection. The description shown in Figure 10-20 is optional.

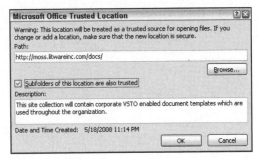

Figure 10-20

That's it; click OK to the Microsoft Office Trusted Location dialog and then work your way back through the OK buttons on each consecutive dialog until you are in Excel. Next, you need to close Excel and all open workbooks. This means that your local machine is now ready, but you need to access the assembly, preferably from SharePoint. Creating a new document from SharePoint's Sales Forecast library won't be possible until after you've completed the next step, which is to assign your Sales Forecast Workbook as the content type on MOSS. Then, when you are ready, you can test this by attempting to create a new Sales Forecast Workbook from the Sales Forecasts document library.

Setting up the Sales Forecast Content Type on MOSS

Finally, it's time to focus on creating a custom content type that will be used to create sales forecasts. One of the key new features of SharePoint v3.0 and MOSS is the ability to identify the types of documents based on a template that should be created in a library. Fortunately, this ability doesn't end with simple templates, but extends fully into customized workbooks that include VSTO assemblies.

To start this process you should begin on the Site Settings page for the Document Center site collection. This page allows you to create a custom content type that will be available to SharePoint only within your Document Center. Figure 10-21 shows the Site Settings page, and the link for customizing content types is located under the Galleries column. Clicking this link takes you to the pages shown in Figure 10-22.

Figure 10-22 shows the Site Content Type Gallery. Reviewing the breadcrumb controls shown in the upper-left corner of the page and just below to horizontal tab bar you see that you are currently viewing the available content types for the Document Center. This is also reflected within the table of available content types. The final column in the grid is the Source column, and in this display it is currently consistently populated with Litware Inc. This column shows the level at which a given content type is defined. These templates are all defined for the entire top-level MOSS.litwareinc.com domain. That means that any newly created sub-site anywhere within the organization can access these existing content types.

The advantage of this is, of course, the idea that a given content type can be reused, and certainly for a certain subset of customizations and baseline templates, this is a good idea. Over time, however, this has scalability issues, because attempting to manage potentially thousands of templates would become problematic. SharePoint allows you to define templates at different scopes; in this case your VSTO-enabled template will be available only to document libraries located within the Document Center site collection. Not only does this manage complexity, but in the case of VSTO-enabled templates it helps with security. By keeping the VSTO-enabled content types limited to a subset of your overall SharePoint site, you reduce the trusted areas of the site and potentially limit who can create this type of application. Because any application, by definition, includes a greater possibility for misuse, having this limited to one or more limited portions of your overall site is a good practice.

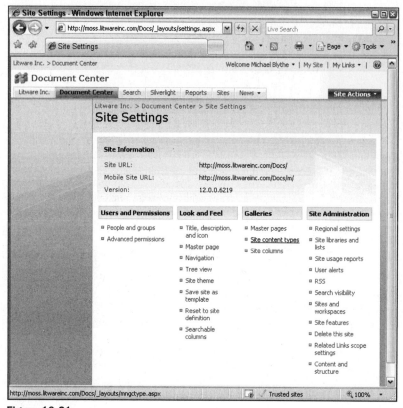

Figure 10-21

It should be noted that if you wanted your template to be available across the entire site you could click one of the Litware Inc. links in this page, and you would be taken to the Site Content Type Gallery for the Litware Inc. site.

Clicking the Create button at the top-left corner of the grid on the Document Center site takes you to the New Site Content Type page shown in Figure 10-23. This page allows you to start the process of defining your new VSTO-enabled content type. The name and description are both reasonably self-explanatory, and the values used in Figure 10-23 are appropriate.

Below the Name and Description is a section for defining the Parent Content Type. Because we are looking to create a custom document type, we have chosen to indicate that our custom content type is part of the Document Content Types collection and that it inherits from the Content Type of Document. Finally, even though we have already indicated that it will inherit from a Content Type in the Document Content Types, we have the alternative of grouping it with other similar content type definitions, placing it in another group altogether, or even creating a new custom group on the fly.

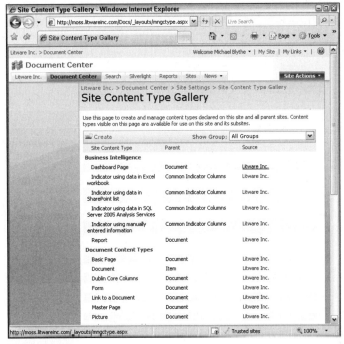

Figure 10-22

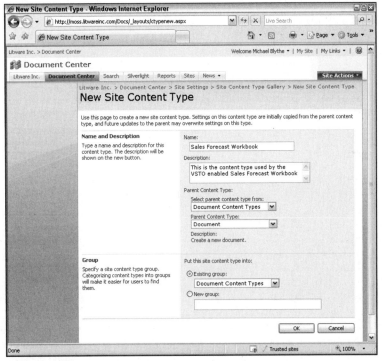

Figure 10-23

Once you have made the associated selections, click the OK button to save your new content type and take you to the page shown in Figure 10-24. The Site Content Type: Sales Forecast Workbook page uses a standard template to display all Site Content Types. In this case, it displays your newly created content type. Though you have a valid content type, you have not yet mapped this content type to your actual `SalesForecastWorkbook.xlsx` file and its related assemblies. To do this you need to select the "Advanced settings" link shown near the middle of Figure 10-24.

Figure 10-25 shows the Site Content Type Advanced Settings page with your newly created Sales Forecast Workbook template selected. This is where you'll specify your document template, which in this case is the `SalesForecastWorkbook.xlsx` file created when you published your Sales Forecast Workbook. Note that you will want to refer to the shared folder path, not a local path, even though the shared folder may exist on your local server. For your MOSS server and OBABinaries shared folder this path was `\\MOSS\obabinaries\SalesForecastWorkbook\SalesForecastWorkbook.xlsx`.

In addition to mapping your custom VSTO-enabled spreadsheet to the content type, this page allows you to make a couple of other optional changes to your content type definition. The first optional change is whether the content type should be read-only. Because it's not necessary to prevent someone from modifying this content type, keep the default setting of No. The other option is whether any content types that inherit from this one should be updated. Keep the default setting of Yes.

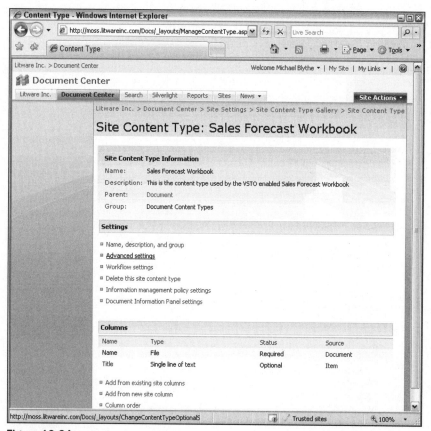

Figure 10-24

Though we don't expect to create any child content types from our custom Sales Forecast Workbook content type, this setting allows you to create a somewhat more generic template. For example, if the Sales Forecast Template was focused on a default budgeting scenario, different departments might all need to refer to the same budgeting logic, but would undoubtedly want to name the template appropriately for their local departments and possibly even customize some non–assembly-related portion of the template. In this scenario, it is reasonable for such departments to inherit from the baseline VSTO-enabled template and then make minor modifications to the accompanying .xlsx file.

Clicking the OK button in this screen completes setting up your content type. You will be returned to the Site Content Type screen for the Sales Forecast Workbook. It should be noted briefly that, though it is possible to associate a custom workflow with a given content type, this was not the direction we took for the sales forecast OBA. Figure 10-24 includes a link with which you could associate one or more workflows with this template. The sales forecast OBA chose instead to associate our custom workflow with the Sales Forecast document library as opposed to the content type.

At this point, you are done creating your content type, however just as you needed to map your custom VSTO-enabled spreadsheet into your content type, you need to map your content type into your Sales Forecast document library. From the Site Content Type screens navigate to your Sales Forecast document library. Once back in the library, you'll see the Settings menu shown in Figure 10-26.

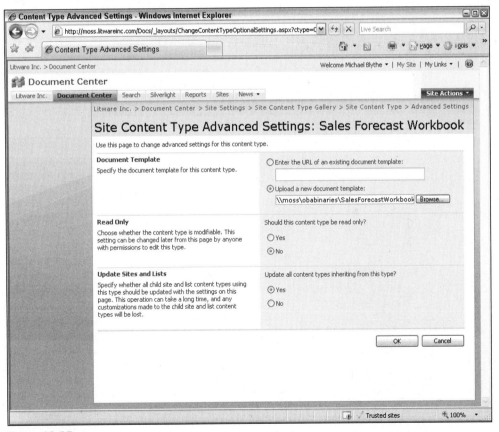

Figure 10-25

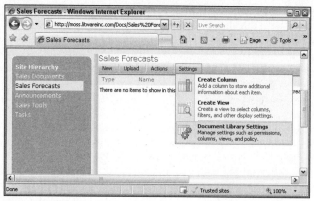

Figure 10-26

Mapping a site content type to a document library requires updating that document library's settings, and you can select this option from the Settings menu in your document library. Selecting this item takes you to the screen shown in Figure 10-27. This page allows you to customize the settings associated with your Sales Forecast document library. As part of the initial creation of this document library in Chapter 3, you customized the settings to allow for modifications to the content type. As long as that step was completed, you'll see the Content Types section shown near the bottom of this screen.

If, for some reason, you don't see a Content Types section in your display, then, for whatever reason, that setting is incorrect in your library's definition. To resolve the issue, click the "Advanced settings" link under the General Settings, and in the resulting screen, shown during the creation process in Chapter 3, switch the setting to allow for customization of your content type.

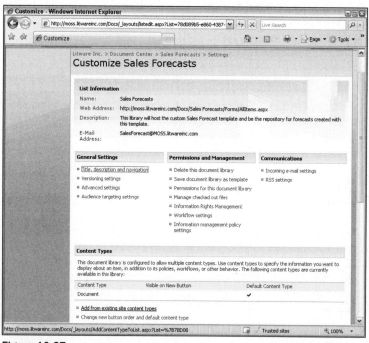

Figure 10-27

Once you have the Content Types section shown in Figure 10-27, you'll want to click the "Add from existing site content types" link shown at the bottom of the figure. This link takes you to the page shown in Figure 10-28. The Add Content Types page allows you to assign content types that are defined for your current site as well as any content types defined at the top level of your site. Actually, if your site hierarchy is more than one layer deep, it will allow you to select from any content type defined at the current or higher level. The list is alphabetical and by scrolling to the bottom of the list we were able to select and then add the newly created Sales Forecast Workbook template.

Because this is the only template you want to associate with this document library, you can click the OK button to complete this action. If you chose, you could, in theory, add multiple different content types to the same document library. In your case, this would call into question your decision to apply the Sales Forecast Approval Workflow to the document library. Instead you might choose to limit the workflow to a specific content type. Our decision was made based on the concept that we wanted to create a specific document library to contain a specific custom business application.

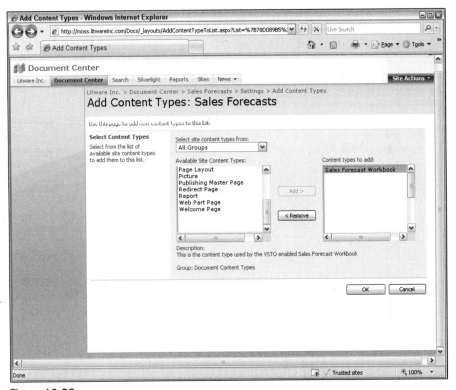

Figure 10-28

Once you have finished working with the screen in Figure 10-28 you are taken back to your Sales Forecasts document library settings screen. Ideally your display will look similar to the one shown in Figure 10-29. The Content Types section now shows that the Sales Forecast Workbook content type is visible on the New button and that it is the default content type for this library. It also makes clear that the original generic document content type is no longer visible on the New menu, effectively hiding it from the sales team.

You can exit from the settings page and return to your document library. You should now be able to click or hover over and open the drop-down menu associated with your new button and then create a new Sales Forecast Workbook. The application should install and allow you to retrieve data from your database and save your customized document to the document library.

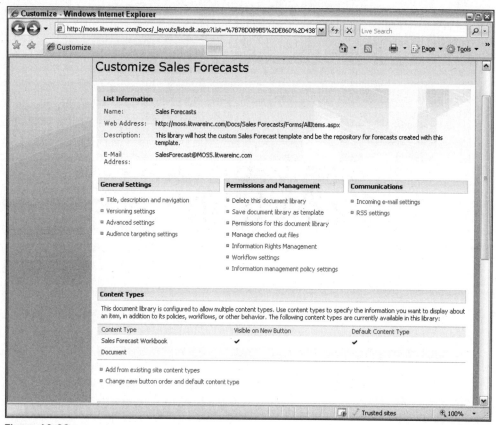

Figure 10-29

Maintaining Your Content Type

Unlike some ClickOnce applications, the custom VSTO-enabled spreadsheet used for sales forecasts isn't automatically updated. When you mapped the current packaged version of the Sales Forecast Workbook to the content type, all of the current assembly information was also mapped with the .xlsx file. When that package was updated, SharePoint did not ever query to determine whether updates were available. Instead, you need to remap your customization.

For the most part all you need to do is return to the Site Content Type Advanced Settings screen shown in Figure 10-25 and reload the .xlsx file. There is one exception — for the file to reload, all references to the current content type must be removed. There are two ways to do this. The first option is simply to remove all of the documents that refer to this content type and then reload the content type. For the purposes of our work we have been following this method of updating the content type.

Alternatively, you can leave the documents in place and then delete the mapping from this library to the content type. Next, delete the entire content type from SharePoint and then start from the top. Go back to the Content Types for the Document Center and create a new content type for the site, repeating your original configuration steps.

If you ever think that, for some reason, your content type is not updating correctly, you will almost certainly find it more efficient to delete and repopulate your custom content type than to attempt to determine what is wrong.

Summary

This chapter looked at the deployment and configuration of your VSTO-enabled client applications. The introduction of Visual Studio 2008 and the ability to deploy Office 2007 customizations via the ClickOnce publishing model has simplified deployment. As noted, when it comes to Trusted Locations, the Office 2007 model essentially requires that each user update his or her own system to trust the local Share-Point server in order to run those customizations.

This chapter covered:

- ❑ Publishing a ClickOnce package
- ❑ Creating a Links list on MOSS to make the ClickOnce installations accessible
- ❑ Setting trust permissions on your local machine to run and debug the client components
- ❑ Creating a custom content type based on the VSTO-enabled Sales Forecast Workbook

Although publishing VSTO-enabled applications has become much simpler, there are still several steps to configuring and exposing these same customizations as a SharePoint content type. The benefits of being able to define a document-level customization as a custom content type within one or more SharePoint document libraries make these additional steps well worth the effort.

Deploying and Securing Your OBA Server Components

Now that you've looked at packaging the client components on the server and installing these packages by the clients, the next step is to examine the custom server components that need to be installed on your server. These are encapsulated in two of the sales forecast OBA applications. The first is the Word Document Generation Web service. This Web service is a custom ASP.NET XML Web service. The second is the custom Sales Forecast Approval Workflow. This involves a custom workflow and three custom InfoPath forms.

Accordingly, this chapter focuses on:

❑   Creating a web deployment project

❑   Deploying the Web service

❑   Publishing the InfoPath templates

❑   Configuring the custom workflow

In general, the process of deploying these server components is reasonably straightforward. Recognizing the simple steps is probably the biggest challenge.

ASP.NET Application Installation

In Chapter 3, "Installing and Configuring MOSS," we focused on setting up a development environment. In this chapter, we're actually reversing that, because for applications, most people have questions related to deployment outside a development environment. In the case of the SalesForecastDocService the way to create the necessary Web service on your local development server is to start with a new XML Web Services project in Visual Studio 2008. Once you have created the necessary project as an HTTP-based XML Web service, you can just copy in the `.cs` and the `.docx` files that are available for download from the CodePlex site (`http:www.codeplex.com/obasales`). This is the recommended method because when Visual Studio generates the web site it will assign a variety of permissions (depending on the operating system) that are more difficult to replicate manually.

The simple file copy works great if you are a developer and are looking to update your development environment for a Visual Studio project. When it's time to move to production, however, you need a method that is a bit more automatic. Sure, if you are a small set of developers who double as IT professionals you might manually move and create your Web service. Given how easy it is to create a basic web deployment package, creating an installation package is the recommended method for deploying your Web services in all cases where you aren't targeting a development environment.

Figure 11-1 shows Visual Studio with the SalesForecastDocService loaded. To simplify the process of creating a new installation package, you are going to add the Web Setup Package to the solution containing your Web service. Accessing the File menu you select Add ➪ New Project to begin creating your installation package. This will open the Add New Project dialog shown in Figure 11-2.

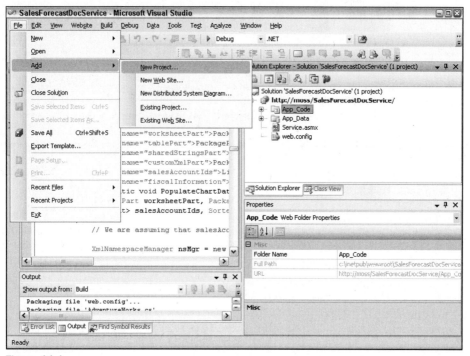

Figure 11-1

Initially, the Add New Project dialog is most likely to default to a language-based solution with a Project Type of Visual Basic or Visual C#. Within the Project Types list box you need to select Other Project Types, and, then, within that you need to select the Setup and Deployment project types. This will result in the list of templates displayed in Figure 11-2. There are two items to note: first, because your Web service leverages LINQ, it is a .NET 3.5 project, so you'll want to keep the .NET Framework 3.5 targeted version option shown in the upper-right corner.

Second, you'll want to name your project. In this case we've chosen to name the project SalesForecast-DocServer_Setup, which allows us to find the Setup project quickly and ensures that it sorts after the project to which it applies. Clicking the OK button returns you to the main Visual Studio 2008 display with your new Setup project selected and the default File System display open, as shown in Figure 11-3.

Figure 11-2

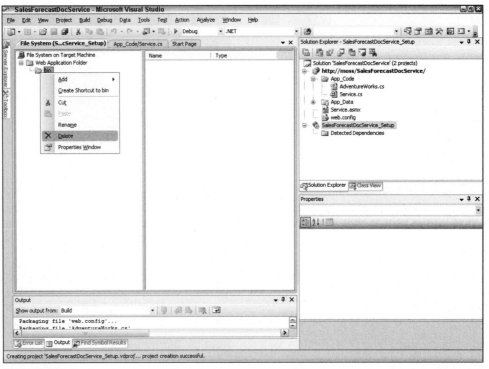

Figure 11-3

Figure 11-3 shows the newly created Web Setup Project after it has been created. By default, Web Setup Projects look to create a new application folder, and within that folder they create a sub-folder called "bin." In this case, there aren't any precompiled binaries that need to be installed in the bin folder, so you can delete that folder, as shown in Figure 11-3.

Once the folder is deleted, you will have a view similar to the one in Figure 11-4. By right-clicking the Web Application Folder you can choose to add the contents of your Web Service project to the Web Application Folder. Doing so will result in the Add Project Output Group dialog opening, as shown in Figure 11-5. This dialog allows you to select from any of the application projects that are part of your solution and add the content files associated with that solution. These content files are then included as part of the package, and, when the setup executable is run, they are placed as-is into the content directory.

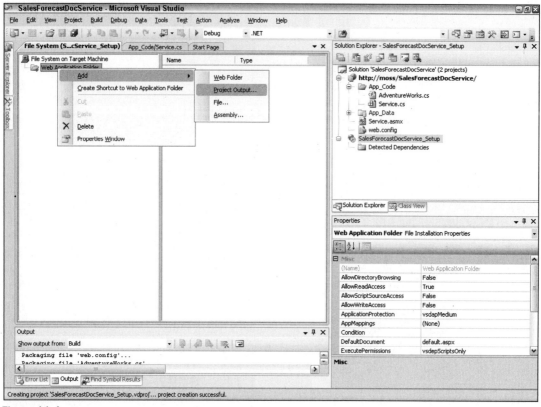

Figure 11-4

Not only will the setup module automatically install files at the top level of the targeted folder, but those files that are in sub-folders in your project will have a matching relative path following installation. This simple action adds not only the `service.asmx` page, but also the App_Code and App_Data folders and their related content.

We should note that the web.config file is also included in the package. As with the other files, it isn't added until you actually build the installation package; however, this is the time to start thinking about disabling the debugging settings and setting up your production connection string. One best practice is to have a different web.config file for each environment where your web application will be installed, and then build the Setup project with that web.config file loaded in the project.

Figure 11-5

Now that you've determined which files will be shipped as part of the installation package, it's time to update the properties of the Setup project. By right-clicking the Setup project in the Solution Explorer it is possible to open the Property Pages for the Setup project. As shown in Figure 11-6, these properties allow you to make changes that help customize your setup process. The first thing to note is that you can, in fact, have different settings for your Debug and Release Setup project builds. Don't forget to account for this when setting up key values.

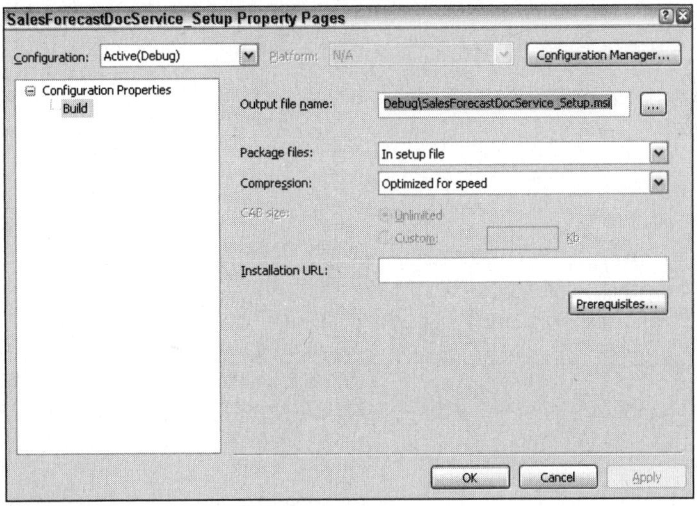

Figure 11-6

In terms of values to change, the only value you want to change here is the Output File Name. This property defaults to the name of your project, however, your project name reflects the name of the installation project, not the product being installed. Therefore, the best practice is to modify this value to reflect the name of what is being installed. The next option, Package Files, allows you to determine whether your project should produce an installation (.msi) file, or, if you prefer, either a CAB file or a set of loose uncompressed files. For the purposes of this project, a setup (.msi) file is acceptable.

The Compression option is available only if you chose either a setup or CAB file as the destination for the application files. Typically, unless you are concerned about size for Web-based delivery of your installation package, selecting Optimized for Speed is acceptable. Similarly, the settings related to CAB size are only related to having selected a CAB-based installation, and are self-explanatory.

The key remaining item in Figure 11-6 is the Prerequisites button. Clicking this button opens the Pre-requisites dialog shown in Figure 11-7. The main reason we are reviewing this dialog is because of the checkbox at the top. When you read that carefully, you find it states that the project will create a "setup program" for installing prerequisite components. This is important because, as you can see, the Web service does have a couple of prerequisite dependencies. The Windows Installer isn't too big a deal, but the fact that your server will need to have the .NET Framework 3.5 is important. When you set up the server, and more important, when you go to a production server, there is nothing to guarantee that the .NET Framework 3.5 will already be installed.

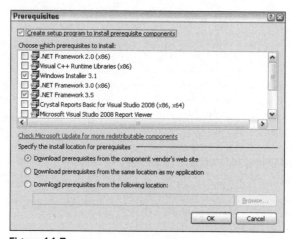

Figure 11-7

Let's say up front, however, that if you make .NET Framework 3.5 a prerequisite, the installer will auto-matically recognize both the 2.0 and 3.0 versions, with their associated patches, as prerequisites. Back to that top line discussion of creating a Setup program — unfortunately, the MSI that is generated does not track these prerequisites. You'll find that when you build your Setup project, the resulting setup.exe and SalesForecastDocService.msi files are of slightly different sizes. This is because only the setup.exe file contains the prerequisite information. As a result, if you run the .msi on a server that doesn't have the .NET Framework already installed, it will not trigger the installation, and your applica-tion will not run.

The only other limitation, you'll notice, is that we keep referring to the `setup.exe` file. Unfortunately, there isn't a way, as part of the build process, to rename that `setup.exe` file to match the name of the `SalesForecastDocService.msi` file, or to give it some other more meaningful name — although you can post build.

Finally, there is some renaming that is optionally associated with preparing to create your Setup project. As part of the Web Application Folder there is a set of properties exposed in the Properties window within Visual Studio 2008, as shown in Figure 11-8. Typically this window is located in the lower-right corner of the display. Most of these properties default to the appropriate values. Figure 11-8 depicts the Properties window when you select the Web Application Folder (shown in Figure 11-4). The very last property, the Virtual Directory to be created to support your project, again uses the Setup project name as its default value. You'll want to edit this value similar to the way that you edited the `.msi` file name to match the name of the installation folder and default directory where the web application should be exposed.

Figure 11-8

Additionally, although not pictured when you select the project in the Solution Explorer, there is a set of properties associated with the project that are loaded into the same frame. In this case, there are properties for the Setup Title and the Setup Product Name. Updating the title is a common practice because, from the standpoint of the person running your installation, that person is running the installer for your product. Similarly, you can modify the product name, but be aware this isn't the product name used by the installed application; it is the product name of the installer itself, and as such can be left unmodified.

To get your actual installation packages you need either to switch to release mode for your solution or to right-click your Setup project to build it explicitly. In the case of setting release mode, by default, when the Setup project was created, it was added to the build list for your solution in release mode. At the same time, however, it was not added in debug mode. Because for most new debug versions of your application you won't need an installation package, this saves you time. In those cases where you do want to test your installation package, all you need to do is explicitly build the Setup project.

Running the Web Installation

Once you've created the installation package, running the installation is very straightforward. As noted earlier, if you run the .msi file, the installation will not check for necessary prerequisites. Therefore, in most cases it is better to deploy the setup.exe file so that the prerequisites are checked and installed as part of the process.

Figure 11-9 illustrates that the setup.exe file, when run, first checks for the installation process for each dependency and calls it, when available. Note that one of the side effects of the installation of the prerequisites is that they are installed as standalone applications. This means that once you've installed .NET Framework 3.5 as part of the installation, uninstalling or removing the SalesForecastDocService will not impact your .NET Framework 3.5 installation.

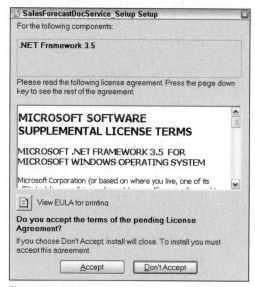

Figure 11-9

Once the prerequisites have been installed, your initial installation screen will appear as shown in Figure 11-10. There isn't much to your installation process. This is the default start screen regardless of whether you start the .msi or the setup.exe file. Once you choose to continue you are given the one setup screen that allows you to customize the installation.

The screen shown in Figure 11-11 is created by the Web Setup Project template and includes the logic to retrieve the list of available web sites and application pools from the server running the installer. In this case, we have chosen the default web site, because the goal is to create an XML Web service that is not part of the SharePoint site. Unfortunately, the default setup logic does not support creating either a new Site or a new Application Pool as part of the installation process. These have to be created in advance. The fact that it does allow you to select from any of the existing Sites or Applications Pools and to rename the default name assigned for the Virtual Directory make it possible for you to customize the installation to fit the requirements of the server.

Figure 11-10

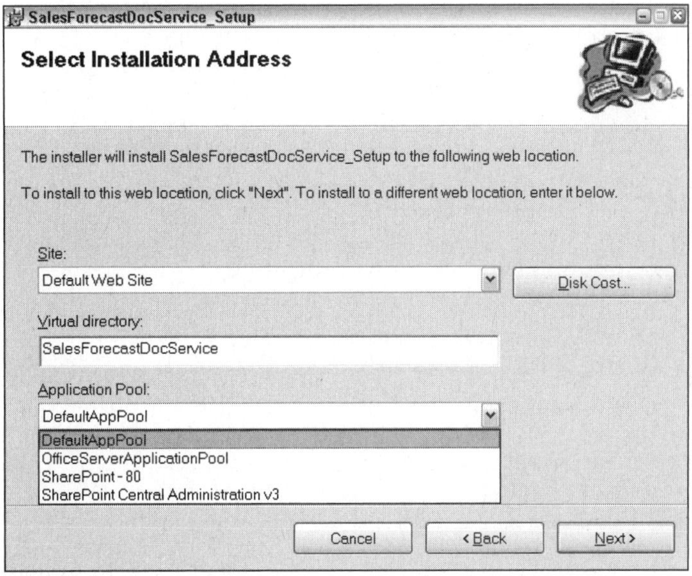

Figure 11-11

At this point your Web service application will finish its installation and be available. Keep in mind that as part of installing the package either at the time of the package or following the installation you need to ensure the settings in your `web.config` file are correct. Potential changes include the need for you to update the connection string for your database to match that of your production database and remembering to adjust your settings for debugging and the display of error messages. Each of these are related to settings within your `web.config` file, and, if you have forgotten to do any of the above, you can edit the `web.config` file in place to make the necessary updates. Perhaps someday Microsoft will enhance the current installation engine to allow the user installing the application to update these settings during the installation. Ideally the packager would have a setting for installation customization. Selecting this setting in the install package would trigger the packager to open and parse the `web.config` file. It would then allow the user to test each connection string defined in the `web.config` for the installed file. Similarly, the installer could detect that settings for debugging and error handling (not logging, but whether errors are returned when a page is requested) are set for a development environment instead of a production environment. For now, just remember to double-check the values in your `web.config` file.

Publishing the InfoPath Forms

The custom SalesForecastStateWorkflow, which is installed in the next section, has a dependency on a set of InfoPath forms. These forms, similar to the workflow itself, need to be installed and maintained on your SharePoint site. This section examines a simple way to update your MOSS site with the forms associated with the workflow. There are a couple of ways you might choose to manage this problem. In this case, using InfoPath itself to update your site seems to be the most straightforward and easiest solution. This method does require you to publish each individual template manually, so the steps described next will be repeated for each template.

As part of the downloadable project files available on Codeplex and Wrox you will find the three Info-Path Form Templates. We suggest storing these in a folder that is located under the solution folder for the workflow project, or in a location appropriate for custom InfoPath templates on your production environment. In many cases the location of the original may in fact be referred to by a network path from your production server. Once you have copied the files, you need to open them in InfoPath to deploy the templates to MOSS.

As shown in Figure 11-12, you can right-click one of the files and select Design from the pop-up menu. The system then raises an informational warning, shown in Figure 11-13. This warning is apparently designed to let you know that the template has, at some point in the history of the template, been published. The warning isn't based on its having been published to one of your servers or on your network, but simply reflects that InfoPath can find a previous path within the .xsn file structure for this template.

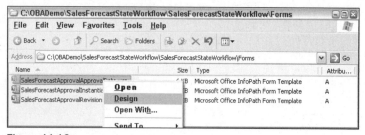

Figure 11-12

Figure 11-13

Once you have gone past the message that this template was published to a location and has been moved, InfoPath will open, as shown in Figure 11-14. If, for some reason, you don't see the Design Tasks pane on the right-hand side of the display, ensure that you are in Design mode. If, instead of choosing to edit the template, you initially chose to open the template, InfoPath will open the template as a form. In this mode, the form will react as if you were running it to collect data. If you do this, you can go to the Tools menu within InfoPath and select the Design this Form option. This menu option will then open the design view that you see pictured in Figure 11-14.

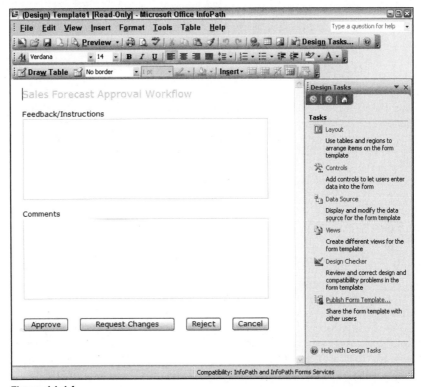

Figure 11-14

Figure 11-14 illustrates one of the three InfoPath forms associated with the workflow. The only thing you need to do is republish the form to the MOSS server, and that task is initiated from the lower-right corner of the display. Clicking the Publish Form Template link will start the process. Note that before you can republish the template you must be in edit mode on the template. By default, when you chose to edit the template, InfoPath opened it in read-only mode. As a result you will be presented with a dialog box and asked to save a copy of the template either to capture changes or to deploy the template.

Unless you have made changes, navigate to the same location from which you opened the template and overwrite the downloaded version of the template. Do not attempt this solution with your development, integration, test, and production environments. Each of these environments will need its own copy of the template.

Figure 11-15 illustrates the first step of the Publishing Wizard. In this case, the default selection to publish this template to a SharePoint site is the appropriate selection. Next, in Figure 11-16, you will need to provide the address of your SharePoint server. The template can be published to the top-level site or to a site you specify, such as the Docs site (shown in Figure 11-16).

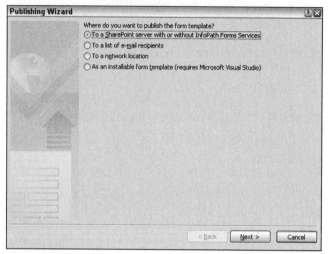

Figure 11-15

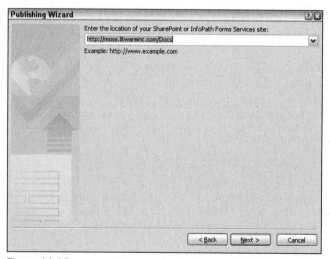

Figure 11-16

At this point, depending on your security model in Internet Explorer, you may be asked to authenticate to that server. Typically, your security settings should allow you to authenticate with your system credentials automatically; however, if the enhanced security configuration of IE is enabled, you may be prompted to enter your password. In either event the next screen is shown in Figure 11-17.

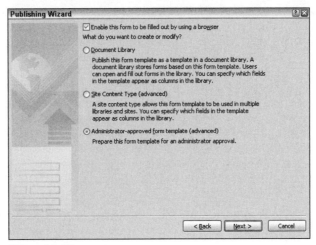

Figure 11-17

You will want to accept the default to allow this form to be accessed from a browser, because the work-flow process will open the form within a browser window when user input is needed. The first option assigns this template as the content type of a Document Library. Similarly, the second option would define this form as a Site Content Type. The difference from the first option is that you could assign this template as the content type for multiple libraries within your site. The final choice is to create the template as an Administrator-Approved Form Template. It is this option that will allow the workflow process to leverage this template to capture user input during the workflow processing.

Clicking Next on the screen shown in Figure 11-17 will open the screen shown in Figure 11-18. This path takes you to the location from which MOSS will retrieve the template. On your local machine, this will be a local path; however, it can also be a network share. By default the system will attempt to use a folder within the default template folder. The folder you select here needs to exist already. If you are working with the developer server you may want to create a custom folder under C:\Program Files\ Common Files\Microsoft Shared\web server extensions\12\TEMPLATE\FEATURES\.

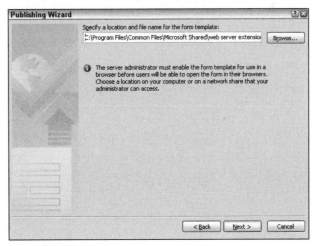

Figure 11-18

Once you have saved the template to a folder that is accessible by your MOSS server, you will be presented with the screen shown in Figure 11-19. Publishing individual columns from your workflow form isn't necessary, and you can move to the final screen in the Publishing Wizard. The final step actually publishes the template as a form on the server. Once the template is published, the screen shown in Figure 11-20 is updated to reflect the location and related information for your form.

At this point, you have published the first of your three custom InfoPath forms to your server. You need to repeat this process for the two remaining InfoPath templates prior to looking to import the workflow.

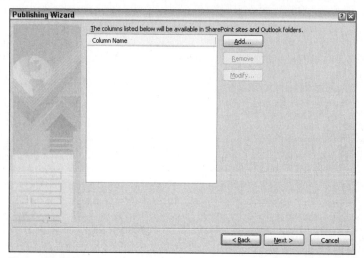

Figure 11-19

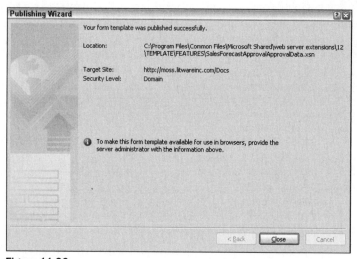

Figure 11-20

Installing the Custom Workflow

Once you have installed the associated InfoPath templates, adding the workflow can be fairly simple. The easiest method, if you are setting up a development environment, is to leverage the built-in deployment capabilities of Visual Studio 2008. When you define the workflow you also define the location of the MOSS server to which it belongs. In fact, you define all of the information necessary to deploy the workflow.

Each time you debug the workflow, you are in fact re-deploying it to the development site. The first option when deploying the workflow project is simply to allow Visual Studio to do it. You can, as shown in Figure 11-21, select the Deploy Solution option from the Build menu in Visual Studio 2008. This will initiate a new build of your workflow, and Visual Studio will then attempt to move the associated binaries to the appropriate location and register the workflow with SharePoint.

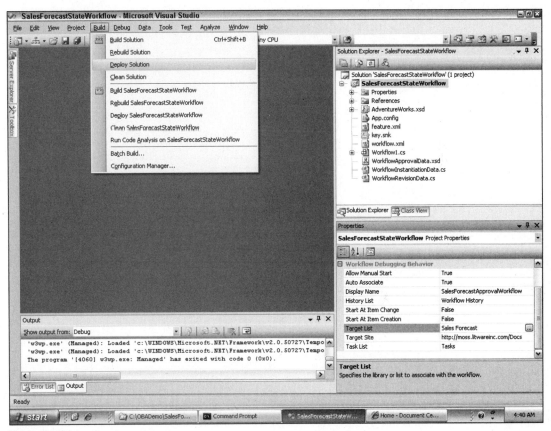

Figure 11-21

The first time that you download the files from Codeplex you may find that the associated files are in fact pointing to a slightly different location from what is available on your site. In this scenario the automated deployment from Visual Studio 2008 will fail, and you will be presented with an error message giving you an idea of the problem. The easiest way to resolve such issues is to access the project properties shown in Figure 11-21.

Within the Properties window, you'll notice that the Target List property is highlighted; on the far right side of this property is an ellipsis button. This property indicates which document library is associated with this workflow. The ellipsis button doesn't just allow you to change this value, but actually restarts the New Office SharePoint Workflow wizard. The first screen of this wizard is shown in Figure 11-22.

You can ensure that the workflow and the local site are defined correctly on the first screen. Even though the screen implies this is the path for debugging, it is used for deployment whether you are in a debug build or a release build. Once you are satisfied with the path to your MOSS server, click Next. You will be taken to the screen shown in Figure 11-23.

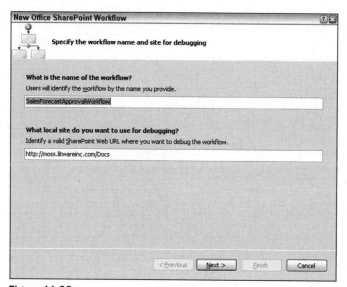

Figure 11-22

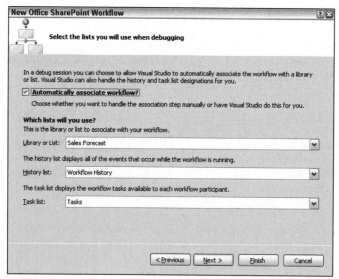

Figure 11-23

The screen shown in Figure 11-23 allows you to define which library to associate with your workflow. By default, the Announcements list will be the default selection, which isn't typically what you want. Opening the drop-down list enables you to select from the list of available document libraries on your server. Additionally, you can create custom history and task lists. For the sales forecast OBA in our example, we relied on the default lists for the values.

The final step in the wizard isn't required to deploy your workflow, however it does allow you to control when the workflow is started. For the sales forecast OBA, we decided that the approval process should begin only when the sales representative is ready to submit it for approval. Therefore, events like checking in an incomplete forecast or changing a forecast that is currently saved to MOSS should not automatically start the approval process. If you wanted to change these defaults you could do so from here.

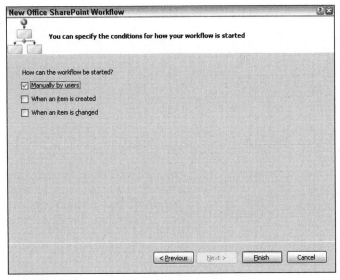

Figure 11-24

At this point, you should again be able to access the Build menu and re-attempt the deployment of the workflow. Deploying from within Visual Studio 2008 is a very simple, straightforward method for incorporating your custom workflow definition with SharePoint.

Deploying a Workflow without Visual Studio 2008

For each of the other projects we have talked about how to deploy without having Visual Studio installed locally. In the case of the workflow, this is also possible. The stsadm tool allows you to import a compiled workflow definition into MOSS. At some point in the not too distant future we expect that creating a deployment package for a custom workflow would become a simple process similar to the Web Setup Project that was used to deploy your XML Web service.

For now, however, the process is handled from the command line. The first step is to take the contents of the Bin directory, where Visual Studio placed the compiled assembly, and copy this folder to the GAC on your server.

Once you have placed the executables on your server, you need to add the `feature.xml` and `workflow.xml` files, which are part of your solution on the server. These do not go in the GAC; instead, they should be placed in the same folder in which you previously installed your InfoPath form templates. The default is under `C:\Program Files\Common Files\Microsoft Shared\web server extensions\12\TEMPLATE\FEATURES\`, with the project name used as a folder name at this location.

Once this is complete, you are ready to run stsadm to install this new feature on MOSS. On the command line, from within the directory hosting your `feature.xml` and `workflow.xml` files, type the following:

```
stsadm -o installfeature -name SalesForecastStateWorkflow
```

Once this command completes successfully, your final step is to activate the associated workflow by typing this:

```
stsadm -o activatefeature -name SalesForecastStateWorkflow -url http://moss
.litwareinc.com
```

This will complete the installation of the workflow on your MOSS server. You can now access the server and start the workflow from within MOSS.

Summary

This chapter reviewed the installation and configuration of the server-side components of the sales forecast OBA. The Web service has a simple, straightforward project type for handling the creation of its installation package. For the InfoPath forms, and, to a limited extent, for the workflow, leveraging the built-in deployment capabilities of the tools involved is the easiest way to deploy your solution.

The installation of the server components is a fairly simple process. The main challenge for most people is just understanding the steps they need to take in order to support deployment. Both deployment and the other projects have settings that may be specific to the environments in which they are installed. Unfortunately, the deployment tools don't currently provide an automated way to update based on the environments in which you are installing your application code.

What's Next?

Now that you've finished this book, you're probably asking yourself "What's next?" As you may have gathered in this book, there are many different sizes and types of OBAs that you could build, so we recommend looking at ways of applying OBA development within your organization. There are many technologies that you will also want to think about as you deepen your OBA development skills. This appendix provides a high-level description of some additional technologies you may want to explore as you move forward with your OBA development. This is certainly not a complete list, but it may be a place a start.

Visual Studio 2008 and VSTO

In the sales forecast OBA, we talked at length about VSTO and showed you some of the VSTO 3.0 technology, but there is much more of VSTO that you'll want to explore. For example, the full set of VSTO project templates are shown in Figure A-1 that not only support Office 2007, but also 2003. We'd encourage you to spend some additional time with each of these available templates to see what they could offer for you in the context of expanding your OBAs.

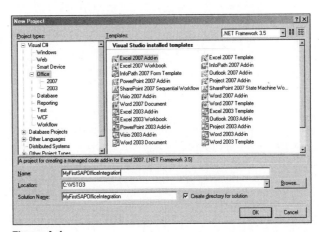

Figure A-1

Social Networking

One of the key themes behind Web 2.0 is social networking. Though the market in some sense is still trying to figure out exactly what that means, there are a few higher-level technologies that come to mind. For example, Facebook and similar sites (LinkedIn, MySpace) are consistently mentioned in conversations about social networking. Many companies are looking to adopt newer, more dynamic ways in which their organization communicates, socializes, and, in some sense, manages relationships. Sites (or technological designs) like Facebook are increasingly becoming an integrated part of the enterprise. What does this have to do with OBAs?

Within SharePoint, which is one of the key pillars of the Office platform, you find many different ways to build social networking natively using the out-of-the-box features, or extend SharePoint by integrating elements of social networking sites into the context of the SharePoint experience. For example, SharePoint ships with the capability to build blogs or wikis, great ways to share unstructured data within the enterprise quickly and easily. You can add another dimension to your OBA by integrating blogs and wikis.

You also have the concept of My Sites in SharePoint; that is, individual sites that can be created in which you house information and documents that are specific to your role in the organization. This information, through your profile and the fact that the My Site is an indexable part of the SharePoint structure, can then be searched. Others in the organization are able to discover key information that pertains to specific projects, technologies, products, and so on.

Further, you can integrate third-party sites (or at least elements of those sites) within your OBA. For example, you can use Popfly technology to integrate elements of Facebook to display your contacts within your SharePoint site and subsequently expose your social network to others in the organization. This is a great way to expose an external (to your organization) social network to your organization. As social networking technology evolves, there will certainly be more opportunities to integrate many different types of technology with SharePoint to create all different types of OBA "mash-ups."

For more information, you might want to check out the following resources:

❑ *Programming Microsoft Office Business Applications* (MS Press), which has a chapter on social networking for your OBA.

❑ "Overview of Microsoft Office SharePoint Server 2007," which provides an overview of the social networking features: `http://technet.microsoft.com/en-us/magazine/cc162511.aspx`.

❑ Microsoft Popfly site, where you can get started building mash-ups that integrate with SharePoint: `http://www.popfly.com`.

Silverlight

Silverlight 2.0 is hot. At every conference we've attended over the past few months, more and more developers are trying to learn this technology. The integration of Silverlight with SharePoint is in its infancy, and you can bet on plenty of integration as this technology matures. (At the time of writing, the Silverlight Beta 2 had just shipped, so by the time you read this, the RTM version of Silverlight should either be available or very close to shipping.)

Silverlight is a browser plug-in that enables developers to leverage the .NET programming model in their web-based applications, so you can build managed code applications (that is, VB.NET and C#) and then deploy these applications to your web site. What is interesting about Silverlight is that it provides a separate but compatible designer and developer experience. For the designer, you have a set of tools at your fingertips in the Expression Blend toolset. For the developer, you can use Visual Studio 2008 (with the addition of the Silverlight SDK and tools for Visual Studio) to begin building richer user experiences for the consumers of your applications. Where this factors into OBA is where you want to really increase the design of the user experience. Think about virtual mapping capabilities, or using multimedia in your applications; this is where Silverlight will really help you design a great interface. You can also create baseline forms and render them with the Silverlight runtime (as opposed to using ASP.NET to build your forms), and you will find some gains in the look and feel of the user interface. You'll really see Silverlight excel when managing multimedia in the user interface.

To get you started, you can check out a couple of resources in this area. The first is the Silverlight Blueprints for SharePoint (see Figure A-2), which provides a rich set of samples that show you how to integrate Silverlight with SharePoint in a number of different ways. For more information, go to `http://www.ssblueprints.net/sharepoint`.

The second resource, and one that you can use to also improve your wider SharePoint developer skills, is `http://mssharepointdeveloper.com`. This is a great new site with many resources for the aspiring SharePoint developer. For example, not only can you find resources on how to integrate Silverlight with SharePoint (there is an entire module dedicated to this topic), but you can also find modules on Web part development, list development, workflow, and integration of services. The screenshot displayed in Figure A-3 shows you all the areas contained within the site.

You'll also want to look out for more SharePoint developer content coming from Microsoft in the coming months.

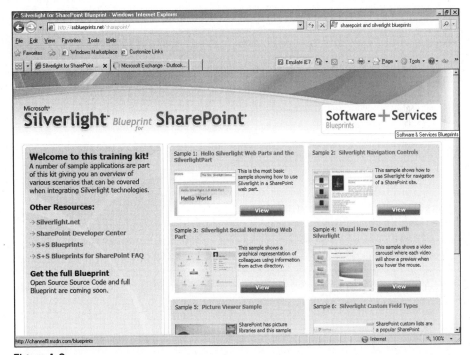

Figure A-2

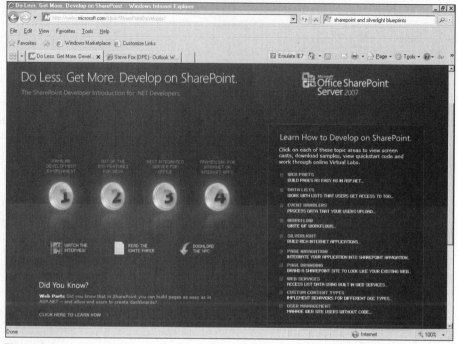

Figure A-3

Integrating SAP, PeopleSoft, and Siebel

Many companies want to create OBAs that specifically integrate with LOB systems, such as SAP, People-Soft, and Siebel, among others. For you, we've released a set of kits called the OBA Sample Application Kits. Using these kits, you can educate yourself on how to integrate these aforementioned LOB systems with the Office system. The landing page is here: `http://msdn2.microsoft.com/en-us/office/cc442491.aspx`. Figure A-4 shows a screenshot of the OBA Sample Application Kit for PeopleSoft, a developer kit that ships documentation and source code. This kit, like the others, provides guidance on how to programmatically integrate with specific line-of-business systems.

The OBA Sample Application Kits are composed of technical walkthroughs, installation guides, and source code. Each kit is also based around a sample scenario that illustrates how the key technology integrates the LOB system with Office. They are great resources for those who want to see working code.

VSTO Plus VBA

The OBA hasn't left those with existing VBA investments behind. As part of Visual Studio 2008, it is possible to take existing VBA-enabled documents and extend them with new capabilities provided by VSTO. VBA is still a viable and supported set of tools for customizing the Microsoft Office experience. There are certain things that VSTO does that VBA wasn't designed to do, and, to a certain degree, is not capable of doing.

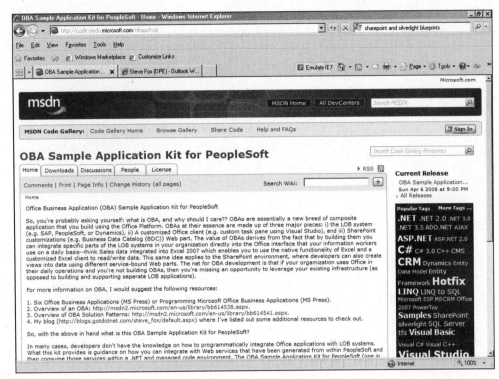

Figure A-4

Just like the WPF interoperability library and the Visual Basic 6.0 interoperability library, VSTO and VBA have an interoperability library. Microsoft suggests that companies with complex VBA solutions update these Document/Workbook style solutions with VSTO features, but not necessarily attempt to convert working code and features. Your new VSTO code may call existing VBA functions. Similarly, your existing VBA code may start calling your VSTO objects.

There are, of course, limitations to this model, and it isn't one that's recommended for new development. To enable VBA in Word 2007, the file is saved as a .docm file instead of a .docx file. The same is true for Excel, where the file type needs to be .xlsm as opposed to .xlsx. By default, documents saved with the extension .docx do not allow macros. Additionally, you need to access the Trust Center discussed in Chapter 10, "Deploying Your Client Components," and ensure that the Macro Settings allow for the automatic execution of VBA code. Also note that when you combine VBA and VSTO, you have to handle permissions for both, so plan to spend a little more time building your installation package and permissions.

To create your project, create a new project using either the Word 2007 document or Excel 2007 workbook template. During the project creation, you need to specify that the project should refer to an existing document/workbook and provide the path to your .docm file. This must be done when creating your project.

When it comes to calling VBA from VSTO, you can call the Run method on the Office object model. This method accepts the name of a VBA method and a list of parameters. There is no IntelliSense, because what you are doing is making a dynamic runtime call. An example of this call follows:

```
Dim result As Integer = Me.Application.Run("MyFunctionAdd", 1, 2)
```

That's it, just a standard call. Of course, your document or workbook needs to include the VBA function MyFunctionAdd, but that should be apparent. The reverse is also available. You refer to the generated method CallVSTOAssembly to create a call from your COM-based VBA code into your newly created VSTO application logic. The CallVSTOAssembly method is generated and added to your existing VBA logic when the project template is created. It is then possible to refer to methods in your managed class from VBA.

More information is available at:

❑ http://channel9vip.orcsweb.com/Showpost.aspx?postid=349570

❑ http://msdn.microsoft.com/en-us/library/bb931201.aspx

OBA Developer Center

Last, and more generally, Microsoft has the OBA Developer Center that you can use to get up-to-date information and technical resources to help support you in your OBA development efforts. You can visit the Developer Center here: http://msdn.microsoft.com/en-us/office/aa905528.aspx.

Index